PLAYS FROM SOUTH COAST REPERTORY

357 W 20th St., NY NY 10011
212 627-1055

PLAYS FROM SOUTH COAST REPERTORY
© Copyright 1993 by Broadway Play Publishing

First printing: September 1993

ISBN: 0-88145-111-8

Editing, design, and production: Marie Donovan
Word processing: Microsoft Word for Windows
Typographic controls: Xerox Ventura Publisher 2.0 PE
Typeface: Palatino
Printed on recycled acid-free paper and bound in the USA.

CONTENTS

FOREWORD

The two of us have the pleasure of working for a theatre where new plays matter; they don't just matter, they stand at the center of South Coast Repertory's artistic life. That means the literary department isn't just a bureaucratic appendage (turn those scripts around, keep those writers and agents off the artistic directors' backs, etc.), but a vital organ in SCR's system.

SCR has been producing new work since its inaugural season in 1965, but the last ten years have brought an extraordinary surge in our new-play endeavors. The main reason is a program called the Collaboration Laboratory (Colab), instituted by artistic directors David Emmes and Martin Benson in 1984 as a comprehensive R&D program for new plays and playwrights. Funded by earnings from its own restricted endowment, Colab comprises an extensive and flexible system of workshops, readings, commissions and residencies, serving as a conduit for new plays on their way to productions here and at other theaters.

All six of the plays included in this volume have benefitted from one or more of Colab's component programs. SEARCH AND DESTROY, SIGHT UNSEEN, and PRELUDE TO A KISS were written under commissions funded by the Colab endowment. The first two were workshopped in NewSCRipts, a Colab series of public play-readings.

The 1989 Mainstage production of ABUNDANCE served as the centerpiece for SCR's first California Play Festival, another Colab initiative. A year later CalFest included the premiere of MAN OF THE FLESH , which had already undergone an intensive workshop in Colab's Hispanic Playwrights Project.

HOLY DAYS needed no development per se, partly because it had received a small, successful British production prior to our American premiere. Nevertheless, under the Colab residency program, SCR brought Sally Nemeth in for rehearsals, just as we do every playwright whose play receives its first production here.

Colab has succeeded because of the philosophy behind it, summed up in two principles: The developmental process must serve the writer, not the other way around; and development must not be an end unto itself, but a means of moving the most promising new plays toward production. Emmes and Benson hold closely to these principles and convey them to everyone who contributes to the evolution of new work at SCR. We all understand—not only the literary staff, but the outstanding actors, directors, and designers whose talents bring the plays to life—that the ultimate goal is to realize the playwright's vision as faithfully as possible.

That attitude, embodied in the Collaboration Laboratory, has enabled SCR to introduce dozens of plays into the American repertory, and to count their creators as honored members of SCR's artistic family.

And it means the two of us get to leave our offices regularly to go sit in rehearsals and throw in our two-cents' worth—which isn't a bad way to spend an afternoon.

Jerry Patch, Dramaturg
John Glore, Literary Manager

PREFACE

"What are you looking for?" That's the question most frequently posed to us by playwrights and their agents. We can't give them the kind of answer they want, so over the years we've developed some stock responses.

We're looking for good writing, we tell them, knowing the answer is so general as to be useless. We don't mean to be evasive; it's just that, looking back at the fifty-or-so plays SCR has premiered in three decades, the only attribute they seem to have in common is good writing—fifty different kinds of good writing.

Of course, the truth is even if we could be more specific we wouldn't want to be. And that's another of our stock responses: If we knew what we were looking for, we tell those inquisitive writers, we wouldn't need you. The plays that most appeal to us are those that take us by surprise. Not only do they transport us to places we've never visited, they transport us to places we couldn't have imagined on our own. Playwrights who ask us what we're looking for are expecting us to guide them toward our center, while all along we want to be guided by visionary writers toward their own centers, toward undiscovered vantage points on the world in which we live.

There's a clue in that last phrase. We aren't just looking for any good play. We prefer a play that is clearly a product of its own time, a play that, by virtue of its subject, form, or point of view, is unmistakably contemporary. By the same token, it shouldn't be limited by its timeliness; it should be capable of delivering its impact to people living in other places and eras. The ideal play, for us, speaks of the here and now in a voice that's large and resonant enough to carry to there and then.

You won't find in this volume any plays about a writer's family and that family's individual quirks, tragedies, and dysfunctions. Some great plays fit that description, but for the most part such works speak in little voices that don't carry beyond the next back yard. On the other hand, neither will you find plays here that take a head-on approach to highly charged topical issues like abortion, or incest, or even AIDS; such plays almost always lose their impact as the immediacy of their subject fades.

You *will* find Craig Lucas's PRELUDE TO A KISS, in which some observers have detected the shadow of AIDS. But to the extent that Lucas may be dealing with AIDS in the play, he does so by means of a fairy-tale metaphor that affords a resonance beyond the immediate issue.

You'll find two plays, Beth Henley's ABUNDANCE and Sally Nemeth's HOLY DAYS, that locate their metaphors in history, taking moments out of America's past to make observations about the enduring American character, and about human nature across all cultures.

You'll find Octavio Solis' MAN OF THE FLESH, which borrows its metaphor from past masters, re-imagining the Don Juan legend in the terms of contemporary Chicano culture, without losing the universality of the original myth.

You'll find Howard Korder's SEARCH AND DESTROY, unquestionably a play about America today, but built on the archetypal framework of the fool's quest. Korder's sharp, jabbing voice, his ear for language and his eye for the details of character, all contribute to a portrait of our society that remains vivid outside its own context.

And you'll find Donald Margulies's SIGHT UNSEEN, which is about an artist who, at some early point in his career, probably asked someone, "What are you looking for?" Only when he turned the question back on himself—"What am I looking for?"—did he become an artist of substance, and now, when he is in danger of losing track of the question, both his artistry and his humanity hang in the balance.

These plays offer six points of reference, six daubs of paint that are part of a much larger canvas which, if one could see it all at once, might tell the world what SCR is looking for...except that the painting is always developing; it has no borders; and it's being created not only by the two of us, but by every artist who has ever contributed, will ever contribute, some color, texture, and shape to SCR's evolving body of work.

David Emmes, Producing Artistic Director
Martin Benson, Artistic Director

ABUNDANCE

Beth Henley

ABOUT THE AUTHOR

Beth Henley was awarded the Pulitzer Prize in Drama and the New York Drama Critics Circle Award for Best American Play for her first full-length play, CRIMES OF THE HEART. This play was also the co-winner in 1979 of the Great American Play Contest sponsored by Actors Theater of Louisville, prior to its move to New York. CRIMES OF THE HEART has since been produced in many leading resident theaters, on a major national tour, and in many countries around the world.

Ms Henley's second play, THE MISS FIRECRACKER CONTEST, has been produced in several regional theaters in the US, and in London at the Bush Theater. It opened in the spring of 1984 at the Manhattan Theater Club, and subsequently transferred for an extended run off-Broadway, and was published in the *Ten Best Plays of 1983-1984.*

Ms Henley's third play, THE WAKE OF JAMEY FOSTER, had its premiere at the Hartford Stage Company prior to its presentation on Broadway, directed by Ulu Grosbard. Ms Henley's one-act play AM I BLUE? was produced at Circle Repertory Company in New York. It is included in *Best Short Plays of 1983.* Her play THE DEBUTANTE BALL was presented in the Spring of 1985 at South Coast Repertory, and was presented in a substantially revised version at the Manhattan Theater Club and the New York Stage and Film Company in the spring and summer of 1988, respectively. Subsequently, it was presented in London at the Hampstead Theater Club in the spring of 1989. Her play, THE LUCKY SPOT, was presented at the Williamstown Theater Festival in the summer of 1986, and had its New York premiere at the Manhattan Theater Club in 1987. It had its London premiere in the spring of 1991.

Ms Henley's newest plays are SIGNATURE, which was given a workshop at the New York Stage and Film Company in the summer of 1990, and CONTROL FREAKS, which premiered at Chicago's Center Theater in 1992 and recently opened at the Met Theater in Los Angeles in July 1993 under the direction of Ms Henley.

Ms Henley wrote the screenplay for the acclaimed film version of CRIMES OF THE HEART, for which she was nominated for an Academy Award. The film was directed by Bruce Beresford, and starred Diane Keaton, Jessica Lange, Sissy Spacek, and Sam Shepard. She also wrote the screenplay for

MISS FIRECRACKER, starring Holly Hunter, Mary Steenburgen, and Tim
Robbins. She wrote the screenplay for NOBODY'S FOOL, starring Rosanna
Arquette and Eric Roberts. She has written a teleplay for the PBS series
TRYING TIMES, as well as a screenplay based on Reynold Price's novel
A LONG AND HAPPY LIFE. Most recently, she has completed a screenplay
for Lewis Gilbert based on her play THE LUCKY SPOT.

She was born and raised in Mississippi, graduated from Southern Methodist
University, and lives in Los Angeles.

ABUNDANCE premiered at South Coast Repertory on 21 April 1989. The cast and creative contributors were:

BESS JOHNSON . . . . O-Lan Jones
MACON HILL . . . . Belita Moreno
JACK FLAN . . . . Bruce Wright
WILLIAM CURTIS . . . . Jimmie Ray Weeks
PROFESSOR ELMORE CROME . . . . John Walcutt

Director . . . . Ron Lagomarsino
Set design . . . . Adrianne Lobel
Costume design . . . . Robert Wojewodski
Lighting design . . . . Paulie Jenkins
Music and sound . . . . Michael Roth
Stage manager . . . . Julie Haber
Assistant stage manager . . . . Delphine Urbien

Dedicated to Robert Darnell
and the spirit of Darnelli Points

CHARACTERS

BESS JOHNSON
MACON HILL
JACK FLAN
WILLIAM CURTIS
PROFESSOR ELMORE CROME

TIME

The play spans twenty-five years, starting in the late 1860s.

PLACE

Wyoming Territory and later in St Louis, Missouri

ACT ONE

Scene One

(Late 1860s. Morning. Spring.)

(Outside a stagecoach ranch in the Wyoming Territory)

(BESS JOHNSON, a young woman, sits on a bench. There is a bag at her feet. She wears a dirty travelling suit that has no buttons.)

BESS: *(Singing to herself)* Roses love sunshine
Violets love dew
Angels in heaven
Know I love you.

Build me a castle forty feet high
So I can see him as he rides by
(BESS stops singing and speaks softly to herself.) The size of the sky. The size of the sky.

(MACON HILL enters wearing green goggles and a cape. She is covered with road dust and carries a satchel and green biscuits on a platter. She is whistling. She stops when she sees BESS.)

MACON: Lord Almighty.

BESS: What?

MACON: You're like me.

BESS: Huh?

MACON: Sure. You're like me. Biscuit?

BESS: Please.

MACON: Go ahead. Help yourself. What's mine is yours; what's yours is mine. After all, you're like me. You've come out west to see the elephant. Hey, true or no?

BESS: Elephant. No.

MACON: To see what's out there; whatever's out there. *(Beat)* What do you guess is out there?

BESS: Don't know.

MACON: Right. Could be anything. I savor the boundlessness of it all.
The wild flavor. I'm drunk with western fever. Have you ever seen a
map of the world?

BESS: Un-huh.

MACON: Well, it stopped my heart. There are oceans out there. Oceans
aplenty, and I swear to you I'm gonna see one and walk in one and swim
in one for sure. I love water, it never stops moving. I want to discover gold
and be rich. I want to erect an ice palace and kill an Indian with a hot bullet.
I'm ready for some sweeping changes. How about you? We could be friends
throughout it all. It's part of our destiny. I can smell destiny. One day I'm
gonna write a novel about it all and put you in it. What's your name? *(She
produces a pad and pencil.)*

BESS: Bess Johnson.

MACON: *(Writing down the name)* Good. That's a good name for a novel.
Bess Johnson. Will you be my friend?

BESS: It'd be a pleasure. A true pleasure. Could I—could I trouble you for
another biscuit?

MACON: Why sure. Sure, I hate stinginess. You'll never get anywhere
watching every egg, nickel, and biscuit. Ya gotta let it go! Let it go! Go!
And I don't give a damn if ya never pay me back.

BESS: Thanks kindly. I'm near pined t'death with famine. These green
biscuits taste heaven to me.

MACON: Why, how long ya been at the ranché?

BESS: Ten days, I been waiting here. My travel money's all spent. Yesterday I
traded French Pete my buttons for an extra night's lodging. I'm at my rope's
end if Mr Flan don't get here real soon; I don't know what.

MACON: Who's Mr Flan?

BESS: He's the man who's coming t'pick me up. We're to be wed.

MACON: Wed? A wedding?

BESS: That's right. It's been arranged.

MACON: Then you're a bride-to-be?

BESS: Yeah.

MACON: Lord Almighty! Angels sing; devils dance! I'm a bride-to-be, too.
It's like I said, you're like me. It's true! It's true! Tell me, do ya know your
husband or is he a stranger to ya?

BESS: We had...correspondence.

MACON: Correspondence. Me too. And he sent you the fare?

BESS: Partial.

MACON: Me too! Me too! (*She whistles a few notes.*) Ya know what I hope? I hope our husbands don't turn out t'be just too damn ugly t'stand.

BESS: You think they'll be ugly?

MACON: Maybe. Maybe. But I hear divorce is cheap and easily obtainable out here in the west.

BESS: I'd never get no divorce.

MACON: Honey, I'd rip the wings off an angel if I thought they'd help me fly! You may find this hard to believe, but back home they considered me the runt of the family. See, those folks are all full, large-bodied people, and to them I appeared to be some sort of runt. But out here I can be whoever I want. Nobody knows me. I'm gonna make everything up as I go. It's gonna be a whole new experience. We're dealing with the lure of the unknown. Yeah, we're hunting down the elephant! Bang! Bang! Bang! What's wrong with you? You're looking morose.

BESS: I...I'm just hoping my husband ain't gonna be real terrible ugly.

MACON: Well, Bess, I hope so too.

BESS: It don't mention nothing about his looks in the...matrimonial ad.

MACON: Well, now that ain't good news. Folks generally like t'feature their good qualities in them advertisements.

BESS: 'Course I know I'm no prize. I got nice hair, but my eyes are too close together and my nerves are somewhat aggravated. Still, I was hoping we'd be in love like people in them stories. The ones about princesses and chimney sweeps and dragon slayers.

MACON: Oh, them stories ain't true. They ain't factual. Catapult them stories out of your brain. Do it! Do it! Catapult 'em!

BESS: I don't know, I...well, I bet he's gonna like me some.

MACON: Sure. Maybe he'll be cordial at Christmas.

BESS: I promise I'll be a good wife, patient and submissive. If only he'd come. I hope he ain't forgotten. He sent partial fare. Three letters and partial fare. Three letters all about the size of the western sky.

MACON: Damn! What size is it?

BESS: The largest he has witnessed.

MACON: Glory be.

BESS: And he loves singing. I can sing real pretty. Oh, I'm betting we're gonna be a match made in heaven, if only I ain't left stranded. See, 'cause, well, I don't know how I'll get by. I can't do nothing. I don't know nothing. I oughta know something by now. I went t'school. They must have taught me something there. But I can't even recall what my favorite color is. Maybe it's blue, but I'm just guessing.

MACON: Well, the fact is, if ya know too much, it's just gonna limit your thinking. Take me, I got this brown dress and I don't even get upset about it 'cause I got no recollection in my mind that my favorite color is blue. I mean, it may be, but I don't know it. Have another biscuit.

BESS: It's your last one.

MACON: I saved it for you. (JACK FLAN *enters. He is handsome, with an air of wild danger.*)

JACK: 'Morning.

MACON: 'Morning.

JACK: I'm looking for.... Is one of you Bess Johnson?

BESS: That's me. That's me. I'm here. I'm here. That's me.

JACK: Uh-huh.

BESS: Are you Mr Michael Flan?

JACK: No, I'm Jack Flan, Mike's brother.

BESS: Oh well, well, pleased t'meet you, Mr Jack Flan. Would you do me the great favor of taking me t'meet Mr Michael Flan?

JACK: Mike's dead.

BESS: What?

JACK: Got killed in an accident and died.

BESS: Are you saying Mr Michael Flan is no longer living?

JACK: That's right; he's dead.

BESS: Dead. Oh my. Oh my. Lord, Lord, Lord.

JACK: What's wrong with you? You never laid eyes on him. You're just some stranger.

MACON: Hey, hey, don't be so grim.

BESS: *(Crying with fury)* I wanna go home. I'll die if I stay here. I don't wanna die in this miserable, filthy territory!

JACK: Look at her crying. She's a woman alright.

BESS: Oh, how can this be? My husband's dead. He's gone. He's dead. I never even got to meet him or shake his hand or say, "I do." "I do, I do." I worked on saying them words the whole way here. Over cliffs, across streams, in the rain, in the dust. "I do, I do." Every dream I ever had I said in them words. "I do, I do, I do, I do..."

JACK: I'm gonna knock her down.

MACON: Don't do that. (JACK *shoves* MACON *aside, then goes and knocks down* BESS. MACON *comes at him with a knife. He takes her by the hair and slings her to the ground.)*

JACK: *(To* MACON*)* You're out west now. Things are different here. *(To* BESS*)* Come on with me. I'm gonna marry you. But I won't have you crying. Never again. You got that clear?

BESS: Yes.

JACK: Let's go. *(They exit.* MACON *gets to her feet.)*

MACON: That was something. I didn't mind that. That was something. (MACON *whistles to herself.* WILLIAM CURTIS *enters. He is neatly dressed. He wears a patch over the left eye. There is a scar down the same side of his face.)*

WILL: Hello. Are you Miss Macon Hill?

MACON: Yes, I am.

WILL: I'm Mr William Curtis. I've come for you. You're to be my wife.

MACON: Well, here I am. I'm ready to ride. *(They exit.)*

(End of Scene One)

Scene Two

(Later that day)

*(*JACK's *cabin.* JACK *sits in a chair.* BESS *is pulling filth-covered blankets off the floor.)*

BESS: This is a beautiful home. Some women get squeamish over fleas and ticks and lice, not me. We'll root 'em out by bathing with plenty of sheep-dip and then we'll add kerosene to the sheep-dip and boil all our clothes and bedding in the sheep-dip and kerosene. That'll root 'em out. Kill 'em all for sure. I'm gonna be happy here. I can feel it coming.

JACK: Don't start messing with things around here. That's not my way.

BESS: Uh-huh. Uh-huh.

JACK: *(A beat)* I'm not used to you being here.

BESS: *(A beat)* I can...I can cook something.

JACK: There's nothing t'cook. Got some dried beef on the shelf.

BESS: I'll fetch it. *(She gets the dried beef and brings it back to the table.)* Here.

JACK: Thanks.

BESS: Welcome. You're welcome. *(They chew on the dried beef in silence.)* Mr Flan.

JACK: Yeah?

BESS: Do you like singing?

JACK: No. *(A beat)*

BESS: Your brother said he liked singing.

JACK: You never met my brother.

BESS: He wrote it in his letters.

JACK: That he liked singing?

BESS: Yes.

JACK: Never said nothing to me about it.

BESS: I got his letters, if ya wanna look at 'em. (JACK *nods.)* Here they are. He wrote three of 'em. (JACK *takes the letters and looks at all three of them.)* In each one of 'em he mentions something about singing. Says there's not much music out here, but for the birds. I was hoping to change things for him. See, me, well, I sing... (JACK *tosses down the letters.)* Pretty letters, ain't they?

JACK: I don't read writing.

BESS: Oh, well, I could read 'em for ya. *(She picks up one of the letters and starts to read it.)* "Dear Miss Bess Johnson, I was overjoyed to receive your correspondence accepting my humble proposal of marriage. I sincerely believe you will not be disappointed living in the west. The skies out here are the largest I have witnessed. The stars hang so low you feel you could reach up and touch them with your hand...." (JACK *grabs the letter out of her hand. He tears up the letters.)*

JACK: Hey! You don't read t'me! I ain't no baby. You ain't no schoolmarm. You got that clear?! Nobody reads me nothing! Nothing! Nothing at all!

BESS: *(Overlapping)* Don't tear 'em! Please, don't tear 'em!

JACK: I did! I tore 'em! They're torn! And I don't want you singing. There'll be no singing. I don't tolerate no singing never. You hear me?

BESS: I do.

JACK: Hey, you better not start crying. Remember what I warned you about crying?

BESS: I won't. I won't never be crying. I'm telling ya. I can do things right.

(End of Scene Two)

Scene Three

(Same day)

(WILLIAM's cabin. WILL and MACON enter.)

WILL: Come on in. Here we are.

MACON: I see.

WILL: What do you mean by that, Miss Hill?

MACON: Nothing. I just see.... Here we are.

WILL: I lost it in a mining accident.

MACON: What?

WILL: No need playing coy. I see you see it's missing.

MACON: Oh, your eye.

WILL: Yeah.

MACON: Oh, well, I did observe it'd been removed.

WILL: Man knocked it out with a mining pick. It was an honest mistake. There was no violence or malice intended.

MACON: Hmm. Well, I bet you wish it didn't happen.

WILL: I intend to order a glass one just as soon as finances permit. It'll be brown, same color as the one I have left.

MACON: Uh-huh.

WILL: You can tell me right now if this makes a difference. I'll send you back if it does.

MACON: I ain't going back.

WILL: Alright. *(Pause)* Miss Hill?

MACON: Yeah?

WILL: I got something for you.

MACON: What?

WILL: It's a ring. A ruby ring. *(He takes out a ring.)*

MACON: Oh, I cherish rings.

WILL: It was my wife's.

MACON: Your wife's.

WILL: Yes, she died.

MACON: Oh.

WILL: Last winter. It was snowing. *(Pause)* She once had a photograph taken of her. Would you like to see it?

MACON: Alright.

WILL: *(He hands her a photograph.)* Her name was Barbara Jane.

MACON: What'd she die from?

WILL: No one could say for sure. She took to bed. A long time I stood by her. One night she coughed up both her lungs. There was nothing to be done.

MACON: She looks pretty sickly.

WILL: I thought she was beautiful.

MACON: Well, I don't think I want her ring.

WILL: Why not?

MACON: Could have her sickness on it. I don't want no part of it.

WILL: She never wore the ring when she was sick. She only wore it the first year of our marriage.

MACON: Why's that?

WILL: She lost three fingers in a sheep-shearing accident. One of 'em was the ring finger.

MACON: Well, y'all certainly seem t'be plagued with all sorts of disfiguring misfortunes around here.

WILL: If the ring won't do, I'll get a piece of tin and bend it around for ya. Maybe in time I can get ya another ring with a stone in it.

MACON: I'd appreciate it.

WILL: The Marrying Squire will be here at the end of the month. At that time we'll be wed.

MACON: Uh-huh. *(They glance at each other, then turn away in silence.)*

(End of Scene Three)

Scene Four

(Three months later. A summer's night. In a field. BESS *is calling out to* MACON, *who has disappeared into the night.)*

BESS: Macon! Macon, you out there? Where are you? Where'd you go? Indians could be lurking! Come back! Macon! *(*MACON *runs onstage, breathless with excitement.)*

MACON: I almost touched it!

BESS: I thought you was lost in the dark.

MACON: I almost did.

BESS: Indians might a' captured you.

MACON: From the top of that far-off hill I almost felt it.

BESS: What?

MACON: That little silver star. The one sitting there so low in the sky. See it?

BESS: Uh-huh.

MACON: Stars send off chills. Closer you get, the more chill you feel. Go on, try it. Go on, reach up for it. *(*BESS *reaches up to touch a star.)* There you go! Jump! Jump! Did ya feel the chill?

BESS: Maybe I might a' felt some sort of small chill.

MACON: The thing we gotta look out for is a falling star. You ever seen a falling star?

BESS: No.

MACON: Well, now, when we see one of them, we gotta run for it. I know I can touch one of them. *(*MACON *whistles.)*

BESS: That's a nice tune. I never heard it.

MACON: It's a good song. You wanna learn it?

BESS: Oh, I don't sing no more. Jack don't like it.

MACON: Jack don't like singing?

BESS: His brother, Michael, liked singing. But Jack don't. *(*MACON *whistles a moment.)*

MACON: I don't mean t'speak out, but your husband, well, he don't seem t'got a whole lot to recommend him.

BESS: Oh, he suits me fine. Why, I ain't sure we ain't a match made in heaven. Soon as we get the inheritance money Mr Michael Flan left. Everything'll be rosy.

MACON: Well, I sure hope things work out for you. I got doubts about my own predicament.

BESS: Don't ya get on with your new husband? He seems a good man t'me.

MACON: Well, I hate to criticize Mr Curtis. I know he does try; but, well, frankly, I'm allergic to him physically.

BESS: Is it 'cause of his eye?

MACON: Could be part of it. But even with one more eye, I might find him repulsive. *(She whistles.)*

BESS: Show me how t'do that.

MACON: What? Whistle?

BESS: Yeah.

MACON: Easiest thing in the world. Just watch me. I'll show ya how. *(She whistles. BESS tries to imitate her. She fails. MACON starts to laugh.)*

BESS: I can't get it!

MACON: You will!

BESS: When?

MACON: Soon! *(Running off)* Come on! I wanna show you the white jasmine. They're in bloom now down by the pond. *(They exit.)*

(End of Scene Four)

Scene Five

(Three months later. Autumn.)

(JACK is walking down a path near his property. He carries a load of mining equipment. He sees something coming. He hides behind a rock. MACON appears, carrying a bundle. She wears a cape and is whistling. JACK takes out his six-shooter, aims it at MACON, and fires. MACON screams in horror and throws the bundle up in the air.)

MACON: Aah! *(JACK saunters out from behind the rock brandishing the pistol.)* You trying to kill me?!

JACK: If I was, you'd be dead. *(A beat)* Better watch out. Bullets make me smile. *(He shoots off the gun and then exits. MACON stands frozen with fear and fury. BESS enters.)*

BESS: Macon, you alright?

MACON: Yeah. It was Jack. He seen a snake.

BESS: He kill it?

MACON: Scared it away. Here, I got two small items for ya. Coffee and some shoes.

BESS: Thank you, Macon, but I don't need t'take things from you no more. Me and Jack, well, everything has turned around.

MACON: You talking on account of Lockwood's mine?

BESS: That's right. Jack purchased it last night with all the inheritance money Mr Michael Flan left. It's sugared with pure gold like a town of fairies been dancing there. (MACON *whistles for a moment, then stops.*)

MACON: Pause a moment, Bess. Use the round thing above your shoulders and tell me why anyone in this world would sell a mine laden with pure gold?

BESS: ...Mr Lockwood's very old. His eyesight's poor.

MACON: Well, his mind is sharp.

BESS: What're you telling?

MACON: I know that mine. It's dry as a parched tongue. Lockwood salted that claim with gold dust just to lead greedy fools astray.

BESS: I hope that ain't so. 'Cause we paid him for it. We paid him all we had. Oh, what's gonna become of us now? Times is already harder than hard.

MACON: I know. I seen it coming. Now it's arriving at the front door.

BESS: Not at your door. Things are going good for you and Will Curtis.

MACON: Maybe in your eyes you see it that way. But me, I've come to a staunch conclusion. We gotta go. We gotta go now. We could leave here tonight.

BESS: Where'd we go?

MACON: West. We'd be going west.

BESS: Which way west?

MACON: Out past the Jack pine and yellow cedar, off through the grass that grows scarlet red across the plains, and on and on and onward.

BESS: We'd die of thirst and famine.

MACON: We'll drink plentiful before starting out, then chew constantly on small sticks to help prevent parching. Wild fruits grow all in abundance. Ripe plums will cool our fevered lips.

BESS: What about the Indians?

MACON: I got a cup of cayenne pepper and a corn knife...t'take care of 'em. Whatever happens. It don't matter. Why limit the limitless. I'll write a novel about it all and put you in it. Go with me.

BESS: I can't go.

MACON: Why not?

BESS: I'm married.

MACON: He don't treat ya no good.

BESS: I'll learn t'make him.

MACON: You can't change his nature.

BESS: I'm here to try. You go on. You go without me. Please. Ya don't need me.

MACON: You're my one friend.

BESS: I ain't special.

MACON: You looked my way.

BESS: I can't go. I gave out my oath.

MACON: *(A beat)* Here's the coffee. It's from parched corn and sorghum sweetening, but better than the dried carrot variety you been drinking. And take these shoes; those flaps of skin will never get you through the winter.

BESS: I'll pay ya back someday.

MACON: Don't mention it. I like giving gifts. It's who I am.

(End of Scene Five)

Scene Six

(A year later. Fall.)

(A clearing)

WILL: *(Offstage)* Hey, let go of that wood! You ain't stealing no more of my wood!

JACK: *(Offstage)* Stealing? I ain't stealing nothing! *(A crack of wood offstage)* Ow! (JACK *is thrown onstage.)*

WILL: I'll kill you, you son of a bitch!

JACK: You calling me a thief?

WILL: That's my wood. Pay me for it fair.

JACK: Miser.

WILL: Shiftless.

JACK: Blind mouse, one-eyed, scar-faced farmer—

WILL: *(Overlapping)* Lazy, no-good, fool's gold miner...(JACK *and* WILL *tear into each other. The fight is brutal.* MACON *enters. She carries a walking stick and wears field glasses around her neck. She dives into the fight, knocking the men apart with her stick.)*

MACON: Hey, hey, what's going on here? Stop it! Please! Hey! We're all neighbors here. Will Curtis, what is wrong?

WILL: He wants to freeload more of our wood. Hasn't paid me for the last five bundles. He ain't getting nothing else for free.

MACON: Will. Please! There's a bobcat caught in the trap line. Better go check on it before it gets loose. I don't want it on our hands.

WILL: *(To* JACK*)* You get off my place. *(*WILL *exits.)*

JACK: Good thing he went off. I might a' had t'kill him.

MACON: You come here looking for wood? *(*JACK *looks away from her.)* You know where the woodpile is. You take some and haul it on home.

JACK: Just so you'll know, I got things in the works; irons in the fire. Nothing worries me.

MACON: You oughta look to salted pork. Last year we put up 1,560 pounds at three-and-a-half cents a pound.

JACK: It don't interest me. I'd rather gamble for the high stakes. 'Afternoon, May Ann.

MACON: What?

JACK: May Ann. It's a prettier name than Macon. Its suits you better. I think I'll call you that.

MACON: Tell Bess she can keep the needle she borrowed. I won't need it back till Monday.

JACK: Uh-huh.

MACON: She's had a hard summer, losing that baby. You need t'watch after her.

JACK: Is that what I need? Is that what I need, May Ann?

MACON: That's not my name.

JACK: It is to me. *(*JACK *exits.* MACON *pauses a moment, then looks after* JACK *through the field glasses.* WILL *enters.)*

WILL: Bobcat got loose. Chewed off its paw. (MACON *quickly stops looking through the field glasses.*)

MACON: Will.

WILL: What?

MACON: I told him t'take some wood.

WILL: You what?

MACON: All they got t' burn is green twigs.

WILL: I don't like that, Macon. Why, that man's a freeloading ne'er-do-well. We don't want nothing to do with him.

MACON: Still I gotta look out for Bess. She's a friend of mine.

WILL: I don't understand about her and you. She's not special. Just some joyless creature with sawdust for brains.

MACON: Don't say that.

WILL: Look, I've observed in her strong symptoms of derangement that just ain't healthy. That ain't right.

MACON: Don't you got one drop of human kindness inside your whole bloodstream. It was just last summer she buried her infant child in a soap box under a prickly pear tree and wolves dug it up for supper.

WILL: Things haven't gone her way, that's true. Still, I cannot agree with her strange and gruesome behavior. How she dresses up that prairie dog of hers in a calico bonnet and shawl; sits there rocking it on the porch, talking to it just like it was a somebody.

MACON: People do strange things t'get by.

WILL: That may be. But everybody's got to make their own way. If they drop down, it ain't for you to carry them. (MACON *turns away from him and looks through the field glasses into the distance.*) I just don't like being exploited. I don't like the exploitation. People should earn what they get. What're you looking at?

MACON: Checking the cows.

WILL: How're the cows? Can you see the cows?

MACON: I see 'em.

WILL: Anyway, what's a load of wood? After all, we seem to be prospering. Last year we sold 1,560 pounds of salt pork at three-and-a-half cents a pound. Friday I'll go into town and see if the copper kettle you ordered from St Louis has been delivered in the mail. After all, they're the ones with problems and burdens. If their luck doesn't change, they won't make it through the winter. They'll starve to death by Christmas. When the copper kettle comes, it will improve the looks of our cabin. You spoke about it before. You said it would add cheerfulness.

(End of Scene Six)

Scene Seven

(Christmas, months later. Night.)

(JACK's cabin. It is snowing. The wind is howling. JACK sits staring. BESS is on the floor, picking shreds of wheat out of the straw mattress.)

BESS: You know what, Jack? Jack, you know what? I think it's Christmas. I've been thinking that all day.

JACK: I don't know.

BESS: I could be wrong. But I might be right. There's not much wheat in all this straw. Not much wheat to speak of. Would you agree it could be Christmas?

JACK: Where's the prairie dog?

BESS: Of course, Macon would have been here by now if it'd been Christmas. She was planning to bring us a galore of a spread. I was looking forward to it. Maybe the bad weather's put her off. The blizzards. Blinding blizzards for weeks now. Keeping Christmas from our front door. Jack, something happened to Prairie Dog.

JACK: It did?

BESS: It was when you went out trying to kill us something this morning.

JACK: Yeah.

BESS: This man came by. Some wandering sort of vagabond dressed in rags. Dirt rags. He wanted a handout. Food, you know.

JACK: We don't have anything.

BESS: I told him. I sent him on his way. "We don't have anything," I said. "I gotta go through the straw in the bed mattress picking out slivers of wheat so we won't starve here to death. I don't have food to spare some unknown wanderer." He asked me for just a cup of warm water, but I said no. Not because we couldn't spare it, but just because I didn't want him around here on the premises anymore. Something about him. His face was red and dirty. His mouth was like a hole. *(About the wheat)* This is not gonna be enough for supper, this right here.

JACK: So what happened to the dog?

BESS: As he, as the vagabond was leaving, Prairie Dog followed after him barking. He picked up a stone and grabbed her by the throat and beat her head in with it. With the rock. She's out back in a flour sack. I'd burn her to ashes, if only we could spare the wood.

JACK: This is your fault.

BESS: Yes it is.

JACK: You're so weak. You make me sick. Christ, you're useless. I may just have to kill you.

BESS: You know what? I think it is Christmas. It's Christmas, after all. And you know what? I got something for you. I been saving it for Christmas. A surprise for you. A present. A Christmas gift. I been hoarding it away for you, but the time has come. The day has arrived. Merry Christmas, Jack. *(She produces a sack of cornmeal.)*

JACK: What is that?

BESS: Cornmeal.

JACK: Cornmeal. What're you gonna do with that?

BESS: Make you some cornbread. Cornbread for Christmas. A surprise.

JACK: Yeah. Yeah, a real big surprise. Boo! Surprise! Boo!

BESS: It's special. It's a treat. Hot cornbread. A lot better than that ash-baked bread we used to have.

JACK: Yeah, sure. But I ain't gonna choke t'death on no ash-baked bread. I ain't gonna turn blue and purple and green till I die eating no ash-baked bread.

BESS: You ain't gonna die eating no cornbread neither.

JACK: You tell that to Mike. You tell that to my brother, Mike, who had himself a big hunk of cornbread and choked t'death on it while riding bareback over the swinging bridge.

BESS: I never knew about that. I never knew how he died. I swear it, I didn't.

JACK: You might not have known it. Possibly you never was told it. But I bet you guessed it. I bet you dreamed it up. First Mike, then the baby, next Prairie Dog, now me. You want us all dead, don't you? You like things dead. You want it all for yourself. Well, here, have it. Take it. *(He throws a handful of cornmeal in her face.)*

BESS: No.

JACK: *(He continues throwing the cornmeal at her.)* There. There you go.

BESS: Stop.

JACK: Take it all!

BESS: I wanted this to be good. I wanted to be your true one.

(End of Scene Seven)

Scene Eight

(Same night)

(WILL's cabin. MACON and WILL are drinking cordials. It is Christmas.)

MACON: I don't think so, Mr Curtis. I don't believe so in the slightest. We're in no agreement, whatsoever.

WILL: Reliance on one crop is too risky. I'll say no more.

MACON: I'm telling you wheat promises the largest cash return and there's nothing comparable to it.

WILL: Besides there're other cautions to attend. We don't wanna expand too rapidly. We oughtn't get ahead of ourselves.

MACON: But there's no way to get ahead of ourselves. Not with the Union Pacific track-laying crew coming through. We gotta look to the future. Did I steer you wrong about the pork prices? No, I did not. We bought up Dan Raymond's east field with the profits from salt pork. Turn that over in your head a minute.

WILL: Listen here—

MACON: Ssh! Ssh. Just turn it over. Churn it around. Let it fester. Here, now, I'll pour both of us another cordial. After all, it's Christmas. *(She pours out two drinks.)*

WILL: You have a nice way of pouring that drink. It looks delicate.

MACON: It's got a pretty color. The liquor.

WILL: Macon.

MACON: Huh?

WILL: There's, there's something for you. St Nicholas left it, I guess. *(He hands her a gift with a card. She starts to open it.)*

MACON: A present for me.

WILL: Wait, wait. There's a card. Read the card.

MACON: Oh, yeah. "Merry Christmas, Mrs Curtis. You are sweet as honey. From Brown Spot." Brown Spot?

WILL: *(He laughs.)* Yeah.

MACON: Brown Spot, the cow?

WILL: She's your favorite one, ain't she?

MACON: Not really, I prefer Whitey.

WILL: Oh, oh, well, pretend it was from Whitey. It was supposed to be from Whitey. Alright, now open the gift. But first, tell me, what do you guess it's gonna be?

MACON: I don't know. I'm hoping for a thing.

WILL: I got a feeling it's what you're hoping for. *(She opens the gift.)* Well?

MACON: What is it?

WILL: It's an eye. A glass eye. It's brown, see?

MACON: Oh, yeah.

WILL: I promised you I'd get one and I've kept that promise. Want me to put it in?

MACON: Alright.

WILL: I need a looking glass. *(He goes to put in the eye.)* I tried it on before, right when it arrived. I been saving it five weeks now. It ain't real...
(He groans.)...comfortable, but it makes a difference in my appearance. I think you'll appreciate it. *(He turns to her, wearing the eye.)* Hello.

MACON: Hi.

WILL: What do you think? Looks pretty real, huh?

MACON: Uh-huh.

WILL: If it wasn't for the scar, no one could guess which was real and which was glass.

MACON: Don't it hurt inside there?

WILL: Sure, but that's part of it. I'll adjust. Give me another cordial. That'll help it. (MACON *pours him another drink.)* I like to watch that pouring. Your hands. Delicate. *(She brings him the drink and starts to leave. He gently holds her arm.)* Say here. *(He drinks the drink.)* Macon, I know most times you don't feel like being nice to me. But I thought tonight, since I got this new eye, maybe you would.

MACON: *(A beat)* Alright. (MACON *unbuttons her top and takes it off.)* Mr. Curtis?

WILL: Yes?

MACON: Have you thought any more about planting wheat in the east field?

WILL: Not much.

MACON: It'd be a good idea.

WILL: Alright, if that's what you think. We'll do it that way. *(There is a loud, desperate knocking at the door.)*

BESS: *(Offstage)* Macon! Macon, let me in. Please. Let me in. Please, please. (MACON *rushes to the door.* BESS *enters. She wears a thin coat. She is covered with snow, wheat, and cornmeal. Frozen blood is caked to her forehead.)*

MACON: Bess, Bess, come in. Get in. Look at you. You've been hurt.

BESS: You've got to help. My husband Jack...he's in an insane condition.

MACON: She's freezing. Bring a blanket. My God. My God, Bess.

BESS: He took a torch and set our cabin on fire. It's burning hot, hot in the snow.

MACON: Will, we gotta go see to Jack Flan.

WILL: I'll see to him. I'll go. Both of you stay here. I'll handle his derangement. *(WILL exits.)*

MACON: Here, get outta these wet boots. How in the world did you get here? How did you cross the gulch in this blizzard and not freeze to death?

BESS: Freeze t'death. Freeze t'death. I like the sound of that prediction. I long for the flutter of angel's wings.

MACON: Calm down. You're in a fit of delirium. Let me wash off your face for you.

BESS: It's all uncoiling. The springs in my mind. In my body. They're all loose and jumping out. Rusted and twisted.

MACON: I should have come to you. I should have braved the storm. I had your Christmas spread all packed up, I just been waiting for a break in the weather.

BESS: I wish you'd come. I been so lonely. I been going outside and hugging icy trees, clinging to them like they was alive and could hold me back. I feel so empty sometimes I eat warm mud, trying to fill up the craving.

MACON: Hush now. You're with me now. Let me brush out your hair. You got straw and sticks in your hair.

BESS: I just wanna say...I just wanna say—

MACON: What?

BESS: Early disappointments are embittering my life.

MACON: I'll draw you a bath of herbs and water. Sleep will fall on you. It'll restore your peace.

BESS: Macon?

MACON: Huh?

BESS: Let's go west.

MACON: West?

BESS: Let's start all over. Let's start from scratch. See, I've tried and I've tried, but I'm starting to believe Jack, he's just not in my stars.

MACON: I have to say...I have to remember...I did, I always thought I'd make much more of myself than this. My husband gave me a Christmas card from our cow. Still, I need to think things out. There's a lot we don't know. Practical knowledge, reality, and facts.

BESS: But we will go?

MACON: Oh yes, we'll go. Soon we'll go.

BESS: I realize now...now that you're brushing my hair, that I love you so much more; so much more than anyone else.

(End of Scene Eight)

Scene Nine

(Over two years have passed. It is spring.)

(Outside WILL's *cabin. Bright sun shines down on* JACK, *who is sitting on a fence eating a large piece of pound cake. He wears dress pants, but is barefoot and bare-chested. His hair is slicked back.)*

*(*WILL *enters, barefoot and bare-chested. He carries two freshly pressed dress shirts.)*

WILL: Here're the shirts.

JACK: Thanks.

WILL: It's gonna be some feast we're having; some celebration. *(*WILL *puts on his shirt.* JACK *eats cake.)* Can you believe it's been four years since the Marrying Squire came through here and joined us all together in holy matrimony?

JACK: Happy anniversary.

WILL: I don't know. Time travels.

JACK: Well, what else can it do?

WILL: Yeah... Have you checked into that new land that's opened up for homesteaders?

JACK: I hear there ain't nothing available that ain't worthless.

WILL: Huh. Well, have you given any more thought to rebuilding on your own property?

JACK: Everything's burnt up over there.

WILL: Then what're ya gonna do?

JACK: About what?

WILL: This is supposed to be the deadline. Our anniversary. We made a deal, remember? You and your wife could stay here until this anniversary, then your time was up.

JACK: Fine. Our time's up. Fine.

WILL: You have been living here over two years now. I know you was sick for a time, but we've been more than generous. That cabin's damn small.

JACK: All right, we'll go.

WILL: When?

JACK: Now. Right now.

WILL: Where're you gonna go?

JACK: Don't know. What do you care?

WILL: Well, don't go tonight. Wait a while more. Tonight's a celebration. Macon's been preparing all week. We best not spoil it.

JACK: Have it your way. *(He finishes the pound cake.)*

WILL: Was that the pound cake Macon brought out for us to sample?

JACK: Yeah. Damn good cake. Warm and moist, right outta the oven. *(WILL hunts around for another piece of cake.)*

WILL: Where's my piece?

JACK: It's all gone.

WILL: She said she left a piece for me. She said she left two pieces.

JACK: Oh, well, I ate both of 'em.

WILL: Both of 'em. You ate both of 'em. But one of 'em was for me. One of 'em was my piece.

JACK: Sorry, I was hungry.

WILL: Well, damnation, I'm hungry, too! I'm hungry, too!

JACK: Look, you don't wanna ruin your supper. We're having a huge supper. It'd be a shame to spoil it.

WILL: Well, you didn't mind spoiling your supper. It didn't bother you none. Damn, I wish I had that cake.

JACK: Well, ya don't. It's gone. I hogged it. What can ya do?

WILL: Nothing. Just nothing. Not a damn thing.

JACK: Here, some crumbs. There's some crumbs left.

WILL: Forget it. I don't want it. Forget it. *(He picks up some crumbs with his fingers and sticks them into his mouth.)*

(End of Scene Nine)

Scene Ten

(Same day)

(Inside WILL's *cabin.* BESS *wears a cape. She is walking around the room whistling and waving a list in the air.* MACON *sits at a table putting a waterfall hairpiece on her head.)*

BESS: The list is complete. Completely complete. The day has arrived. The time has come. We have it all here: tallow, rice, tea, chip beef, grease bucket, water barrel, one kettle, one fry pan, powder, lead, shot.... Check it out. See for yourself. The list is complete.

MACON: Do we have heavy rope?

BESS: Yes, we do. There it is right there.

MACON: And a tar bucket.

BESS: Tar bucket, tar bucket, right there. Right there. *(A beat)* We should go tonight.

MACON: On our wedding anniversary?

BESS: Why drag things out?

MACON: It would be a cruel blow to our husbands, leaving them on our marriage day.

BESS: They'll adjust. They have each other.

MACON: I think we should wait a little.

BESS: It's just we've been waiting so long.

MACON: I wanna see what the pumpkin patch produces. I suspect, it's gonna yield a phenomenal crop.

BESS: I don't care about the pumpkins.

MACON: And I got that rainbow-colored petticoat ordered. I can't leave before it arrives. And next month I'm to be the judge of the baking contest.

Last year I won first prize. I got t'stay here and judge. It's your duty if ya win first prize.

BESS: I got this feeling that you're putting me off. You swore last time soon as I got the new items on the list we'd go. Please, I can't stay here no longer.

MACON: Things aren't so bad for you now that you and Jack have moved in here with us. You seem content most of the time.

BESS: I try not to show my hurt. I hide it in different parts of the house. I bury jars of it in the cellar; throw buckets of it down the well; iron streaks of it into the starched clothes and hang them in the closet. I just can't hide it no more. We got t'go now. You promised. You swore.

MACON: Stop pushing at me. I got things here. Out there, I don't know what. (JACK *enters, wearing his clean shirt. He is still barefoot.*)

JACK: *(To* MACON*)* Hi.

MACON: Hi.

JACK: Good pound cake.

MACON: Thanks.

JACK: Will's out there upset. Says I ate his piece a' cake.

MACON: I told you one was for him.

JACK: I was hungry.

MACON: Shame on you, Jack Flan. I'll go take this bowl out to him. He can lick the batter. (*She exits. There is a horrible moment of silence.* BESS *gets* JACK's *boots and takes them to him.*)

BESS: I polished your boots, Jack. (JACK *puts on a boot.* BESS *stands, staring at the floor.*)

JACK: I can't see myself in the toe. (BESS *kneels down and slowly starts to shine the boot.* JACK *gives her a glance filled with cold-blooded disdain.*)

(*End of Scene Ten*)

Scene Eleven

(*That night*)

(WILL's *cabin, after the anniversary supper.* WILL, MACON, JACK, *and* BESS *are all gathered.*)

JACK: Listen to me. I'm asking you. I'm making a point. Why do we have to be hungry? Why do we have to be hot or cold? Why do we have to stink? If someone could find a cure, a potion, an elixir for one of these conditions or possibly all four of 'em, that person could make a whole lot of money. Picture a killing. Picture money to burn. The facts are simple. Nobody wants to stink. Not really. Not if they thought about it. They'd come to me; I'd give them the potion; they'd cross my palm with silver; thank you very much, next customer.

MACON: It sounds like an exciting prospect.

JACK: It's how my mind works.

WILL: Well, he's right about one thing, nobody wants to stink.

BESS: I know I don't. I used to put vanilla behind my ears, but Jack said I smelt like food.

JACK: I'd love another piece of that delicious pound cake. It melts like butter in my mouth. (MACON *takes the last piece of cake and pushes it onto* JACK's *plate.*)

MACON: Well, I'm delighted nothing's going to waste.

WILL: Was that the last piece?

MACON: *(Nods)* Uh-huh.

JACK: *(Biting into the cake)* Mmm, mmm. You cook better than anybody I ever knew.

MACON: Thank you, Jack, but Bess helped out a lot.

BESS: Not much really.

JACK: She's good at scrubbing dishes, but all her cakes fall flat as nickels.

MACON: Why, that's not true, Jack Flan. Why, that two-layer strawberry cake she made for my birthday was a sensation.

BESS: Oh, no, Macon, you don't remember. It was a five-layer carrot cake I made for you, but it only rose half an inch high. We all got such a big laugh out of it.

MACON: Oh, that's right. I remember now.

WILL: Your wife sure is good for a laugh, I'll say that. Remember when she asked me, "How'd I get my eye t'grow back?" *(Everyone laughs.)* She thought this glass eye was a real eye that just sprouted back there in the socket like a radish.

JACK: She's a howl alright.

BESS: *(Cheerfully)* I guess I've just been dreadfully stupid all my life.

MACON: Don't listen to them. They're only having fun. It's all foolishness. Why, no one's even noticed the bow in Bess's hair. Turn around, please. Now isn't that a lovely sight?

JACK: Yes, it is. She's got pretty hair. Her eyes are too close together. But she's got pretty hair. *(To* MACON*)* What about you? Your hair looks different tonight. What happened to it?

MACON: Waterfall curls. I ordered them from Boston. They're the latest sensation.

JACK: Ain't they something.

WILL: Delicate.

JACK: Lovely, lovely, lovely.

BESS: The ribbon's my favorite color. It's blue. Macon lent it to me. It's her favorite color, too. We're alike, us two. *(She points to a bucket of daisies.)* Both of us love daisies. They're our favorite flower.

MACON: Oh, daisies aren't my favorite flower. My favorite flowers are tulips.

BESS: Tulips?

MACON: They grow in this small country called Holland. They're the most beautiful flowers in the world. Daisies don't compare. Why, daisies are really nothing more than common weeds.

BESS: Well, I'm sure, if I ever got to see a tulip, they'd be my favorite flower, too.

MACON: Maybe someday we'll all go over to Holland and pick rows and rows of tulips. That would be a time to remember. Filling our skirts with golden tulips and tossing 'em up in the sky! Ho! Oh, I feel like being boisterous, let's have some celebrating! I wanna dance!

JACK: Alright!

WILL: Go ahead!

BESS: *(Overlapping)* Me too! Me too! I love to dance!

MACON: I have a step I know. It's from the quadrille. It's the latest dancing fashion.

JACK: Let's see it!

MACON: Everyone's gotta clap! (MACON, BESS, *and* WILL *all start clapping.)* Come on, get the rhythm going! That's good! Keep it going! Jack Flan, why aren't you clapping?

JACK: I don't do anything to music. I don't dance to it. I don't clap to it. I like to watch it, but I won't join it.

MACON: You are as ridiculous as ever, surely more so. Here, hold my combs for me. Hold them, silly. Hold my combs. *(She gives her hair combs to* JACK. *He holds them for her. To* WILL *and* BESS:*)* Clap for me now. Louder, please! Louder! (MACON *does some fancy dance steps to the clapping.)*

BESS: Bravo! Bravo!

WILL: She's delicate! Look how delicate!

JACK: Look at her go! Swing them curls.

BESS: Oh, I wanna join in!

MACON: Come on, Bess! Take a turn! *(BESS starts dancing wildly.)* That's it! Go now! Wow! What a dancer!

WILL: Watch out! Watch out! Oh, let it ride! Yes sir, yes sir, let it ride! *(BESS kicks her foot up high and falls on her butt.)*

BESS: Oops!

MACON: Oh, well, that was good! That was good! Give her a hand!

BESS: I fell down. I can't do things right. I think I'm clumsy.

WILL: You took a spill alright. Up in the air you went and down again.

JACK: Try to be more ladylike. Everyone saw all your things under there.

MACON: Come on, take another spin.

BESS: I don't wanna dance anymore.

MACON: Come on. You can do it.

BESS: No, please, let me be.

MACON: Well, I know, why don't you sing for us?

BESS: I don't sing. You know I don't sing.

JACK: That's right. She told me when we got married that she never sang. Didn't you mention that the very first day we met?

BESS: That's right. At one time I did sing, but I don't anymore.

MACON: Well, if you sang once, you can sing again. Why, I believe I've even heard you singing when you wash the clothes.

BESS: Oh, that's not singing; that's more like humming.

MACON: Well, if you can hum, you can sing. Please, sing a song for us. I'd like to hear it.

BESS: Can I, Jack?

JACK: I don't know, can you?

BESS: Well, I do remember this one tune.

MACON: Good, let's hear it. You're on stage now. The stage is set for your song. The curtain is rising on you. Welcome Bess Flan and her singing! *(She claps.)*

BESS: *(Singing)* Down in the valley
The valley so low
Hang your head over
Hear the wind blow
Hear the wind blow, dear
Hear the wind blow
Angels in Heaven
I love you so

Roses are blue, dear
Roses are blue
Roses are blue
They're so, so blue
Blue, real, real blue...

MACON: That was wonderful.

BESS: I...I guess I've forgotten the song. Some of it. How it goes.

WILL: I know that song. I've heard it before. It didn't sound right.

MACON: Do you know another one?

JACK: She didn't know that one.

MACON: She knew most of it and she's got such a lovely voice.

JACK: I don't know a thing about singing, but it seems to me, if you're gonna sing a song, you need to know the words to the song you pick.

BESS: I used to know a lot of songs. I knew 'em all by heart. It's just I haven't sung ever since I come out here. It felt funny opening up my throat to sing. Like it was somebody else who was singing. Somebody else who wasn't me. I think I'm gonna go outside in the moonlight and pick some night-blooming jasmine out by the pond. Their fragrance draws me to 'em. The smell of 'em and the moonlight. (BESS *exits.)*

JACK: For no apparent reason, she seems to have lost her mind.

MACON: I think you hurt her feelings about her singing.

JACK: What? I did not. I didn't say anything against her singing except she should brush up on the words.

MACON: Maybe you should go see to her.

JACK: She don't want me to see to her.

MACON: Why not?

JACK: She's mad at me about her damn singing.

WILL: All the cake's gone, I suppose.

MACON: Yes.

WILL: My eye's burning. I'm ready to take it out for the evening. (MACON *starts for the door.*) Where're you going?

MACON: Out to see to her. (MACON *exits. Offstage.*) Bess...Bess...(*Etc.*)

WILL: (*A beat*) Think they'll be alright out there in the dark?

JACK: I don't know.

WILL: There're wild animals out there this time of night. Coyotes for sure. Bears and wolves.

JACK: Indians, maybe.

WILL: Macon! Macon! (WILL *exits.*)

MACON: (*Offstage*) What? Huh?

WILL: (*Offstage*) Macon, come back in here. I'll get Bess. (JACK *gets up, goes and pours himself a drink.* MACON *enters.* JACK *looks at her, then downs the drink.*)

JACK: Whiskey?

MACON: No.

JACK: (*Pouring himself another drink*) Are you sure...May Ann?

MACON: Don't you call me that. Ever.

JACK: Alright. Here're your combs back. I been holding them for you. Pretty combs. Lucky, too. Lucky to be running all through your hair.

MACON: Don't talk to me. Sit there and don't talk to me.

JACK: (*A beat*) May Ann; May Ann; May Ann.

MACON: Shut up.

JACK: You been circulating in my head. All through my head. You're more vivid to me than any other thought. I can't get you outta here. Can't knock you out; can't drink you out; can't scream you out. Never, never. You always here.

MACON: Stop it. Don't do this. Stop it.

JACK: Can't you see that I am outta control of my feelings over you?

MACON: Look, I don't want anything to do with you. I got a husband, Will. You got a wife, Bess, who is my dearest friend of mine. I would never, ever imagine betraying her feelings. Never, ever, even if I did care for you, which I do not and never will and never could; 'cause in all honesty, there's absolutely not one thing about you I can bear to stand. You're mean and selfish and a liar and a snake; I spit on your grave, which can't get dug up fast enough and deep enough to suit me just fine.

JACK: *(A beat)* Well, I just wanna know one thing. You tell me one thing. Why did you ask me to hold your combs for you? You chose me to hold your combs. You placed them in my hand. Why'd you do that? Huh?

MACON: Because I... You were standing there nearest to me, and I realized how I was afraid when I danced the combs would fly out of my hair and get lost in some faraway, far-off corner of the room. You must know, I mean it is common knowledge, that you can have somebody hold your combs for you and still believe with your whole being and heart that you hate them and they're worse than bad, but you just need your combs held and they happen to be standing in arm's reach.

JACK: You certainly are talking a lot. Rambling on. Why's that?

MACON: I...I don't know. I'm just talking. I just feel like talking. I got this sensation that keeps on telling me that silence ain't safe.

JACK: Hush now.

MACON: No, I can't allow no silence 'cause then something real terrible's gonna happen. The world might stop moving and that could start the earth shaking and everything'll just fall into cracks and openings and horrible holes—

JACK: Just hush a moment.

MACON: No, I won't, I can't, the world will break open; the oceans will disappear; the sky will be gone; I won't; I can't; I won't—

JACK: Hush or I'll have to gag you.

MACON: It won't do no good. I'll still go on mumbling and moaning all under the gag.

JACK: Maybe then, I'll just have to break your neck. *(He grabs her and holds his hand to her throat.)* There now. Be very still. *(MACON freezes.)* Hear that? The world's not falling apart. Hear that? *(She nods her head.)* You can handle it, can't you?

MACON: Yes.

JACK: *(He removes his hand from her throat.)* You can handle it just fine. *(He puts his hand on her breast.)* Tell me how you can handle it.

MACON: I can.

JACK: Just fine.

MACON: Yes. *(They embrace with a terrible passion, tearing at each other like beasts. Finally, she breaks away. Tears of rage stream down her face.)* Stay away. You viper. You twisted snake. (JACK *looks at her helplessly. He goes to get a drink.* MACON *straightens her dress and hair, then sits in a chair with her arms folded.* WILL *comes in the door carrying* BESS's *cape and an arrow. His face is white. He is in a panic.)* Will?

WILL: She's not out there by the pond. She's disappeared.

MACON: That's her cape.

WILL: I found it on the ground. And this. *(He produces an Indian arrow from under the cape.)*

MACON: Oh my God. Where is she? What's happened?

JACK: Whose is it?

WILL: Looks like Oglala.

JACK: You think Indians got her? *(*MACON *runs to the door and calls out in the night.)*

MACON: Oh God! Bess! Bess! *(*WILL *grabs* MACON *in the doorway.)*

WILL: Macon!

MACON: Please, God! Bess! *(Blackout)*

(End of Act One)

ACT TWO

Scene One

(Five years later. WILL's cabin. A spring night.)

(MACON is drinking whiskey. WILL and JACK are eating huge pieces of cake. JACK has a mustache.)

JACK: I love this cake.

WILL: It's got a delicate flavor.

MACON: I know it's both your favorite. Happy anniversary, everyone.

WILL: Happy anniversary.

JACK: Happy anniversary.

MACON: Can you believe how fast time travels? Nine years I been living out here on this plain. Youth isn't really all that fleeting like they say. I mean, it seems solid, like it was there, the time you spend being youthful. The rest here, it just flies by, like everything'll be over before you can breathe.

JACK: I don't like to discuss time. It's not my favorite subject, I'd as soon not hear about it.

MACON: I'm sorry, Jack. I know anniversaries are hard for you. Here, let's hand out the presents.

WILL: They're some major presents this year. Some major surprises. *(MACON hands out two gifts that are wrapped identically.)*

MACON: Here you go. I ordered them from the catalogue. I hope you like 'em.

JACK: Thanks.

WILL: Thanks, Macon. *(After opening the gift)* Well, that's nice. A fancy cup.

MACON: It's a mustache cup. So you won't get your mustache wet when you drink.

JACK: Well, that's a crafty idea. It oughta come in real handy.

WILL: I ain't got no mustache.

MACON: Oh, well, maybe you'll grow one. Jack's looks real nice on him. I think mustaches are the coming thing.

JACK: Here, pour me some cordial. Let me test mine out.

MACON: Alright, let's see.

WILL: Anyway, I could still use it. I'll just drink out of this other side. (MACON *pours* JACK *a cordial. He drinks from his mustache cup successfully.*)

MACON: Oh, look!

JACK: Pretty handy. Pretty handy.

WILL: Macon, I know there's concern now that the railroad's being rerouted, but I went on and splurged. I got these for you. I know they're what ya wanted. (*He presents* MACON *with two red pillows.*) Scarlet plush sofa pillows. Two of 'em.

MACON: Oh, thank you, Will! Thank you! They're so pretty; aren't they pretty!

WILL: They'll cheer up the place.

MACON: They will. Oh, I appreciate it, thank you. Now, if only I could get a new room built, I'd be satisfied. But perhaps not. Seems like I've always something to wish for.

WILL: You do like the pillows though?

MACON: Uh-huh.

JACK: I got a gift for you May Ann.

MACON: You do? Why thank you, Jack.

WILL: (*About the gift*) It looks kinda small. (MACON *opens the gift.*)

MACON: A ring. It's a ring. I cherish rings.

JACK: It's sapphire blue. The color you like best.

MACON: (*Trying the ring on*) Look, how it fits.

JACK: Just right.

WILL: I don't like him giving you a ring. I'm your husband. You're supposed t'wear my ring.

MACON: Will, I wore that tin band ya gave me till it tore right off.

WILL: I always figured to get ya another one. And now he comes in with this sapphire ring, knowing blue is your favorite color just like you was his wife or something. (*To* JACK) It's not right! You set your own house on fire, set it aflame, burn it t'ashes, and then move in here with us. Just come t'stay and don't ever leave; start giving out rings. Rings are what you give to your wife and she's not your wife. She's my wife. She don't want this ring. Save it for you own damn wife.

MACON: Will, what's wrong with you? You know he ain't got no wife.

WILL: I wouldn't be so sure about that.

MACON: I don't wanna be sure about it. I sure don't wanna be sure. But we've hunted all over for her for years.

JACK: We sent out searching parties.

MACON: We put articles in broadsides, and made inquiries to U.S. Army officers.

JACK: I never wanted to give up hope, but when that hunter from the trading post brought us that scalp....

MACON: She had such beautiful hair.

JACK: It's all I got left of her. My darling Bess. How I miss her apple butter cheeks now that they're gone.

WILL: People don't always die when they're scalped. You know that, don't ya?

JACK: Yeah.

WILL: Sometimes, they take the scalping knife and cut just a small tuft off at the crown of the head. People recover. It happens a lot. Happy anniversary, Jack. (*He hands an official-looking letter to* JACK.)

JACK: What's this?

WILL: A letter from the U.S. Army. They got your wife. They're gonna deliver her to ya in an Army ambulance. (JACK *grabs the letter. He realizes he can't read it.* MACON *grabs the letter.*) A Mexican fur trader tipped off a Captain Patch at Fort Sully. The Captain says they had to threaten the chief, Ottawa, with a massacre 'fore he'd sell her back. They got her for two horses, three blankets, a box of bullets, and a sack of glass beads.

MACON: I don't believe this. She's alive.

JACK: I wonder what she'll look like? How do people look when they've been scalped?

MACON: It says here, she's been tattooed on her arms and on her chin.

JACK: Tattooed?

MACON: It don't matter. She won't have changed that much. She's alive. They're bringing her to us and she's still alive.

(*End of Scene One*)

Scene Two

(A few days later. BESS stands rooted in the center of the room. She is barefoot. Her skin is dark and burnt; her hair is thin and sun-bleached; her chin has been tattooed. She wears an enormous dress that was lent to her at the fort. MACON and WILL stand around her. JACK stands alone, gazing at her from the corner of the room.)

MACON: Bess. Bess. Welcome back. Welcome home. We've missed you. We've prayed for your return and here you are back from the vale of death. Fresh from pandemonium.

WILL: I don't think she likes being inside. I bet, you ain't used to having a roof over your head? It agitates ya, don't it?

JACK: No point in pumping her. She don't wanna talk.

MACON: Well, I'm sure it was an awful experience but it's over. Right now you probably could use a bath. Will, go bring a couple of buckets of water for me from the well. Jack, you go fetch the washtub.

JACK: Alright, but I bet she don't remember what a bath is. *(WILL and JACK exit.)*

MACON: Everything's gonna be fine. Just fine. Just very fine. In honor of your homecoming we're having a big juicy ham. *(BESS retches.)* What's wrong?

BESS: Thought of hog eaters make me choke.

MACON: What's wrong with hog? It's just pig. It's just pork.

BESS: *(Fiercely)* Mud and water animal, bad.

MACON: Well, we could have something else. Vegetables. A lot of vegetables and pumpkin pie for dessert. You remember our pumpkin patch? Well, anyway, it's doing real well. People come by at Halloween time and pick out their own jackerlanterns. We make a little money from that venture. It comes in handy. It's not like times are flush around here. Wheat prices have dropped and the railroad's been rerouted. We're in bad debt 'cause of purchasing three fields we don't have the resources to work. But like they say, trouble comes in twos. I'm hoping someday things'll be different and we'll have an abundance. Don't you remember me at all? I'm your friend. I taught you how to whistle. *(She whistles.)* Don't ya remember? *(She whistles again; she stops. BESS looks at her. MACON whistles with a desperate intent. BESS whistles back to her, very softly.)* Bess.

BESS: Friend.

MACON: Right. Yes. It's gonna be alright. Everything'll be just like it was. Sour milk will help bleach down that dark skin, and we'll get ya a brand-new dress. A blue one.

BESS: Blue.

MACON: Yeah, one that'll fit ya just right. Lord, that captain's wife musta been bigger than a mule. A real mud and water animal, that captain's wife.

BESS: Oh, big. *(They laugh.)*

MACON: I don't know but somehow, you survived it.

BESS: I picture you.

MACON: What? You pictured me?

BESS: Hunt the elephant.

MACON: The elephant?

BESS: Bang, bang, bang.

MACON: Oh, Bess. I think you're gonna need some false curls. And maybe some cornstarch over that chin. Or veils. Sweet little net veils. (BESS *feels her chin.)*

BESS: Ottawa.

MACON: What?

BESS: To be his bride. They mark me.

MACON: You were a bride?

BESS: *(She nods.)* Two...two children. Chante, Hunke-she. Ottawa. I thought he was true one. He gave me black horse.

MACON: No, no. He was bad. He was an Indian. He was bad.

BESS: Yes, bad. Sold me. Sold me cheap. Two horses, blanket, beads, bullets. Cheap.

MACON: Bess, you can't...don't ever tell Jack.

BESS: No.

MACON: No one else. Don't tell anyone else. (JACK *enters with the washtub.)* Jack. Jack, she's talking. She don't like pork, but she's talking.

BESS: Jack.

JACK: Look at her. She's disgusting.

MACON: Jack, don't—

JACK: *(Running on)* She smells like old cheese.

MACON: Stop it!

JACK: *(Running on)* I wish they'd never found her.

MACON: Hush up! Hush! *(JACK grabs MACON passionately in his arms, smelling and caressing her. He rams his fingers through her hair, tearing out her combs.)*

JACK: I want you. Not her. Only you. Understand me?

MACON: *(Overlapping)* Let me go. Let go. Get away. *(MACON pushes him away.)*

JACK: She may be back. But nothing's changed. *(JACK exits. MACON turns to BESS, who stares at her with anguished eyes.)*

MACON: Bess, please, he...I'm sorry. I never....You must believe me. I thought you were dead. They brought us your scalp. You were gone so long. So many years.

BESS: No. You. I saw. *(Pointing to MACON's combs)* Combs. You gave him. He held them. I saw.

MACON: It'll be over now. I promise. I'll make it up to you. I'll make it right, I swear. Everything will be just the same.

(End of Scene Two)

Scene Three

(A week later. A hot summer night.)

(WILL sits outside the barn hammering together a chain. He now has a moustache.)

(MACON enters.)

MACON: Have you finished?

WILL: Not yet.

MACON: It's always hot. Summer's almost over and it hasn't rained once. There's no relief.

WILL: I think you're working the ox too hard. It needs more rest. More water.

MACON: We have to work the fields.

WILL: If the ox gets sick, it'll be over for us.

MACON: What do you want? The bank is breathing down our necks. When will you finish that?

WILL: I don't know.

MACON: I need it by morning. I can't chase her and be in the fields. Not in this heat.

WILL: I don't like the idea of this.

MACON: I don't know how else to stop her from running away. She bites through rope.

WILL: Why not let her go?

MACON: She's my friend, I have to save her. We got to be patient. We got to wean her from her savage ways. She'll come around in time. God, you look—

WILL: What?

MACON: I don't know, old, I guess.

WILL: Maybe it's the moustache.

MACON: Oh yeah. You have a.... You grew one. (MACON *exits.* WILL *continues hammering on the chain.*)

(End of Scene Three)

Scene Four

(A month later. A hot day.)

(Outside WILL's *cabin.* JACK *aims his six-shooter at an offstage target. He fires the gun. He misses his target.)*

JACK: Damn. *(He shoots two more bullets. He keeps missing his offstage target. This puts him in a rage.)* Damn, hell, damn. (MACON *appears from the direction of the barn.)*

MACON: What are ya shooting at?

JACK: Playing cards. I used t'could split 'em at thirty paces.

MACON: Stop wasting powder. (JACK *turns around and points the gun at her.)* You don't scare me anymore.

JACK: And you don't make me smile. *(He lowers his gun.)*

MACON: Your wife's here for that.

JACK: Uh-huh.

MACON: *(Softly, intensely)* It's all over between us.

JACK: It wasn't over in the barn last night.

MACON: Well, now it is.

JACK: You been telling me that for some time. I'm starting to doubt your word.

MACON: Go clean out the chicken coop. Earn your keep.

JACK: I still smell you. *(He embraces* MACON. *She responds.)*

MACON: *(With loathing)* I wanna be rid of you. Why can't I be rid of you? *(BESS appears. She wears a blue dress and is barefoot. She has a shackle around her foot and is chained to an offstage stake.* MACON *and* JACK *break apart. They stare at her for a brief moment before* JACK *exits toward the barn.)* Where're your shoes? You have to wear shoes. We all wear shoes around here. And you need to keep that veil on to cover your face. Those tattoos are not proper. People frown on 'em. *(WILL enters. He looks very glum.)* Will! Will, you're back. How'd it go? Not good? Not so good? What? Huh? Speak! Will you speak!

WILL: They won't renew the note. They're repossessing the steeltipped plow and the barbwire. They want our horse and mule and hogs, even our ox. Everything we used as security.

MACON: They can't take our livelihood. The last two years, there's been a drought.

WILL: They've heard all about the drought.

MACON: I'll go into town. I'll fix this myself. You can never get anything done. You're incapable. I'll get my hat and gloves. I'll get this settled. *(She goes into the cabin.)*

WILL: *(To* BESS*)* I understand why you wanna run away. I'd let you go, but she keeps the key. Me, I'm not sure why I stay. I don't know what I expect to get. She used to be nice to me sometimes for very short intervals of time. Not anymore. I don't know what I expect to get now. I mean, from now on. *(MACON appears from the cabin wearing a hat and gloves. She carries* BESS's *shoes and veil.)*

MACON: Have you hitched the wagon?

WILL: Not yet.

MACON: Go do it. *(WILL exits for the barn. Throughout the following,* MACON *dresses* BESS *in the shoes and veil.)* Will Curtis is a very commonplace type man. Really, anyone who would spend money to buy a glass eye makes me laugh. You'll see, I'll go into that bank and come out with a loan for a windmill, a gang plow, and twenty cord of barbwire. Great invention, barbwire. Keeps what you want in and all the rest of it out. There, that's better. That blue dress looks good. You look pretty in it. I sacrificed a lot to get it for you. I want to make you happy. I'd take these chains off, if only you would stay. Will you stay? Bess. Bess. *(A beat)* I wish you'd speak to me. *(A beat)* No. Alright. I'll bring some daisies back for you, if I see them on the road. *(MACON exits.* BESS *jerks violently at her chain. She struggles with fierce rage, pounding the chain. She moans with unbearable despair and finally sinks to the ground, exhausted.* JACK *and* PROFESSOR ELMORE CROME, *a distinguished-looking young man, enter from the barn road.* JACK *holds money in his hand.)*

JACK: *(Indicating* BESS*)* Here she is. Right there. Go ahead. Look at her. *(He removes her veiled hat.)*

ELMORE: Why is she chained up?

JACK: We've had to restrain her to prevent her from returning to the wilds.

ELMORE: I see. Mrs Flan?

JACK: I didn't say you could talk to her. *(*ELMORE *hands* JACK *another bill.)* Alright. But she don't talk back.

ELMORE: How do you do, Mrs Flan. I'm Professor Elmore Crome. It's an honor to make your acquaintance. I read about your brutal capture in a broadside. What an amazing feat to have survived such an ordeal. You're a remarkable woman. I'm in awe of your strength and courage.

JACK: She don't understand nothing you say.

ELMORE: One more word, please. I just...I just wish so much I could hear about your experiences from your own lips. I was hoping we could write a book together. A book that would help prevent others from falling prey to similar atrocities.

JACK: Write a book. Why she ain't spoke one word since they brought her back. *(Sympathetically)* She's just a pitiful specimen.

ELMORE: Please, I have a gift for you. I brought a gift. *(He hands her a silver mirror wrapped in a handkerchief. She looks at herself in the mirror. She touches the tattoos on her chin.)* I know people would want to read about you. People all over the world. I'm sure you have so much to tell. So many adventures to impart. You must know a great deal about Indian ways. About their lives; about their treachery.

JACK: That's enough now.

*(*BESS *looks* ELMORE *in the eye. He looks back at her.)*

JACK: I said time to go.

ELMORE: Good afternoon, Mrs Flan. In all honesty, I must say, you have the bravest eyes I have ever witnessed. *(*JACK *and* ELMORE *start to leave.)*

BESS: Don't—

ELMORE: *(Stopping)* What?

BESS: Go.

ELMORE: Yes.

BESS: I do. I know treachery. I could write book. A big book. All about treachery.

ELMORE: Excellent.

(End of Scene Four)

Scene Five

(Two months later)

(The yard in front of WILL's cabin. WILL rushes onstage. He is breathing hard. His eyes are grief-stricken. He stops, sits down, and puts his hands over his face.)

(JACK appears from the cabin carrying a pitcher of cool punch and two tin cups.)

JACK: 'Morning, Will. How're things going?

WILL: The wheat's burnt dead. There's no saving it. The ox just collapsed down in the dirt. He's alive, he's struggling, but he can't get back up. Could I have a drink? I'm parched.

JACK: I made this beverage for the Professor and Bess. They get real thirsty working on the book.

WILL: I just want a sip.

JACK: Sorry. *(MACON appears from the fields. She hauls a load of wilted corn. She is in a state of mad frenzy.)*

MACON: Christ. Will. The ox. The look in his eyes. God, how he's suffering. Did you get the gun?

WILL: Not yet.

MACON: Go get it. Shoot him! Kill him! Blow out his brains! I can't bear it! He keeps looking at me like I owe him something!!! *(WILL goes into the cabin to get a gun.)* Where were you last night?

JACK: I didn't come.

MACON: I waited for you.

JACK: I couldn't get away.

MACON: Why not? *(BESS is heard singing "Down In The Valley.")*

JACK: Because of her.

MACON: Her.

JACK: Yeah.

MACON: Did you stay with her?

JACK: What could I do? She's my wife. (BESS *and* ELMORE *enter.* BESS *carries a parasol. She wears a cape and new shoes. She doesn't wear her veil. We see her tattoos.* ELMORE *has a pad and pen. He is constantly taking notes.)*

ELMORE: What a voice you have! Like an angel!

BESS: Every time the Oglalas raised scalps on a pole and threatened to slay me, I'd sing for them. They'd fall to their knees and listen to my song, entranced, like charmed wolves. Ottawa, the head man, gave me strings of beads; others gave me acorns, seeds, ground nuts, feathers. Any treasure they possessed so I would favor them with my singing.

ELMORE: Amazing. Quite a provocative tale. Ah! The punch! Please serve Mrs Flan a glass. I'm sure she must be parched. (JACK *serves punch, then holds* BESS's *parasol to shade her.)*

BESS: Oh, no. Why I often went months without a drop of any drink during my stay in captivity.

ELMORE: Fascinating. How did you survive?

BESS: I'd chew constantly on a small stick to help prevent parching, or I'd hunt for wild fruits that grow all in abundance. (*She whistles softy.)*

ELMORE: You are an amazing creation. How anyone could have endured such hardship.

MACON: She pictured me.

ELMORE: What?

MACON: She pictured me. (WILL *comes out of the cabin with a gun.)*

WILL: Macon, I have the gun.

MACON: Not now.

WILL: I...I'm going to shoot the ox. It has to be done. He's suffering. *(He heads toward the field.)* Won't you please come?

MACON: Shoot it by yourself.

WILL: I'll need somebody to help me slaughter it. Jack, would you?

JACK: The Professor pays you for our room and board. I'm no hired hand. (WILL *exits.)*

MACON: Bess, tell the Professor how you pictured me when you was captured.

BESS: I thought about ya. I thought about all my loved ones back home.

ELMORE: It must have been unbearable...your sorrow.

BESS: It's true, I've suffered. But I come out here drunk with western fever. I wanted to see the elephant. To hunt down the elephant. Bang! Bang! Bang! I savor the boundlessness of it all! The wild flavor!

ELMORE: You take my breath away. How powerfully you speak in your simple, unadorned language. When your book comes out we must send you on the lyceum lecture circuit. What a sensation you'd make.

BESS: You flatter me, really.

MACON: My Lord, yes. Just imagine Bess on a big stage in front of a whole room full of people. Such a shy little thing. She'd die of fright. You need somebody who's got a real knack for that sort of thing. Ya know, I once played the Virgin Mary in a Christmas pageant. I had such a saintly face, an unearthly glow. I cried real tears when the innkeeper told us there was no room for us at his inn.

ELMORE: (*A beat*) It seems to me, the sun's very bright here. Why don't we go work in the willow grove down by the pond.

BESS: Yes. I'll tell you all about how the horrid hell hounds tattooed my face with sharp sticks dipped in weed juices and the powder from blue mud stones.

ELMORE: Monstrous savages. Godless perpetrators of butchery. (*He and* BESS *exit.*)

MACON: I wore a blue robe as the Virgin Mary. Blue looks good on me. It's my best color, although I did not know it at the time.

JACK: Something about you's changed. You've lost the stars in your shoes. You used to run everywhere you'd go.

MACON: Well, what about you? Look at you. Serving punch, toting parasols, bowing and scraping.

JACK: I do, what I do.

MACON: You live like a leech.

JACK: Would you give me back the ring I gave you? I want to give it to my wife. (*An offstage gunshot is heard.*)

MACON: Take it. Here, take it.

WILL: (*Offstage*) God, it's still alive. Macon!

MACON: Good, it's over. Good.

WILL: (*Offstage*) It's looking at me.

MACON: I'll kill it. I'll blow it dead. I'll do it! (MACON *exits.* JACK *looks after her. He tosses the ring up in the air and starts offstage. As he goes toward* BESS *and the* PROFESSOR, *we hear one last shot.*)

(End of Scene Five)

Scene Six

(The following spring)

(WILL sits alone in the yard. BESS and ELMORE are gathered in WILL's cabin. ELMORE is looking through a portfolio taking out letters, contracts, illustrations, etc. BESS is waving a check through the air.)

ELMORE: A phenomenon. Your book is a phenomenon!

BESS: I've hit pay dirt!

ELMORE: *(Looking at a sheet of figures)* It's astonishing! No one can believe it!

BESS: I must have a pet song bird! We'll sing a duet together!

ELMORE: Over sixty thousand copies sold!

BESS: Oh, and get me a giant harp with gold cherubs and an ice palace to keep it in.

ELMORE: Whatever your heart desires.

BESS: *(Singing)* Roses are blue, oh, roses are blue....

ELMORE: *(Overlapping)* Now I have some correspondence that requires your attention.

BESS: Yes, yes, proceed; proceed.

ELMORE: *(Presenting a letter)* The President of Indian Affairs wants to dine with you at the White House the day you arrive in Washington.

BESS: Oh, delightful. I'm delighted. How thrilling! I hope they don't serve any pig.

ELMORE: No, of course not. I'll alert them to your wishes. All pig shall be banned. Now here's an inquiry from actor-manager-playwright Dion Boucicault. He wants to adapt your book into a hit play.

BESS: Dion Boucicault? Who's that?

ELMORE: He's very famous.

BESS: Oh, alright then, I consent. *(JACK enters, carrying some luggage. He has shaved his moustache.)*

ELMORE: *(Handing her an illustration)* Now here's the portrait of you that we want to include in the second edition.

BESS: Oh, dear.

ELMORE: I find it very sensitive, yet I feel there's a deep sense of inner strength.

BESS: Hmm. My eyes are too close together. I've got beautiful hair, but my eyes are too close together. *(To* JACK*)* Don't you agree?

JACK: No.

BESS: But they're closer together than an average person's eyes, wouldn't you say?

JACK: I don't know. No.

BESS: Well, how close together do you think an average person's eyes are?

JACK: I don't know.

BESS: Then stop offering opinions on subjects you're completely stupid on.

JACK: Alright.

BESS: Don't be so agreeable. Finish fetching our bags and move them out to the carriage. We don't want to miss our train. *(*JACK *exits into another room.)* Do we really have to bother with him?

ELMORE: Of course, it's entirely your decision, but I'm afraid an anguished, adoring husband makes for excellent pathos.

BESS: Yes. Well, then. I'll manage.

ELMORE: Good. Excellent. Now, according to this schedule, you'll be doing up to one hundred and fifty lectures this season. You stand to profit over twenty-five thousand dollars from the lecture circuit alone.

BESS: Angels sing, devils dance.

ELMORE: Mr William Sutton is the promoter for the tour. He's a very successful land speculator who is deeply devoted to western expansion and the concept of manifest destiny. He'd like for you to sign this contract agreeing to expound certain philosophical beliefs from the podium.

BESS: Philosophical beliefs? I'm not sure I got any of them. Here, let me see the paper. *(She takes the contract and reads it thoroughly.* MACON *enters the area in front of the cabin. She spots* WILL.*)*

MACON: Repossession. Repossession. That one word they clung to like a pack of sick dogs. They're taking our home. There's nothing to be done, unless they get fifty dollars. Fifty dollars. I asked the man with the red beard if he'd accept potatoes as partial payment. He laughed at me like I was a brand-new joke.

WILL: I told you how it come out. Things are finished here. We'll have to go somewhere else. Start fresh.

MACON: I'd rather choke to death right here in the sun. *(Inside the cabin,* JACK *enters with the bags. He starts for the cabin door.* BESS *stops him.)*

BESS: Jack, don't forget that basket there, I packed us some food for the road.

JACK: Great. What is it?

BESS: Cornbread. *(*JACK *nods, picks up the basket, and leaves the cabin. He goes into the yard.* MACON *spots him.)*

MACON: Jack, where're you going?

JACK: The Professor's come for us. Bess's book's selling like wildfire. We're going on a lecture circuit. We've become important people.

MACON: You're leaving right now?

JACK: That's right.

MACON: How long will you be gone?

JACK: For good, I hope.

MACON: God. How will I ever stand living in this great wasteland all alone.

JACK: *(Indicating* WILL*)* Ya still got him.

MACON: Yeah. Listen, Jack, I'm in trouble. I need fifty dollars to save the homestead.

JACK: I ain't got no money.

MACON: Well, would you talk to Bess for me? Would you put in a good word?

JACK: You talk to her. She's your friend.

MACON: That's right. You're right. She's my friend. I done a lot for her. A whole lot. Goodbye, Jack.

JACK: So long, May Ann.

MACON: I'll always remember you as the possessor of a very handsome pair of eyes. *(*JACK *exits.* WILL *stares ahead, trying to decide why he doesn't care about killing these people.* MACON *goes into the cabin.* WILL *exits.)* Bess. I need to talk to you. It's concerning a personal situation. Good afternoon, Professor.

ELMORE: Yes, well...good afternoon, Mrs Curtis. *(*ELMORE *gets up and goes into the yard.)*

MACON: I heard you're leaving. You're off. You've made it in the big time.

BESS: That's how it appears.

MACON: I don't begrudge you. I saw it coming. People lap up them atrocity stories. They read 'em all the time in them penny dreadfuls. Now you go and give 'em the real factualized version. Ya even got the marks t'prove it.

People'll get up outta their homes and come down to them big halls to see them marks. Them tattoos. People thrive on seeing freaks.

BESS: Well, I'm glad you don't begrudge me.

MACON: No. Why would I?

BESS: No reason. I just thought you wanted to write a book, a novel. You spoke about it. But I guess that was more like a pipe dream, a childish fantasy. Nothing to be taken seriously.

MACON: I had a book in mind at one point. I was gonna write about my adventures.

BESS: I guess, you just never had any, did ya?

MACON: I had some. Some things happened to me.

BESS: Not that much, though.

MACON: Well, I never got my face scarred.

BESS: Do you wish you had?

MACON: Why would I?

BESS: Because, maybe you would like to be...remarkable. But you're not. You look forward to things by decades. You're settled, staid, and dreamless. I see it haunts you how ya just can't compare t'me. To Bess Johnson, the woman who survived five adventurous years of Indian captivity. Who returned to write the book of the century and be adored by throngs all over the globe.

MACON: You don't fool me. I know how ya done it all. You pictured me. You stole from me. You stole me. I showed you how to walk and speak and fight and dream. I should have written that book. People should be clamoring t'meet me; t'talk t'me. I'm the real thing; you're just a watered-down milktoast version. Them Indians stole the wrong woman.

BESS: Is that a fact?

MACON: Yeah, it is.

BESS: Well, maybe it ain't too late. Maybe you've got one more chance. Here, take this knife. Take this ink. Go ahead. Cut open your face. Pour in the ink. Go be me, if you think you can. If you think you're so brave. I'll let you be me. You can do my tour. People will rise to their feet and clamor for you. Go ahead. The Oglalas rejoice in wounding themselves. They do it for prayer. They do it to celebrate grief. Come on, do it, celebrate, rejoice, do it...all it is is your face.

MACON: Bess, please...I always cared for you. I always did.

BESS: Then do it. Cut it. To shreds; all to shreds.

MACON: I did, you know. I always did.

BESS: Then do it. Cut it; do it. (MACON *takes the knife. Holds it to her face, then sets it down.*)

MACON: I'm not gonna cut myself up. I don't wanna be scarred for life.

BESS: *(A beat)* No. That would cost too much. And you've gotten so measly you watch every egg, nickel, and biscuit. *(She starts putting on her hat and gloves.)*

MACON: I know we don't like each other. We used to be friends. But somehow we drifted apart. Still, you have to admit, you have to see, that you owe me something.

BESS: What do I owe you?

MACON: You...well, you owe me...fifty dollars. At least, fifty dollars. I gave you shoes when you had none and food and coffee and clothes and lodging. I even brought you blue ribbons and a blue dress. Whatever your heart desired, I gave to you.

BESS: Maybe it never occurred t'you. Maybe you never realized the fact, but people don't like being beholding. They resent always needing and always owing. And pretty soon they come to resent whoever it is they been taking from.

MACON: I do. I know that. You've resented me all along.

BESS: Yeah, I believe I have and I don't want you resenting me. So why don't we just call it even.

MACON: But I gotta have it. The fifty dollars. I need it to save my homestead. They're gonna throw me out on the dusty road. You can't do this to me.

BESS: Honey, I'd rip the wings off an angel if I thought they'd help me fly. *(She leaves the cabin and goes out into the yard. MACON follows her.)*

MACON: You owe me! I'm due! You can't deny me what's mine! I gave you green biscuits; I combed your hair; I taught you to whistle!

ELMORE: Are you ready?

BESS: Yeah.

ELMORE: Did you read the contract?

BESS: They want me to demand the immediate extermination of all Indian tribes.

ELMORE: That's correct.

BESS: I got no problem with that. Just make sure wherever we go I have a basket of golden tulips to greet me. They're my favorite flower, tulips. *(She and ELMORE exit as MACON screams after them.)*

MACON: You thief! Robber...thief! Tulips are mine! They belong to me! I seen the picture! You never did! (WILL *enters wearing his eye patch and carrying a satchel.*) God, Will. God. She wouldn't give me the money. She wouldn't give me nothing. She owes me, too. She knows she does. I was her friend. God, I'd like to kill her. I'd like to tear off her head and feed her brains to rabid rats. The selfish, back-biting, stuck-up, black-hearted Indian whore!

WILL: Macon, I'm leaving here. I'm heading west.

MACON: West? Where west?

WILL: Don't know.

MACON: Maybe we'll try Idaho. They got that Turkey red wheat in Idaho. It's a hard-kerneled wheat. You can grow it all spring.

WILL: I don't want you with me.

MACON: What?

WILL: My first wife, Barbara Jane, well, I loved her. And I remember she loved me. But you never loved me and I never loved you. That's all it's been. I don't want it no more.

MACON: You leaving me here? With nothing?

WILL: This is yours. Catch. (WILL *throws her his glass eye. She catches it.*) I bought it for you. It never done me no good. (WILL *exits.* MACON *paces around the yard tossing the glass eye back and forth, from hand to hand.*)

MACON: I got nothing. Nothing. After all this time. (*A beat*) Nothing.

(*End of Scene Six*)

Scene Seven

(*Fifteen years later*)

(*A hotel suite in St Louis.* BESS *drinks a glass of whiskey.* ELMORE *holds a copy of the* St Louis Chronicle.)

ELMORE: Are you sure you want to hear this?

BESS: Uh-huh.

ELMORE: It's not very good.

BESS: That seems to be the trend.

ELMORE: It's appallingly written.

BESS: Go ahead, Elmore, it's the last one I'll ever get.

ELMORE: The *St Louis Chronicle* says, "Mrs Bess Johnson delivered her speech with impassioned fervor. However, the story seemed excessive and outdated like a worn-out melodrama one would read in a dime novel. The text lacked all orderly progressions and seemed to ramble and roam incoherently, as though perhaps Mrs Johnson had had a drop too many."

BESS: A drop too many! They can't actually expect me to deliver those speeches sans intoxication. What a tight-lipped powder puff. What a worm-ridden toad.

ELMORE: *(Folding up the paper)* Yes, well, let's put it away.

BESS: God. I can't tell you what a relief it will be to never again to have to rhapsodize about writing with fish blood and being scantily clad in a thin bark skirt.

ELMORE: Yes. I'm well aware we have played ourselves out. People are no longer interested in hearing about the untamed savages. Times have changed. Indians today are beloved circus performers. Yesterday, I read in a broadside that they finally arrested your old friend, Ottawa, down by the Pecos River. They'd been hunting him for years. He was the last holdout. The lone one.

BESS: Ottawa, I didn't know he was still alive.

ELMORE: He's not. He drank a lantern of kerosene the night they captured him.

BESS: Oh.

ELMORE: *(Presenting her with contracts)* Well, here are the final papers disbanding our long and lucrative union. They're all in order. You'll find everything's as we discussed.

BESS: I'm sure they are. I'll just have my attorneys read it over before I sign it.

ELMORE: I admire your consistency, Bess. All these years and you've never trusted me once.

BESS: Sorry, Elmore. I tried that. It never really worked out for me.
(JACK enters smoking a large black cigar. He is dressed dapperly.)

JACK: 'Afternoon.

ELMORE: Hello, Jack.

BESS: What's that awful thing?

JACK: A ten-cent cigar. I won it betting on the comic mule races down at the tent show.

ELMORE: Ah, yes, how was the tent show?

JACK: Pathetic, small-town dredge. The freaks were even third rate: armless boy; electric girl; skeleton dude. Oh, but you'll never guess who I ran into. What's her name? We used to know her back when. Her husband wore an eye patch.

BESS: Macon?

JACK: Yes, I think that was it.

BESS: Macon Hill.

JACK: You should see her. Disgusting. She's got some syphilitic disease. It's broken out all over her face. She was working at a little booth dispensing whiskey and tobacco and raisins. I bought some raisins from her. She didn't recognize me. I had to laugh when I saw she had newspaper stuck in her clothes to stay warm. I remember her always thinking she had it so good.

BESS: Your cigar is foul. Put it out. Get it out. *(JACK puts out the cigar.)* God, you're an imbecile. Coming in here, filling the room with your vile smoke. You've given me a sick head. I'm going out for some air. Clear out this room before I get back. *(She exits.)*

JACK: Christ, why am I ever nice to that woman? You're lucky you're getting out from under her. I'm stuck with her for life. Tomorrow we leave for our White Plains estate. We'll retire there together till the end of our days. What will it be like?

ELMORE: She can be difficult. But I think, underneath it all, she has real affection for you.

JACK: You think she does?

ELMORE: It's the sort of thing that's only apparent to an outsider.

JACK: Well, I'll say one thing, she'll never find anyone who'll treat her better than I do. She oughta know that by now. I'm her one true one.

(End of Scene Seven)

Scene Eight

(A few hours later. Early evening.)

(MACON's tent. MACON sits alone in the dimly lit tent, drinking and playing solitaire. There are sores on her face.)

BESS: *(Offstage)* Hello? Anybody here?

MACON: Yeah. *(BESS enters.)*

BESS: Macon?

MACON: Bess?

BESS: I heard you were here.

MACON: Jack tell you?

BESS: Yeah.

MACON: I seen him this afternoon. He bought some raisins. He wouldn't speak to me though.

BESS: Well, you know him.

MACON: Yeah. Why'd you come?

BESS: I—don't know. I was—remembering....

MACON: Uh-huh.

BESS: So much.

MACON: Well.

BESS: How you been?

MACON: Great. Just great. Yeah, for a time I was raking in the green selling this Indian Remedy. A cure for your opium, morphine, liquor, and tobacco habit. Hell of a cure it was, too. Then I got this stuff coming out on my face and people kinda eased off purchasing the cure. But for a time there, I was flush. How 'bout you?

BESS: I don't know. Maybe other people's lives have made more sense than mine.

MACON: It's always a possibility.

BESS: Oh, well. There it is, I guess.

MACON: Yeah, laid right out behind you like a lizard's tail.

BESS: Today I—Well, today I heard that Ottawa, the head man—my husband—was captured. He, ah, poisoned himself on a lantern of kerosene. I don't know why, but it's hard. I'd always thought I might—but now I won't—ever see him once more.

MACON: It's a shame how things turn out. I swear to God, I wish I knew how it could be different.

BESS: Uh-huh. Me too.

MACON: 'Least ya got out there and saw the elephant.

BESS: Yeah. Yeah, the Oglalas knew such beautiful places. I saw rivers that were so clear you could see every pebble and fish. And the water was any color you could dream: pink and turquoise; gold and white; lime green.

MACON: Hell of a time you had with the Oglalas.

BESS: Beautiful time I had. Hey, you ever hear from Will Curtis?

MACON: Nah. Will got caught in a threshing machine back in '87. Got his leg cut off in the blade. Bled t'death in a field. Funny, I always figured he'd go piecemeal.

BESS: Yeah.

MACON: You know, when I was younger, I never knew who I was, what I wanted, where I was going or how to get there. Now that I'm older, I don't know none of that either.

BESS: Well, one thing I wanted, one thing I know I wanted was, well, I don't know, I guess you'd call it true love. And when I got them three letters from that man, that man, Michael Flan, who wrote to me about the size of the sky, I thought it was all right there, all within my grasp and all I had t'do was come out west and there it'd be.

MACON: Thought you'd just reach up and touch it like a star.

BESS: Yeah. Thought I might. (BESS *reaches her hand up as if she were grabbing a star.*) Aah!

MACON: Feel a chill?

BESS: Just a small one.

MACON: Bess?

BESS: Huh.

MACON: I, well, I've had a bad pain in my heart all day today. I'm scared and it troubles me, but I expect I'll die soon.

BESS: ...What can I do?

MACON: Nothing t'do. I just wanted somebody t'tell, that's all. Someone to tell.

BESS: Well, you can tell me.

MACON: There ain't much t'tell.

BESS: Maybe not, but I'm glad you looked my way.

MACON: Uh-huh. Well. Yeah.

BESS: Hey, do you still whistle?

MACON: Me? I...God...I... (*Then definitely*) No. (*A long beat, then she whistles a tune,* BESS *whistles back. The women both laugh from deep in the bottom of their hearts. The lights fade to blackout.*)

END OF PLAY

HOLY DAYS

Sally Nemeth

ABOUT THE AUTHOR

Sally Nemeth was born in Chicago and worked extensively in the Off-Loop theaters there, founding Chicago New Plays, a playwrights' collective. She subsequently relocated to New York, and now resides in Brooklyn.

HOLY DAYS premiered at the Soho Poly Theatre in London. Critically acclaimed, the production won three awards at the Fringe Theatre Awards and later was produced in Dublin, Ireland and Auckland, New Zealand. Its United States premiere at South Coast Repertory won four Los Angeles Drama Critics Circle Awards. HOLY DAYS has been published by Broadway Play Publishing in a single edition.

Nemeth's play MILL FIRE premiered at the Goodman Theater in Chicago, and later moved to New York under the auspices of the Women's Project. It premiered in London at the Bush Theatre at Riverside Hammersmith, and is included in the Applause Books anthology WOMENSWORK.

Nemeth's one-act WATER PLAY was included in the New Works Festival at the Mark Taper Forum and was produced in New York by Road Theater at the Downtown Art Co. An evening of one-acts and monologues titled SALLY'S SHORTS was recently produced in New York by One Dream Theater. Her full-length SPINNING INTO BLUE, commissioned by South Coast Repertory, was part of the Showcase of New Plays at Carnegie-Mellon, and was produced in January 1993 at Victory Gardens Theater in Chicago.

She is a 1989 recipient of a National Endowment for the Arts grant, and a 1990 recipient of a New York Foundation for the Arts grant.

Her television work includes writing on staff for the Wolf Films/NBC TV show LAW AND ORDER. A film version of HOLY DAYS is currently in post-production.

HOLY DAYS premiered in London on 16 March 1988. It was produced by the Soho Poly Theater (Sue Dunderdale, Artistic Director; Annette Clancy, Administrative Director) in association with Alexander E. and Dina Racolin.

HOLY DAYS premiered in the United States at South Coast Repertory on 26 January 1990. The cast and creative contributors were:

ROSIE .... Jeanne Paulsen
GANT .... Richard Doyle
WILL .... John K Linton
MOLLY .... Devon Raymond

Director .... Martin Benson
Set design .... John Iacovelli
Lighting design .... Tom Ruzika
Costume design .... Ann Bruice
Music and sound .... Michael Roth
Stage manager .... Andy Tighe
Assistant stage manager .... Christine Santmyers
Dramaturg .... John Glore

CHARACTERS

ROSIE, GANT's *wife, age thirty-five*
GANT, WILL's *brother, age thirty-seven*
WILL, *age thirty-five*
MOLLY, WILL's *wife, age twenty-six*

The action of the play takes place in ROSIE and GANT's kitchen. WILL and MOLLY's farmhouse is adjacent to ROSIE and GANT's house. The farm is in western Kansas. The time of the play is Good Friday to Easter Sunday, 1936.

(Scene: 1936, western Kansas, Good Friday. ROSIE *stands outside the back screen door, scanning the horizon.* ROSIE *is wearing a cotton dress with a cardigan over it. It is a little past lunchtime, and a small dust storm has just cleared.)*

ROSIE: There was a time I recall when things was just beginning to come green all around. My daffodils come up early. Then it snowed—not heavy, but enough to make me certain they'd gone. And I went out to cut the flowers that already opened. If I couldn't have daffodils out front of the house, I'd sure have them all over inside. Anyway, I went out with my shears and all of them had opened—they was sitting in snow and they was open as you please. I started cutting at them, and it seemed I'd brought in armfuls and there was still more to cut. Almost like they was opening before my eyes. Opening and growing all around me. I didn't have but one or two pitchers, so I left them be and went back inside to put the ones I'd cut in water. I swear I'd brought in enough to cover the table, but all it came out to be was barely a pitcher full. Well, I went back out to cut more, but there weren't no more to cut. I'd just seen them out there—dozens of yellow flowers in the snow—now there weren't none. And the stems and leaves was all black—not like they'd frozen, but—dry. Dry as a bone.

*(*ROSIE *turns and enters the kitchen. There is a table with six chairs in the middle of the kitchen. A large wood stove occupies one wall; sink and cabinets take up another. There is a back screen door near the stove and a window over the sink. A hallway leads to the rest of the house. There is an icebox and a door to the pantry. A cloth covers a completely set and laid-out table. Dust covers the cloth and everything in the room.* ROSIE *picks up a rag and slaps it on her thigh to knock the dust out of it. She takes the rag and ties it over her nose and mouth, picks up a broom, and starts to clear the dust off the chairs, then begins to sweep.)*

*(*GANT *and* WILL *enter from the screen door.* GANT *is* WILL'*s older brother and is* ROSIE'*s husband. Both are dusty and are wearing hats and rags over their faces. They turn as they enter, go out to the steps, and knock some of the dust off themselves. They re-enter.)*

ROSIE: Doesn't much matter. You weren't going to make it any dirtier than it already is.

GANT: I suppose.

ROSIE: Thought you'd be later with the blow and all.

GANT: We saw it coming before it hit. Got part-way home before it met us.

WILL: Just a little blow anyway. Didn't last.

(ROSIE *starts to fold the cloth over the table in on itself to keep it from spilling dust on the food.*)

GANT: Let me help.

ROSIE: I got it. You'll just spill it.

(GANT *and* WILL *sit down at the table. Bread, chicken meat, butter, milk, and some potato salad are laid out.* ROSIE *takes the cloth to the door to shake it out.*)

ROSIE: I'm sorry it's all cold food but I didn't know how long it would storm and I didn't want to be cooking.

WILL: This is fine. Just fine. *(He removes his hat.)*

ROSIE: I know Molly usually makes a hot lunch. *(She sits at the table.)*

WILL: When we get caught out there it just gets cold anyway. This is just fine.

GANT: Molly should have been back by now, shouldn't she?

WILL: No. You know she's always back late. She has to wait at the doctor's office, then she usually takes her sweet time, looking at store windows and all.

ROSIE: She loves to shop.

WILL: I know it. If we had any money we wouldn't have any money.

ROSIE: No worse off than when you started.

WILL: That's right.

GANT: Aren't you eating anything, Rosie?

ROSIE: No. I'm not very hungry.

GANT: You ought to eat something.

ROSIE: I had a little something when I was fixing it.

GANT: I wish you wouldn't do that. I always feel funny eating when there's someone at the table who isn't eating.

ROSIE: Well, Gant, then I'll just go find something to do. *(Starts to rise)*

GANT: Sit down, Rosie. Come on. I didn't mean for you to leave. I just wish you'd eat with us.

ROSIE: I do have things to do.

GANT: They can wait until lunch is over.

WILL: Your wash out on the line ain't going to get any dirtier.

ROSIE: Oh no. I forgot it was out there.

WILL: You probably didn't have time to bring it in.

ROSIE: No, I had the time. I just forgot. Now I'm going to have to do every bit of it again. I don't know what I was thinking about. *(Rises and gets the laundry basket by the door and heads out)*

GANT: Rosie—it can wait!

WILL: Sorry. I wouldn't have mentioned it.

GANT: I figured she knew about it, too.

(MOLLY enters from the hallway door. She is about seven months pregnant. She looks tired and bedraggled.)

WILL: *(Stands and kisses her)* Honey, I didn't even hear you pull up.

MOLLY: *(Sits and puts her feet up on a chair)* That's because I didn't.

WILL: What happened?

MOLLY: I pulled off when the dust started to blow—decided I'd sit it out instead of trying to drive through it. Well, when I went to start the truck again—nothing. Wouldn't start for nothing. So this nice man pulls over and tries to start it and he can't get it started. So, he give me a ride to the driveway and I walked from there.

WILL: You should have had him take you to the door. That's like a half-mile from the mailbox to the door.

MOLLY: He was nice enough to bring me as far as he did. Anyway, I didn't think he'd make it. He was in a little two-seater and I knew for sure it would never make it over the wheel ruts.

WILL: You rode in a two-seater?

MOLLY: Yes, I did. With California plates.

GANT: I'd have loved to see you get out of it.

MOLLY: I required a lot of help.

GANT: How far away is the truck?

MOLLY: About halfway between here and town.

WILL: Why didn't you go back into town and get someone from the gas station out to help you?

MOLLY: The man wasn't going that way. Besides, gas station's closed.

WILL: Closed? Why? Someone die or something?

GANT: Well, yeah, sort of—

MOLLY: Gant—don't you dare. *(Pause)* It's Good Friday, Will, remember?

WILL: Oh, yeah. Right.

MOLLY: Heathens.

GANT: Was the doctor open?

MOLLY: Of course.

WILL: How are we doing?

MOLLY: We're all doing just fine, thank you. And we all may be doing even better very soon.

WILL: How's that?

MOLLY: Well, while I was waiting for the doctor, one of the men working down on the railroad smashed up his hand real bad and one of his buddies brought him in. I sat out there and passed the time with this man's buddy. Joe was his name, and he told me the Santa Fe is going to hire a whole bunch of men through the WPA to build a bridge over the Cimmarron River Valley.

WILL: We should head down to the railroad office. Head down there right away.

GANT: Santa Fe's hiring through the WPA?

MOLLY: That's what the man said.

GANT: Then all we got to do is stay put. We're both registered with the WPA. There's any work and they'll let us know.

MOLLY: That ain't so. Joe said you got to be there when they start hiring.

GANT: Molly, that can't be right. That's not how they do things.

MOLLY: Right or not, that's what the man told me.

WILL: We should still go see.

MOLLY: Never hurts to check up on these things.

GANT: We got to go get the truck, anyway. All right—we'll take the tractor to the truck and then I'll go ahead and take the truck into town.

WILL: I hope the WPA's open—you know, if the gas station's closed—

GANT: They can't be closed—it's a government office.

MOLLY: Don't be too sure.

GANT: You were in town, Molly—couldn't you have found out?

MOLLY: It sounded to me like you just had to show up when they were hiring.

GANT: And when's that?

MOLLY: I don't know. All I know is what I already told you.

WILL: It can't hurt to try. The loan 's due soon and we need some cash.

MOLLY: That's for sure.

WILL: And a WPA job is the only cash around.

GANT: Sounds like a lot of nothing to me, but I'll go check on it.

WILL: I'll go into town if you don't want to.

GANT: It's not that I don't want to. It's just that I don't really think there's any reason to.

MOLLY: Sounds like a real long-term job. Building a bridge.

GANT: Those things usually are.

MOLLY: Well, if there is some work it could mean a good deal of time away from the farm.

GANT: Molly, neither Will or I are heading off to build any bridges yet, so let's not worry about that, all right?

MOLLY: Just thinking out loud. *(Pause)* Where's Rosie?

WILL: Taking her wash off the line.

MOLLY: *(Gets up and goes to the door)* Gant, she's just standing there with the basket in her arms.

GANT: *(Joins MOLLY at the door)* Oh, no. *(Goes out the door)*

MOLLY: She been out there long?

WILL: As long as you've been here.

MOLLY: Her wash is still all out on the line.

WILL: Come here and sit down. Gant will take care of her.

MOLLY: I should go out and help her.

WILL: Leave them alone for a bit. She gets embarrassed when you do things for her.

MOLLY: I know, but when is she going to start doing things for herself again? *(She sits next to him.)*

WILL: I don't know.

MOLLY: I don't mean to be mean or anything. I don't mind doing for her. I just know she doesn't like it. She doesn't like to be this way.

WILL: I don't know anyone that would.

MOLLY: Another couple months and I won't have the time to help her out as much.

WILL: By that time I'm sure she'll be helping you. It'll make her feel good to have a baby around.

MOLLY: I'm not so sure about that.

WILL: What do you mean?

MOLLY: Nothing. I just hope the baby's a girl. I think having a little girl would be the best thing, don't you?

WILL: A girl would be all right.

MOLLY: Well, I think it would be nice. Come on. You can still play catch with a girl.

WILL: But I'll never teach her to throw.

MOLLY: I can throw.

WILL: You throw like a girl.

MOLLY: I do not.

WILL: Do too.

MOLLY: I was the best pitcher the Methodists ever had.

WILL: So, you threw better than the rest of the girls. But you still throw like a girl.

MOLLY: Five cents says I can strike you out.

(GANT *and* ROSIE *enter,* GANT *carrying the laundry.*)

MOLLY: Hey, Rosie.

ROSIE: Hello. You get caught in the storm?

MOLLY: Sure did. Sat it out in the truck. Then the truck wouldn't start, so I got a ride back here.

GANT: We need to get to that truck.

ROSIE: Did the doctor say everything's all right?

MOLLY: Yes. I checked out all right.

WILL: Why don't I pull the tractor around and you go get some tools.

GANT: What did the truck sound like when you tried to start it?

MOLLY: Not much. It would turn some but it wouldn't catch.

GANT: I bet it's just clogged with dust.

MOLLY: I'd have no idea.

GANT: I'll bring all the tools, anyway. Let's go, Will.

WILL: See you at dinner, ladies.

(He kisses MOLLY *on top of her head, and they exit.* ROSIE *starts to clear the table, then stops.)*

ROSIE: I'm sorry. You have any lunch yet?

MOLLY: No, I haven't. I'll just fix myself a sandwich here. You leave it all out, I'll put it away when I'm done.

ROSIE: All right. *(She continues to clear dirty plates from the table.)*

MOLLY: Rosie, just leave it.

ROSIE: I'm only clearing what's dirty. Let me do that much. *(She continues to clear and sets the dishes in the sink but does not rinse them.)*

MOLLY: You collect eggs yet today?

ROSIE: No, there was a storm. I couldn't see the coop from here.

MOLLY: Must've blown worse here than where I was. I had trouble seeing but it wasn't that thick.

ROSIE: I really couldn't see it.

MOLLY: I don't doubt it.

ROSIE: Anyway, the hens get so scared when it blows like that they don't lay many eggs.

MOLLY: They better have laid some. I want to color some eggs.

ROSIE: It's Easter already?

MOLLY: On Sunday.

ROSIE: I thought it was another week or so. I didn't even make any plans for supper. What are we going to have?

MOLLY: I don't know. I haven't given it much thought either.

ROSIE: We have to have an Easter supper. We can all go to church with you in the morning.

MOLLY: You're more than welcome to join me, but I know you'll never get Gant or Will anywhere near a church.

ROSIE: I know. Well, whatever they want to do, but we're going to have an Easter supper. Oh, I don't even know what we have in the pantry.

MOLLY: Nothing exciting, but enough for a respectable meal.

ROSIE: We've got a hundred things to do. Baking pies and things and...

MOLLY: *(Pause)* We've got time to do it all. You want to invite anyone over to join us?

ROSIE: No. I don't know who I'd ask.

MOLLY: Probably just as well. Short notice and all.

ROSIE: Well, I've got to re-do my wash. It got caught out in the storm. I didn't have time to go out and get it. *(Goes to door and picks up basket)* I think having an Easter supper will be nice, don't you?

MOLLY: It'll be real nice.

(ROSIE exits.)

(While MOLLY delivers the next speech, she clears the table. There will be a shift of time during the speech, and when she is through, it will be evening.)

MOLLY: It never occurred to us to leave. We'd all heard of people who did go only to find that things were tough all over. This was our home—it had been passed on to Will and Gant by their folks to keep as it had been kept before, and when things were good they were very good. When everyone's land was full of wheat I can't think of anything more beautiful. Far as you could see, the wind would make waves through the wheat and you could fool yourself and play like your house was a ship on the ocean and you were on your way to China or somewhere. That was a favorite game of his. A Sunday afternoon game. Barbary pirates on the high seas. We got very elaborate. I made him an eye patch and Gant or Will, I don't remember, made swords from some old lumber. Then he got it in his mind that he wanted a parrot. All the pirates in the books had parrots. Aren't many parrots in this part of the world. (MOLLY *should be finished clearing the table. She takes a deck of cards out of a drawer of the table. The lights dim. It is evening, after dinner. She sits and shuffles the deck.)* Will! You done with that cigarette yet?

WILL: *(From outside)* Just about.

MOLLY: I'm tired of playing solitaire.

WILL: *(Grinding out cigarette with heel)* You wouldn't have to play solitaire if you'd let me smoke inside.

MOLLY: You know that ever since I've been pregnant the smell makes me sick.

WILL: You got sick once and that was a long time ago.

MOLLY: Better safe than sorry. You know how much I hate throwing up.

WILL: I don't know anyone that enjoys it.

ROSIE: *(Entering from hallway)* Enjoys what?

WILL: Throwing up.

ROSIE: Why are you talking about that?

MOLLY: Will's tired of smoking outside, but I won't let him smoke inside because since I've been pregnant it makes me sick.

WILL: Once.

MOLLY: It still makes me sick.

ROSIE: Sometimes I think feeling sick and queasy is worse than actually getting sick.

WILL: I can think of a couple instances when I was happy to get sick.

MOLLY: I'm sure you can.

ROSIE: I was sick the whole time I was pregnant.

MOLLY: Don't tell me that.

ROSIE: Everybody told me something different about when it would end, but it never did.

MOLLY: I've heard all sorts of things. Everybody's got an opinion and a remedy.

WILL: You going to deal those cards or are you going to let us watch you cheat at solitaire?

MOLLY: I was waiting for Gant.

WILL: He'll be back any time now.

ROSIE: Maybe the truck's broke down again.

WILL: We got it started right up. He probably just ran into some people in town.

ROSIE: That's not like him.

WILL: Maybe not, but I'll bet that's what happened.

MOLLY: What do you want me to deal?

WILL: How about seven-card stud?

MOLLY: Will—

WILL: All right then. Five-card draw.

MOLLY: *(Hands him deck)* You deal.

WILL: *(To MOLLY)* You'll play?

MOLLY: How about it, Rosie?

ROSIE: You'll have to remind me of the game.

WILL: All right. *(Shuffles the deck)* Could you get the matches off the stove? *(ROSIE goes to the stove.)* Both boxes. *(She returns with them and sits.)* OK. The red tips are five cents and the blue tips are ten. You get five cards face down. You bet on them. You get to discard up to three and get new ones from me, your dealer, and then you bet on that hand. Then we show hands and the winner takes the pot.

ROSIE: What beats what? I can never remember.

MOLLY: Royal flush beats flush beats four-of-a-kind beats straight beats, uh, don't tell me—full house? Full house beats three-of-a-kind, no, two pairs beats three-of-a- kind beats a pair. Right?

WILL: *(Shuffling)* Something like that.

MOLLY: I'll help you with your first couple hands.

WILL: Cut the deck. *(Sets the deck in front of* ROSIE *and she cuts.)* Take some matches, ladies, and ante up.

MOLLY: I'd forgot about this part.

WILL: Pay to play, pay to play.

MOLLY: All right, fine, deal the cards.

(They all ante. WILL *deals the cards and* MOLLY *counts along to herself as he deals. When the cards are dealt and the hands picked up,* GANT *enters.)*

ROSIE: Gant. Where have you been?

GANT: In town.

WILL: Sorry, this hand's dealt. You'll have to wait until the next to get in the game.

GANT: What are you playing?

MOLLY: Five-card draw.

GANT: You're kidding.

ROSIE: Why don't you take my hand, Gant? I'll get your dinner out of the oven.

GANT: No, Rosie. I want to see you play this.

ROSIE: I have no idea what I'm doing.

GANT: Then it's a good thing you're playing for matches.

WILL: How many you want?

ROSIE: I don't know.

WILL: It's Molly's turn.

MOLLY: I'm not ready yet.

WILL: Well, it's still your turn.

MOLLY: Aren't we supposed to bet first?

GANT: None of you have any idea what you're doing.

WILL: Gant, I knew that.

GANT: Then, how come you asked her how many she wanted before you found out how much she was spending?

MOLLY: I'll bet five cents.

GANT: Match the bet, Rosie.

ROSIE: I'll match.

WILL: I'll meet that and raise it a nickel.

MOLLY: Call.

GANT: Call.

ROSIE: Call.

MOLLY: I'll take three cards.

WILL: *(Dealing out)* There you go. Rosie?

ROSIE: *(Points out a card in her hand to* GANT. *He nods.)* One.

WILL: There's some daring. And the dealer takes three.

ROSIE: Well, I didn't get anything. *(Lays down her hand)*

GANT: Rosie, you still could have bet on it.

ROSIE: I know that, but I don't feel like betting on nothing.

WILL: Smart lady. Molly?

MOLLY: What?

ROSIE: I'll get your dinner.

WILL: Bet.

GANT: Just sit. It'll wait.

MOLLY: I'll bet a dime.

WILL: A dime? I'll call that and raise you a quarter.

MOLLY: I'll call that.

GANT: Let's see the cards, Molly.

MOLLY: Full house.

GANT: Sure is. Jacks high. Will?

WILL: There you go. *(Lays hand down)*

GANT: Pair of eights?

MOLLY: *(Raking in pile)* It's a good thing you're playing for matches.

WILL: How's the truck?

GANT: Truck's fine.

WILL: Sounded pretty good after we got it going.

ROSIE: Why did you go into town if you got it started yourself?

WILL: Gant wanted to—

GANT: It hasn't been looked at in a while. Just making sure.

MOLLY: I want to play another hand. That was fun.

ROSIE: So what took you so long in town?

GANT: Oh, you know. Ran into some people in town. Hadn't seen them in a while.

WILL: What's the news?

GANT: The usual. Some rumors about a WPA job with the Santa Fe. Building a bridge in the Cimmarron River Valley.

MOLLY: Just rumors?

GANT: No. This one seems to be happening. I went over to the WPA office.

ROSIE: I don't know how they expect farmers to work WPA. When you leave to go work for them you aren't doing anything for your land.

GANT: What land, Rosie? All our topsoil is probably halfway across the country by now.

ROSIE: So what are you and Will doing out there on the tractor every day? You know you have to work it to keep it all from going.

GANT: I'm not so sure I know that anymore.

WILL: Bad time of year for them to be taking people from the farms.

MOLLY: When are they going to build, Will, in the winter?

WILL: There's never a good time, but—

ROSIE: I think it's ridiculous. Trying to hire people out when they know people are planting. *(Gets up to get plate out of oven)* I'm sure this plate of food is all dried out from being in the oven too long.

GANT: It's all right, Rosie.

ROSIE: Oh, it is. It's all dried out. You want me to scramble you some eggs?

GANT: No. I got some dinner in town.

ROSIE: You shouldn't have done that. You know I always keep a plate for you.

GANT: Rosie, I signed up.

ROSIE: *(Puts plate on stove)* No.

GANT: Yes, Rosie. I had to.

ROSIE: No.

GANT: If we have a summer like the last one we'll never make our loan. I got to make the cash.

(MOLLY lights a match and watches it burn, then blows it out.)

GANT: Rosie?

(ROSIE leaves, running up the hall.)

GANT: Oh, damn.

MOLLY: It's better you let her know right away so she has time to get used to it.

GANT: Ain't no time. I leave Sunday.

MOLLY: Sunday?

GANT: Even if she had time it wouldn't be any easier. *(He exits hallway.)*

MOLLY: Come on. Let's go home.

WILL: I'm going to stay for a minute. I want to talk to Gant.

MOLLY: About what?

WILL: I just want to talk with him.

MOLLY: If you think you're going to talk him into letting you go instead, you're wrong. I ain't having this baby alone.

WILL: Go on. I'll be home in a little bit.

MOLLY: Will—

WILL: Don't worry. I think he's half-relieved to be going.

MOLLY: That's a terrible thing to say.

WILL: That doesn't change the fact that it's true.

MOLLY: No, it doesn't. Don't be too long.

WILL: I won't.

(MOLLY exits screen door. WILL shuffles cards and deals himself solitaire. GANT re-enters hallway door.)

GANT: You still here?

WILL: I didn't guess she'd feel much like conversation.

GANT: *(Goes to sink, gets a tin from under the sink. Opens it and takes out a pint bottle of whisky.)* Join me?

WILL: Molly will smell that on me a mile away.

GANT: *(Takes a swig)* So?

WILL: *(Laughs)* Right. *(Reaches for bottle and drinks)* How long have you had that hid?

GANT: I don't know.

WILL: If I even thought about having a bottle in the house, Molly would know where I was thinking about hiding it.

GANT: This bottle could have sat on the stove and I don't think Rosie would have even noticed it.

WILL: She's seemed better to me.

GANT: Maybe. I can't tell.

WILL: She was having fun playing poker and all.

GANT: She was?

WILL: You saw her.

GANT: All I saw was her fussing about my dinner.

WILL: No, she was having fun.

GANT: And then I came home.

WILL: Gant, you know that's not—

GANT: Just as well I'm going. I don't feel like I'm doing any good here one way or the other.

WILL: That ain't true.

GANT: Come on. We go out there every day trying to put something in the ground to just hold it down—and nothing. For nothing.

WILL: We haven't had as bad luck as some of the others.

GANT: You seen anything grow out there in a while? Have you?

WILL: Gant, this ain't just rough on you.

GANT: Far as I can tell it's going to be a good deal rougher on you.

WILL: What do you mean?

GANT: Whole farm—what's left of it—and just you to take care of it. *(Takes a swig)* Seems hardly worth hanging on at times, don't it?

WILL: I'm not sure what you're getting at, but I ain't selling out for nothing and hitting the road like those poor stupid sons-of-bitches—everything but the cow tied onto their car.

GANT: Hold on.

WILL: You know you can't sell without my OK.

GANT: I've said nothing about selling.

WILL: Then what the hell are you saying?

GANT: *(Takes a drink)* You've got a baby on the way. I'd never think of putting you on the road. *(Offers the bottle;* WILL *drinks.)* I may not be the one to put you there.

WILL: Oh?

GANT: I don't know if this job's going to make us enough money, that's just it.

WILL: Any money is more than we got.

GANT: I'll tell you, they say they got close to three years of work out there. That's a long time for you to be the only one here, but I'll work as long as you need me to and I'll make us some money.

WILL: You won't have to work any three years. Some money will do us. They'll take part of a loan payment in good faith.

GANT: We'll see.

WILL: The money you send us will make us more money, too—I'll see to that. Weather won't be bad forever, you know. You'll be back here sooner than you know it.

GANT: *(Takes a swig)* You want any more?

WILL: No. Yeah. One more. *(Takes a drink)*

GANT: *(Closes bottle and returns it to its hiding place)* Bedtime.

WILL: Yeah. *(Stands and stretches)* You got anything to take this whisky off my breath?

GANT: Try brushing your teeth.

WILL: I mean before I go home.

GANT: Go on home, Will. What's she going to do, shoot you?

WILL: It's your fault if she does. Goodnight. *(Exits screen door)*

*(*GANT *watches him leave, then retrieves the bottle from its hiding place. He drinks as he speaks to us, leaning on the sink, then sitting at the table. When the speech is done it will be Saturday morning.)*

GANT: When I'm on the tractor and the land starts to blow—that's when it comes back the hardest. Can't hear nothing but the wind in my ears. Can't even hear the tractor running, not even sure that it's moving, as I can't see but a yard in front of me. Then, the dust fills my ears and eyes and clogs the rag tied over my nose and mouth. And time stops. I can't be sure if I've been in the blow five minutes or five hours. Just can't tell. And that's when he comes to me the clearest. Trying to get home from the school. Sure he's on the right path, but not sure how much farther. Times I think I see him myself, and come close to jumping off the tractor to lead him the rest of the way. It's not far. Not too much more. There's two of us. Two of us won't get lost. I come back to, crawling off my tractor seat and know the tricks the storm can play. It ain't settled with him—it wants me, too. And it has crossed my mind how easy it would be to let it have what it wants. Easy as stepping off the tractor and setting my feet on the wind.

(GANT *puts his head on his folded arms and sleeps as morning comes.*)

(*Saturday A.M.*—GANT *asleep on kitchen table, head on arms. The bottle is in front of him.* MOLLY *enters from screen door, sees* GANT, *and keeps the door from slamming, closing it gently. She carries a bowl of hard-boiled eggs with her. She sets the eggs silently on the table, picks up the bottle and looks at it. She carries the bottle over to the sink, dumps the contents, brings the bottle back to the table and puts it down loudly.* GANT *jumps, then rubs his face.*)

GANT: Rosie, I'll be to—

MOLLY: It's morning, Gant.

GANT: (*Sitting up quickly*) Molly. Oooohf. (*Realizing how stiff he is, he rubs his back.*)

MOLLY: Stiff?

GANT: Yeah.

MOLLY: Serves you right.

GANT: (*Sees the bottle in front of him and looks up at her*) I didn't drink that whole thing.

MOLLY: I know, Will helped you.

GANT: (*Picks it up*) No. There was some left.

MOLLY: Well, there isn't now.

GANT: (*Sets bottle down, stands and stretches*) What time is it?

MOLLY: Close to seven.

GANT: I wonder why Rosie didn't wake me up.

MOLLY: Probably because she's not up.

GANT: She's always up at the crack of dawn.

MOLLY: So are you.

GANT: *(Goes to icebox and gets a pitcher of water)* You've made your point, Molly. *(Pours a glass)* I drank some whisky last night. So did Will. I know you think we do it just to annoy you, but I promise that wasn't on our minds at all. *(Drinks some water)*

MOLLY: There's no need to be so cross.

GANT: There's no need to pour half a bottle of perfectly good whisky down the sink. *(Pours the rest of the glass of water over his head, leaning over sink. Rubs his face.)*

MOLLY: I did no such thing.

GANT: Righteous people make rotten liars, Molly. *(Pours another glass of water)* Where's Will?

MOLLY: He's messing with the cow. She's got no milk.

GANT: She ain't been steady for a while. Got nothing decent to feed her.

MOLLY: We'll have to get something. I won't be able to do without her.

GANT: We sure as hell won't get another feed and seed loan. Not until we make good on the last one.

MOLLY: You know what the pay schedule on this railroad job is?

GANT: Every two weeks. They'll hold the first check two weeks, though. It'll be a month before we see any money.

MOLLY: We can keep her alive for a month. But she may go dry completely.

GANT: Then just keep her alive and get some issue powdered milk in the meantime.

MOLLY: I hate to do that.

GANT: You've got it coming. It's paid for.

MOLLY: I just hate to start taking things that other people probably need more. We've done all right.

GANT: You ain't taking nothing that we didn't pay for. That's why we pay taxes—so when we can't afford things the government can. And there's a hell of a lot of things we can't afford right now. For starters, we can't afford to feel like a charity case.

MOLLY: I don't feel like a charity case.

GANT: I do. *(Gulps down the rest of his water)* I'm going to find Will. We've got a lot to do before I leave tomorrow.

MOLLY: When exactly are you leaving?

GANT: Morning.

MOLLY: Morning? It's Easter Sunday.

GANT: I got to be at the railroad office in the valley Monday morning and Will's got to get me to a line that connects there.

MOLLY: Can't it wait until evening?

GANT: I don't know when the line runs and I don't want to chance missing it.

MOLLY: I can't believe they'd have you travel on Easter.

GANT: They don't care what day it is. It really don't matter to me either. The job starts on Monday. I'll be there Monday morning sharp.

MOLLY: Rosie was making some Easter plans.

GANT: I can't do anything about that. You and she can still have your Easter.

MOLLY: It's the first time in a long while she's made any kind of plans.

GANT: I got work to do, Molly. I'll see you all at lunchtime.

(Exits from screen door. MOLLY *watches him go then goes to stove and checks the teakettle. She stokes the stove, then goes to the cupboard and gets four bowls. She goes to another cupboard and gets a bottle of vinegar, then fishes around in another cabinet and finds the food coloring.* ROSIE *enters from the hallway in a long flannel nightgown and a housecoat clutched around her.)*

MOLLY: Morning, Rosie.

ROSIE: Molly.

MOLLY: I just put some water on to boil. You want some tea?

ROSIE: Maybe. *(Sits at the table, looks at the bowls, the eggs, and the whisky bottle, but does not see any of it.)* I'm not feeling so good.

MOLLY: I figured. You're up a good deal later than usual.

ROSIE: I just couldn't even lift my head off the pillow. I hope Gant got Drew to school on time.

MOLLY: Rosie, look at all the eggs I hardboiled. After you have your tea, we'll color them.

ROSIE: What day is it?

MOLLY: Saturday. The day before Easter.

ROSIE: There ain't no school today.

MOLLY: We've got so much to do today. We got to get ready for that Easter supper we talked about yesterday.

ROSIE: We should have ham for Easter.

MOLLY: Wouldn't ham be nice? I wish we could. I don't remember the last time we had ham.

ROSIE: What's in the pantry? What do we have?

MOLLY: I know we have some beans and corn we canned a couple years back.

ROSIE: It was so hot when we did that canning. For days and days.

MOLLY: It's turned out to be worth it. Lots of people ran out of their canning a long time ago.

ROSIE: We got any fruit canned? We should bake a pie.

MOLLY: I don't know. We might. I still have some brown sugar though, so at least we can bake something. And we can have chicken. We should get rid of some of those hens that haven't been laying. They're just using up feed.

ROSIE: You sure?

MOLLY: It'll only be one. We can do with one less hen.

ROSIE: One won't be enough.

MOLLY: One will be fine. (Checks teakettle) Water's hot.

ROSIE: I don't think I want any tea.

MOLLY: You should have some. Make you feel better.

ROSIE: No. Thank you.

MOLLY: (Picks up kettle and pours some hot water into bowls) You want to pour some vinegar in these?

(ROSIE adds vinegar. MOLLY follows with drops of food coloring.)

MOLLY: This will be our yellow bowl, and the blue bowl and the red bowl and let's make a green bowl.

ROSIE: That vinegar is making me a little sick.

MOLLY: I always liked the smell.

ROSIE: It's just not setting right with me.

MOLLY: I'll move it over by the sink. How's that?

ROSIE: No, no just leave them there. I'll be fine.

MOLLY: Let's put an egg in each bowl. Get them started so we can get them finished.

(WILL *and* GANT *enter from screen door.*)

MOLLY: I just wanted them, you know. I think they look so pretty all different colors.

WILL: What is that godawful smell?

MOLLY: Vinegar. For the eggs.

(WILL *looks into the bowls.* GANT *goes to the icebox and takes out the bowl of potato salad.*)

MOLLY: How's the cow?

WILL: Don't know. Gant thinks it's the feed but I think she should be looked at.

GANT: *(Eating out of the bowl of salad)* Vets don't make free calls.

WILL: It would be cheaper than losing her in the long run.

GANT: Well, none of that means nothing since we don't have any money anyway.

MOLLY: Gant, why don't you sit down and I'll fix you a plate.

GANT: Because I don't want to get any closer to that evil-smelling shit.

MOLLY: I swear! I'll just pack them up and take them on over to our house.

GANT: Now Molly. You don't have to do that.

MOLLY: *(Grabs a cookie sheet and puts bowls on it)* No, the smell is making Rosie sick, and you and Will both have to comment on it. *(Picks up tray and bowl of eggs)* I just thought it would be nice to have colored eggs for Easter. Things have been so turned around here I thought it would be nice to do something the way it's supposed to be done. *(Finds she can't open door, as both hands are full.)*

WILL: Let me help you. *(Tries to take the tray)*

MOLLY: Just get the door for me.

(*He does and she exits.*)

GANT: Wonder what's wrong with her.

WILL: I'm not finding out.

GANT: Nobody asked you to. What were you girls talking about?

ROSIE: What?

GANT: You and Molly.

ROSIE: We were just coloring eggs and I didn't feel so good. I still don't.

GANT: What's wrong.

ROSIE: I had one of them headaches this morning. Couldn't lift my head.

GANT: You too, huh?

(WILL *slips out the door and sits on the steps. His departure goes unnoticed.*)

ROSIE: You didn't come to bed last night.

GANT: I didn't quite make it.

ROSIE: I don't sleep good when you're not there. Feels funny. I get cold.

GANT: Rosie. I need for you to do some things for me today.

ROSIE: I should feel better if I lie down for a bit.

GANT: Well, you do that, and when you're feeling better, I'm going to need you to make sure I've got at least two of everything clean and mended— socks, shirts, everything.

ROSIE: I know it's clean. I did my laundry twice yesterday.

GANT: That's right. You did.

ROSIE: I'll check it for holes. I can darn socks in bed.

GANT: One more thing. You know where that old duffel is? The one I had in the service?

ROSIE: I believe it's in the big closet off the front room. I can go look.

GANT: I'll go check on it. You just go lie down. Will?

WILL: Yeah? (*Standing and stepping inside*)

GANT: I'll be with you in just a minute.

WILL: We got a lot of things yet to do. (*Sits and leans back*)

GANT: You could go get started on them.

WILL: Nah, I'll just wait for you.

GANT: Come on, Rosie. Let's put you back to bed.

ROSIE: I got to get my wash off the line first.

GANT: Hadn't you ought to get dressed first?

ROSIE: (*Rising and getting basket by door*) Who's going to see me that already hasn't?

GANT: You're absolutely right. (*She exits.*)

GANT: I just need to hunt something out.

WILL: Go ahead. I'll be here.

(GANT *exits hallway door.* WILL *makes himself very comfortable.* GANT *re-enters some moments later with a duffel over his shoulder and a cardboard box in his arms.*)

WILL: What's that?

GANT: It's for Molly.

WILL: *(Stands and opens box flaps)* For Molly? *(Peers inside, takes an item out)* Gant, these are Drew's baby clothes.

GANT: Give them to Molly.

WILL: I thought you gave all his clothes away.

GANT: I thought we had, too.

WILL: Rosie's gonna—

GANT: I don't want them in the house when I'm away. I don't know why she kept them, but so long as she did, they shouldn't go to waste.

WILL: She'll see them on the baby.

GANT: I'm going to go tell her right now I'm giving them to you. She's apparently been taking them out and looking at them all along.

WILL: You think?

GANT: I don't know. I'll meet you over at your house. *(Exits screen door)*

WILL: *(Watches him go, then picks up the piece of clothing he took out and holds it up. During the speech he will fold it, and close the box up and exit.)* I know that it was a traditional thing to do, but I thought it was cruel and I told Molly so. Molly told me that it was part of Rosie's mourning and if she weren't allowed to wash and dress Drew for that last time she'd feel as though she hadn't properly said goodbye. Gant and I brought him to the kitchen and laid him on the table. That little boy and that big old table. Gant went to the living room while the rest of the search party brought him whisky and talked low. I wasn't being of any use there, so I went back to the kitchen and hauled in a big pan of water. I had to change it three or four times—they couldn't seem to get the dust off of him to Rosie's liking. When he was clean enough and they started to dress him, I helped them to roll him to his side and his mouth fell open. And his mouth was full of dirt, too.

(*It is nighttime and* MOLLY *comes to the screen door with a sweet-potato pie in her hands. She opens the door and comes in quietly. She sets the pie on the kitchen table, and turns to leave as* ROSIE *enters from hallway, dressed in her cotton dress and cardigan.*)

ROSIE: What's this?

MOLLY: What?

ROSIE: *(Pointing at pie on table)* This.

MOLLY: Oh, it's a sweet potato pie for Easter supper. We were out of any fruit in the pantry so it had to be sweet potato.

ROSIE: Sweet potato's fine. With the chicken and all it'll seem more like Thanksgiving, won't it?

MOLLY: I suppose it will.

ROSIE: Is your icebox full?

MOLLY: Pretty full.

ROSIE: I'll just keep it in mine then.

MOLLY: Well, I brought it over so Gant could have some if he wanted it—since he'll be missing supper tomorrow and all.

ROSIE: Yeah.

MOLLY: I was surprised when he told me he was leaving so early, but I suppose he's got to.

ROSIE: It's just going to be you and me then—for supper?

MOLLY: Will should be back by suppertime. Will better be back by suppertime.

ROSIE: You want some coffee? I got some on the stove.

MOLLY: No, thanks. I got a cup getting cold over at our house.

ROSIE: I'm sure Gant will appreciate the pie.

MOLLY: It's not the best one I've ever made.

ROSIE: It's a wonder you could even find all the things to make it with.

MOLLY: I did substitute and scrimp on a thing or two. *(Pause)* Rosie, I don't know how to say this, but I want to thank you for the baby clothes.

ROSIE: *(Unconvincingly)* I meant for you to have them.

MOLLY: I just—we really didn't know how we were going to provide anything like that when the time came.

ROSIE: I'm glad they'll be useful.

MOLLY: We do appreciate them. Well, I guess I'd better get back to my coffee, then off to bed.

ROSIE: Goodnight. See you in the morning.

MOLLY: Goodnight. *(Opens door and starts out)* Oh, do you still want to go to church with me?

ROSIE: How we going to get there?

MOLLY: Oh, no. Will and Gant will have the truck.

ROSIE: If they're not leaving first thing you could ride into town with them and ride back with someone else.

MOLLY: I do want to go.

ROSIE: Doesn't hurt to ask.

MOLLY: Gant down at the shed?

ROSIE: He might be.

MOLLY: I'll just drop by there on my way back. See you in the morning. *(Exits screen door)*

ROSIE: Night.

(ROSIE goes to the icebox and gets a small pitcher of cream, then gets a cup and spoon and sets it all on the table. She pours herself a cup of coffee and sits, with her back to the screen door. GANT enters.)

ROSIE: Did Molly catch up to you?

GANT: Yes, she did. *(Sits at table)*

ROSIE: And?

GANT: We got to leave early. I can't take the chance of missing that train.

ROSIE: You want any coffee?

GANT: I don't think so.

ROSIE: Some of it's real.

GANT: Where'd you get real coffee?

ROSIE: Been saving it.

GANT: What for?

ROSIE: I don't know. Rainy day.

GANT: I guess you've had it for some time.

ROSIE: You want some?

GANT: Yeah. I'll have some.

(ROSIE gets up, gets cup and pours.)

GANT: You bake the pie?

ROSIE: No, Molly did. She dropped it by so you could have some since you'll miss supper tomorrow.

GANT: That was nice of her.

ROSIE: You want a piece?

GANT: What kind is it?

ROSIE: Sweet potato.

GANT: I hate sweet potato.

ROSIE: I thought you liked it.

GANT: No. I like pumpkin.

ROSIE: I can't tell the difference.

GANT: I can.

ROSIE: I'll put it in the icebox then so the bugs don't get to it. *(Gets up, picks up pie, looks through her drawers and finds some cheesecloth and wraps the pie)* Why didn't you tell me you were leaving in the morning?

GANT: I did tell you.

ROSIE: No. I'd have remembered.

GANT: I told you the night I signed up.

ROSIE: No. I wouldn't have been making all these Easter supper plans.

GANT: You probably just didn't hear me.

ROSIE: You just didn't tell me. *(Puts pie in icebox. Stands and folds her arms.)*

GANT: Come on, Rosie. Why would I do a thing like that?

ROSIE: You tell me.

GANT: I told you. I know that. I told you when I was leaving and where I was going and why. And none of it has seemed to really make any sense to you. Molly says you've gone on with your plans tomorrow like I was going to be there when you knew I wasn't.

ROSIE: I've known you were going. I packed your socks and shirts and pants and underwear. I packed you a towel and some soap and something to keep you warm. And I knew why I was doing it. I'm not some—

GANT: All right. I didn't mean that.

ROSIE: What did you mean?

GANT: I didn't mean anything. I want—would you sit down for a minute? I can't talk to you when you're standing in the middle of the room. *(She sits and toys with her coffee spoon.)* I know that you still get your headaches and all and that sometimes you have to take things slow.

ROSIE: This morning was the first I've had in a long while.

GANT: I know. What I'm saying is with me gone and with Molly having the baby soon, there's going to be a lot more to do around here.

ROSIE: I pull my weight.

GANT: Yes, you do. But you'll have to do that and then some.
And you'll have to keep Molly from doing too much.

ROSIE: You know I'd do that anyway. Without having to be told.

GANT: Rosie, this ain't—

ROSIE: I've got a shirt of yours to mend yet. *(Heads toward hallway)*

GANT: Bring it in here so you can finish your coffee. *(Takes a pocketknife out and starts to clean his nails)*

ROSIE: *(Enters with chambray work shirt and sewing box)* You got a big hole in the arm of this. See?

GANT: I caught it on the tractor the other day.

ROSIE: You should have told me. I'd have patched it before I washed it. Hole just got bigger.

GANT: Slipped my mind.

ROSIE: Seems to be happening a lot.

GANT: What?

ROSIE: Things slipping your mind. Like when you'll be leaving.

GANT: Rosie—

ROSIE: And how long you'll be gone.

GANT: There's a reason why I didn't tell you that. It's because I just don't know.

ROSIE: You're just working long enough to pay the loan.

GANT: What if this summer's as bad as the last one? So we pay off the loan but we still don't have anything. No money, no food—nothing. They've got three years worth of work out there—

ROSIE: Three years! Three years!

GANT: I didn't say I was staying out there for three years.

ROSIE: But you didn't say you weren't.

GANT: Would you be—

ROSIE: If this summer's no good and next summer's no good and the next—

GANT: Rosie, would you stop it! Now why do you think I'm doing this? Why? You think I'm doing this to leave my home?

ROSIE: I think there's some truth in that.

GANT: Christ, Rosie! *(Stands and walks around)* I'm doing this so I have a home to come home to...so you have a home and Will and Molly and their child have a home.

ROSIE: So, how long will you be gone?

GANT: I don't know. I just can't say.

ROSIE: It's hard to wait for a day when you're not sure when that day will come.

GANT: I'll be waiting for the day I come home, too.

ROSIE: I suppose that you will. *(Picks up the shirt and looks at it)* I don't think I can just mend this. I'm going to have to patch it.

GANT: Patch it, then.

ROSIE: It's real close to the elbow. I think I've got some denim in here. *(Digs around in box, pulls out denim)* Here it is.

GANT: Your coffee cold?

ROSIE: No, I'm fine. I'll just—oh— *(She has held up the piece of denim to smooth it and cut a piece from it. It is a pair of child's overalls.)*

GANT: Oh, Rosie. Please. I'll just tear the shirt again. Leave it.

ROSIE: No. No. *(She has smoothed out the overalls on the table, stroking them, the scissors in hand.)* I can't send you off with holes in your shirt. Can I? *(Begins to hack at overalls with scissors—they aren't cutting.)*

GANT: It's not important—I'll....

ROSIE: *(Hacking away—getting a bit out of control)* The scissors are dull. They just don't want to—

GANT: Rosie.

ROSIE: *(Picking up overalls and trying to tear them)* They won't cut. They won't cut.

GANT: *(Moving toward her)* Rosie, please.

ROSIE: *(Holding overalls to her)* It's your shirt. I need to fix your shirt.

GANT: *(Moves to hold her)* Rosie.

ROSIE: I can't. Oh, God. *(Hugs him back)* I want him back. Damn God, I want him back with us.

GANT: *(Rocking her)* Hush. Hush, now. Hush.

ROSIE: I want my child.

GANT: I want him, too.

ROSIE: I want you to stay.

GANT: I want to stay, Rosie. I wish that I could.

(They kiss and hold one another. Arms around each other, they walk into the hallway. The sound of the wind gets louder and the lights slowly brighten. As day breaks, the wind subsides. It is dawn, Easter Sunday. WILL knocks at the back door.)

WILL: Gant? Rosie? You all ain't up.

ROSIE: *(Enters from hall, picks up a kerchief and knocks the dust out of it)* Morning, Will.

WILL: Morning. Happy Easter.

ROSIE: Happy Easter.

WILL: Gant about ready?

ROSIE: He's packed.

WILL: Well, we've got to get going soon. Got a way to go. You got any coffee going?

ROSIE: Last night's on the stove.

WILL: *(Goes over to pot, lifts lid and decides it's OK. Pours some.)* You're about out. *(Drinks some)* This is real. Where'd you get this?

ROSIE: Had it for a while, but there's no more.

WILL: That's a shame.

MOLLY: *(Comes to door with a pan full of hot cross buns in one hand and the bowl of colored eggs in the other)* Happy Easter, Rosie.

ROSIE: Morning, Molly.

MOLLY: I baked some hot cross buns for Easter morning. I hope you haven't had breakfast yet.

ROSIE: None yet.

MOLLY: Good. *(Sets them on the table)* You want me to fix some eggs? I'll fix some.

ROSIE: No. These will be fine.

WILL: Hey, Molly—there's some real coffee on the stove.

MOLLY: No kidding. Where'd you get it?

ROSIE: I'd saved it.

MOLLY: *(Looking into the pot)* Wasn't that smart. Looks to be only a cup or so left. I don't want to take the last of it.

ROSIE: Drink it. I'm not going to save it again.

MOLLY: *(Pours herself a cup)* I'll make a fresh pot. *(Pours out the rest of pot into* WILL's *cup)*

ROSIE: You know where everything is.

MOLLY: Should I make a full pot?

ROSIE: I don't know. I don't want any. Will, you want any?

WILL: Not really. Not after this.

(GANT enters from hallway.)

MOLLY: Gant, you want some coffee?

GANT: Any more of the real coffee?

MOLLY: No.

GANT: No, thanks.

WILL: Here—finish mine—that's the last of it.

GANT: I'll just have some milk.

MOLLY: I don't guess I'll make any coffee.

GANT: *(Seeing the buns on the table)* You bake these, Molly?

MOLLY: Yes. For Easter.

GANT: That's right. *(Goes to icebox, pours a glass of milk, and gets butter)* Hot cross buns for Easter.

(Comes to table and sits. ROSIE *gets up and gets plates and knives for everyone. Everyone starts passing food.)*

MOLLY: I got an Easter bunny this morning.

GANT: All the rabbits that's been around here—how do you know you've got the Easter bunny?

WILL: He told her so.

MOLLY: *(Glares at him)* Well, I haven't seen a rabbit since that last time everyone went out shooting them. I thought we'd got 'em all.

WILL: Not a chance.

MOLLY: So, I step off the back steps this morning and there's a rabbit just sitting there. Wasn't all still, but it didn't look like it wanted to run away either. So I walked over and reached down and picked it up.

GANT: Come on.

WILL: It's true.

GANT: Did it have an egg under it?

MOLLY: Now you're making fun of me.

WILL: She came walking into the house with it under her arm.

MOLLY: He asked if it was for breakfast. I nearly hit him.

GANT: Had to be something wrong with it.

MOLLY: Well there was. It's eyes and ears were just full of dust. Poor thing couldn't see or hear.

ROSIE: *(Drops her knife and it clatters on her plate)* Excuse me.

WILL: I was surprised it didn't smell her. Rabbits have real good sense of smell.

GANT: You keep it, Molly?

MOLLY: I washed it up as much as it would let me and put it in a box in the kitchen. I was going to bring it over to you, Rosie, but I wasn't sure you'd want a rabbit. Even if it is the Easter bunny.

ROSIE: I'm not sure I'd know quite what to do with a rabbit.

GANT: How long you going to keep him?

MOLLY: I don't know—just until he's better, I guess.

WILL: I bet it will be longer than that.

MOLLY: What do I need with a rabbit?

WILL: She's already named him.

GANT: What?

WILL: Guess.

GANT: Not Peter?

MOLLY: Of course I named him Peter, what else are you going to call a rabbit?

WILL: *(Laughing)* Peter Rabbit.

GANT: Or Peter Cottontail?

MOLLY: Go on and laugh. Either of you looked in on Elsie this morning?

WILL: No.

MOLLY: Anyone's got a cow named Elsie doesn't need to make fun of me for naming a rabbit Peter.

GANT: Oh, I should go out and check on her. Late as it is.

WILL: We need to get moving. Molly or Rosie can do that.

GANT: It'll take a minute. Leaving can wait a minute.

ROSIE: Go on. I'll take care of her.

GANT: It will only take a minute.

ROSIE: You need to get going. You'll miss the train.

WILL: Go on, Gant. Get your bag and let's go.

GANT: You put that shirt in?

ROSIE: It's on the bed. I mended it this morning.

(GANT *goes to room to get duffel.*)

MOLLY: I'll clear. *(Gets up and clears the plates, etc.)* You think you'll want something to take with you? Some food?

WILL: Probably. Pack something up.

(ROSIE *gets up and goes out the screen door.*)

MOLLY: Rosie—I'll take care of the cow.

ROSIE: I'm not going to take care of the cow, yet.

MOLLY: *(Sotto voce)* She's been real quiet.

WILL: What did you expect?

MOLLY: I never know.

GANT: *(Returns with duffel)* I'll just go put this in the truck.

WILL: I'm right behind you.

MOLLY: Will, you wait. I'm packing up some food for you. *(She's putting hot cross buns and Easter eggs in a paper bag.)*

WILL: Bring it out.

MOLLY: Will, just wait for it.

(WILL *takes the hint and sits down. Focus shift to* ROSIE *and* GANT *outside door.* MOLLY *continues to pack food.*)

GANT: *(Sets duffel down next to him)* Rosie. *(Puts his hands on her arms and turns her to face him)* I will let you know as soon as I can how long I'll be.

ROSIE: Fine.

GANT: It will only be as long as it absolutely has to be. *(Reaches up and takes kerchief off her head)*

ROSIE: Gant, don't, my hair is dirty. *(Reaches for the kerchief that he keeps out of reach)*

GANT: Your hair looks better than this rag on your head.

(Holds it up, then behind him, forcing her to reach around him)

ROSIE: Gant—cut it out.

GANT: *(She is reaching all the way behind him and he kisses her.)* There—that's all I really wanted.

ROSIE: Sometimes, Gant—can I have my kerchief back now?

GANT: *(Stuffs it in his back pocket)* No.

(WILL and MOLLY come out. WILL's got a paper sack in his hands and MOLLY's got a fistful of eggs in both hands. She tries to put them in the already full bag.)

WILL: Molly, that's enough. That's fine. Leave some for the two of you.

(MOLLY manages to get one handful in, but is left with two eggs in her hand.)

WILL: All set?

GANT: All set.

WILL: *(Kisses MOLLY on the cheek)* All right now. You girls take care of yourselves. I'll be back tonight.

MOLLY: Drive careful. *(Hugs GANT)* We'll be seeing you sooner than you know it.

(The men walk off and the women watch.)

MOLLY: Egg? *(Offers the ones in her hand to ROSIE)*

ROSIE: Sure.

(MOLLY sits on the steps. They roll the eggs between their hands.)

MOLLY: It's true. He'll be back before you know it.

ROSIE: I know.

MOLLY: And maybe with enough money to hold off the bank for a while.

ROSIE: I'm sure he will. *(She starts to walk off.)*

MOLLY: I'll take care of the cow.

ROSIE: Molly, I'll take care of the cow.

MOLLY: You should go over and have a look at my Easter bunny.

ROSIE: I will as soon as I take care of the cow.

MOLLY: I'll get started on the supper then.

ROSIE: You've already done all the baking. I don't know what you've got left to do.

MOLLY: The chicken. I've got to take care of the chicken.

ROSIE: Will won't be back until after dark. It can wait.

MOLLY: Well, I just thought....

ROSIE: God in heaven, Molly! Will you just sit still for five minutes and eat your egg.

(ROSIE *exits toward direction of shed.* MOLLY *sits and peels her egg.*)

MOLLY: It seemed at times like things was all coming to an end. That there wasn't going to be a hole to crawl out of when it was all said and done. If it wasn't the blow it was the storms the land couldn't soak up. And then the floods. And the grasshoppers. And the land burning. So much gone that what was left hardly looked like a place a person could call home. A lot of people thought it was their fault—their punishment for one thing or another. I don't know. What could folks do that would be so bad they'd deserve this? I couldn't imagine. Well, I never believed we were being punished—maybe measured—just to see how we'd stand up to it all. That seemed more like it. And I never believed I'd never see good weather again. I never believed we wouldn't see things growing here again. But a lot of people never believed. And they left. Sure, there was a point where even I thought things couldn't get any worse. Then it did get worse. Again and again. But after a while there wasn't nothing left that could surprise us. And that was the beauty of it all. (*She bites into her egg and the lights fade to black.*)

END OF PLAY

MAN OF THE FLESH

Octavio Solis

MAN OF THE FLESH
© Copyright 1993 by Octavio Solis

ABOUT THE AUTHOR

Octavio Solis is a playwright from Texas currently residing in San Francisco. After receiving an MFA degree from Trinity University in San Antonio, Texas, he spent ten years in Dallas working at the Dallas Theater Center, the Arts Magnet High School, and the University of Texas at Dallas. He has studied under Paul Baker, John O'Keefe, and Maria Irene Fornes. His plays MAN OF THE FLESH and PROSPECT have been produced at El Teatro Campesino, San Diego Repertory, the Magic Theater, the Latino Chicago Theater Company, and Teatro Dallas. He has also written SCRAPPERS, a play for young people which toured area high schools for South Coast Repertory's Fall Tour '92 and '93.

He is currently working on the AENEID PROJECT for SCR, and on BURNING DREAMS, an original opera collaboration with Gina Leishman and Julie Hebert for San Diego Repertory. Octavio has received the Barrie and BC Stavis Playwriting Award from the National Theater Conference (1992), and grants from the Lila Wallace/Reader's Digest Fund (1992-93), and The Wallace Alexander Gerbodie Foundation Playwriting Award (1992).

MAN OF THE FLESH was originally commissioned by Teatro Dallas, Cora Cardona, Artistic Director.

MAN OF THE FLESH opened at South Coast Repertory on 4 May 1990. The cast and creative contributors were:

JUAN TENORIO .... Vic Trevino
DON DIEGO TENORIO/FORREST DOWNEY .... Jarion Monroe
ROMELIA/ANNE DOWNEY .... Teresa Velarde
LORENA/HEATHER DOWNEY .... Lucy Rodriguez
MARTINA/DORA DOWNEY .... Joan Stuart-Morris
CONCEPCIÓN/FLOR .... Rose Portillo
FRACAS .... Geoffrey Rivas
LUIS .... Patrick Roman Miller

Director .... José Cruz Gonzáles
Dramaturg .... Jerry Patch
Set design .... Cliff Faulkner
Costume design ....Shigeru Yaji
Lighting design ....Tom Ruzika
Composer/musical director .... Marcos Loya
Movement .... Linda Kostalik-Boussom
Stage manager .... Christine Santmyers

To my mentor and my muse, Jeanne Sexton

CHARACTERS

JUAN TENORIO, *the rake*
DON DIEGO TENORIO, *his father*
ROMELIA,
LORENA, *and*
MARTINA, *three women wronged*
LUIS, LORENA's *brother, a landscaper*
ANNE DOWNEY, *the young* DOWNEY *daughter*
HEATHER, *her older sister*
FORREST DOWNEY, *the feeble patriarch of the house*
DORA DOWNEY, *the mistress of the house*
MAID/FLOR
WOMAN/CONCEPCIÓN, *the ghost of* JUAN's *mother, La Calaca Flaca*
FRACAS, JUAN's *friend, landscaper, and narrator*

Various revellers, masked and costumed

ACT ONE

Prologue

(Music. Lights come up on a large neighborhood pavilion, gaily decorated with streamers, balloons, and various comical incarnations of the Merry cadaver. A Day of the Dead altar is set conspicuously in a central area. Other articles of furniture and set-pieces to be used later in the play are also strewn about. As the music swells, a group of revellers dressed for the holiday charge in. Laughter and song. When they discover the audience, they freeze in place. The music stops. One of the revellers, attired in an ill-fitting skeleton outfit, cautiously approaches the audience and slips his mask off.)

FRACAS: Don't be scared. Don't be fooled. It's only me. Fracas.
I'm not so accustomed to looking like these calacas,
But this holiday fever has made us all kinda raucous.
These are some of my friends, so don't get so nervous,
All of us work at the Pronto Lawn Service.
But Don Diego, the boss, drove up in his Honda
And gave us the weekend off, es la mera onda!
So we drink, we eat, we dance, we sing,
We make a little love, we have a little fling,
But don't even suppose this is Halloween.
This is something more in between.
A holiday, my friends, strictly reserved
Not for the living, but the dead and disturbed.
The second night of November they'll be among us,
Covered with maggots and withering fungus.
I don't like to promise, but this much I know—
If spirits can walk, they'll walk in this show.
Well, we're off, man, we'll leave Don Diego there.
See you later at the party, come if you dare!
En la pachanga, cabrones, alli los quiero ver!

(He puts on his mask and rejoins his group. Music resumes as they raise an unearthly howl and stumble off. As if by magic, DON DIEGO is revealed standing at the altar for his wife, adding decorations to it.)

Scene One

(ROMELIA *enters, quietly. Hardly a girl of fourteen and dressed in simple schoolgirl clothes, she tugs at her sweater to draw it over her prodigious belly.*)

ROMELIA: Don Diego.

DON DIEGO: *(Without turning to see her)* I'm closed for the weekend, Romelia.

ROMELIA: Quiero hablar con usted.

DON DIEGO: See me on Monday. El lunes.

ROMELIA: But this is important.

DON DIEGO: So is the altar. All it needs now is the wine, the eggs, and the picture of Kennedy.

ROMELIA: Es sobre Juan.

DON DIEGO: ¿Y en que se metió? What's he got into now?

ROMELIA: Me.

(DON DIEGO *peers up at her.*)

DON DIEGO: Oh my God.

ROMELIA: ¡No tengo ni quince años!

DON DIEGO: ¿Pero cómo? I saw you at the store yesterday. You weren't like this!

ROMELIA: I know. Everything was fine, as far as I knew. But last night, when I went to bed, I couldn't sleep. I felt so hot, and I kept hearing the house creak and groan and shift. The lights came on all by themselves and the clock fell off the wall. I sat up in bed, pulled back the sheets, and saw this!

DON DIEGO: ¡No lo creo! ¿Es una panza real o es de pan?

ROMELIA: Of course it's real. Why don't you ask Juan?

DON DIEGO: How far along are you?

ROMELIA: Four months and twelve days.

DON DIEGO: How can you know exactly?

ROMELIA: All it took was one try. ¡Me siento cambiada! ¡Diferente!

DON DIEGO: *(Guiding her to a seat)* Ay, nina. Sientate. Tell me how it happened.

ROMELIA: How does it usually happen, Don Diego? All he had to do was look at me and my dress was on the floor!

DON DIEGO: Weren't you afraid this was going to develop?

ROMELIA: He had some protection, but when he found out I was still a virgin, he popped it in his mouth like chewing gum.

DON DIEGO: Disgraceful! I don't know what to say!

ROMELIA: He said if I ever got pregnant, I should thank him for it, 'cause a baby born on this side is a sure way to get a green card.

DON DIEGO: ¿Eso te dijo el cabron?

ROMELIA: It's true, isn't it? They won't deport me if my baby's born here, will they?

(He stammers helplessly for a while as angry shouting from off interrupts. LUIS storms in with his pregnant sister LORENA in tow.)

LUIS: Where is he! Where is that bastard!

DON DIEGO: Luis! ¿Que te pasa, hombre?

LUIS: Look at this, Don Diego! Look at what that scumbag has done to my sister!

DON DIEGO: You, too?

LUIS: He knocked her up! He took her purity! My own goddarned sister! Her reputation, Don Diego, is ruined!

LORENA: Oh, it's not that big a deal. He said he'd marry me.

LUIS: Shut up! I don't want to hear a word out of you!

LORENA: Luis, it's my body! I can do with it what I want!

LUIS: Apparently, he thinks so too! You know what else she did? She gave him all my savings! All the money I had in the world!

LORENA: Cool it. He needed to buy the wedding ring.

LUIS: That money I was saving for her Confirmation. I had already ordered the invitations and the flowers. I spent weeks working on it. Only this pops up overnight like a weed! That very same day, five reliable witnesses swear they see tears of motor oil dripping out of the virgin's eyes at San Xavier.

I call that a bad sign, man.

DON DIEGO: And I suppose my son's responsible.

LUIS: Who else would lift my sister's skirt with one hand and take my money with the other? He's brought my life to a screeching halt!

LORENA: Ay, Luis, I'm having a baby, not a flat tire!

DON DIEGO: If it will make you feel any better, Romelia here has a similar problem.

LUIS: Did he get you, too?

ROMELIA: Kind of.

LUIS: ¿Vez? ¡Es una maldición sobre todas las mujeres del mundo! *(More commotion off. They turn to see* MARTINA *plow in, also pregnant. She is an older, plainer woman.)*

DON DIEGO: Who is it this time?

MARTINA: Oh, when I find him! Oh, when I get my hands on him! I'll tear him to pieces! I'll rip his balls off one by one!

DON DIEGO: Take a number.

MARTINA: *(Gazing at the others)* What's going on here? Who are they supposed to be?

ROMELIA: Oh no!

LORENA: I don't believe this!

MARTINA: You're not also...

ROMELIA: We are.

MARTINA: But it wasn't Juan who....

LORENA: Oh yes it was.

LUIS: If I were a woman, I'd be pregnant, too.

MARTINA: ¡Pero cómo! What kind of infernal seed does that man have? I've gone from a size six to a size sixteen in twelve hours!

DON DIEGO: All right, Martina. Calm down.

MARTINA: How the hell am I supposed to calm down? I'm having a baby! It was hardly three months ago at my wedding, and my husband is about to say "I do." What happens? The Migra shows up and drags his ass off. That night Juan shows up to lend a shoulder to cry on. He promises this, he promises that, he gets into this, he gets into that, and before I know it, my skirt's clear over my head! Now that my husband is back and ready to dig in his heels, what happens? This balloons like an empanada!

DON DIEGO: How far along are you?

MARTINA: I'm three months pregnant!

LORENA: I'm four!

ROMELIA: I'm four and twelve days!

DON DIEGO: ¡Bueno pues! But what do you want me to do?

ROMELIA: Find him!

LUIS: Beat the living shit out of him!

LORENA: Give him my love!

MARTINA: Put his balls in a bread basket!

DON DIEGO: Look, there's no need to get vulgar. I realize what kind of man my son is, I know what he's capable of, and believe me, there'll be restitution!

(JUAN, *who has been surreptitiously watching the previous scene, finally makes his entrance, nonchalantly, gracefully. He is young and virile, clad in dark tight-fitting garments that flatter his sinuous figure: Boots and steel tips. A belt with a silver buckle. Dark hair slicked back from his even darker eyes, which glint with their own perverse wisdom. The bearing of a nobleman comfortably draped in a slouch. He smiles with perfectly white teeth.*)

JUAN: Like hell. (*Everyone falls silent as he strolls in.*)

JUAN: ¿Qué tal, jefe?

MARTINA: You've got a hell of a nerve.

JUAN: I guess I must.

LUIS: Came to see the damage you've done?

JUAN: No, just came by to get some change. Papa, can you break a hundred for me? (*He casually slips a hundred-dollar bill from his sleeve.*)

LUIS: That's mine! That's my money! (*He reaches for the bill.* JUAN *puts it away.*)

JUAN: Calmate, Luis. This is from my holiday fund. (*Directing his gaze toward the women*) ¡Orale! ¿Qué onda? What's this? ¿La Niña, la Pinta, y la Santa Maria?

ROMELIA: It's not funny, Juanito.

MARTINA: My husband's left me on account of you.

JUAN: Flattery will get you nowhere, chica.

LORENA: How could you do this with them? You said you loved me!

JUAN: That was before I found out he was your brother.

LUIS: I don't look forward to being your in-law either, mano.

JUAN: Don't worry. You won't be.

LUIS: ¡Desgraciado!

JUAN: Hey, say what's on your mind, vato.

LUIS: You think they're all here for your amusement, don't you?

JUAN: ¿Qual es tu pinchi pedo, Luis?

LUIS: I'm going to tell everyone you're nothing but a damn louse! Thoughtless, heartless—

JUAN: —And politically incorrect.

LUIS: Son of a bitch!

DON DIEGO: *(Coming between them)* ¡Basta! Call him what you like pero no en frente del altar de mi esposa! Don't come in here slurring the name of my wife and expect me to take it sitting down! She was a good woman and she worked like a dog to raise him well, even if it hardly shows now. Don't blame her character for his.

LUIS: Lo siento, Don Diego. No quise ...I didn't mean....

DON DIEGO: I know, I know. Juan, you really stunk up the works this time. How the hell do you do it? Why can't you stick to one woman for a change?

JUAN: *(As he makes change out of the till)* I will when I find her, Papa.

MARTINA: Is that your excuse for rape?

JUAN: Rape?

LUIS: That's right! Violación, cabrón!

LORENA: I'm only sixteen!

ROMELIA: I'm fourteen!

MARTINA: That makes you a felon!

JUAN: ¡Pero no las viole! *(He shifts his tone as he approaches each of the women.)* I may have enjoyed the sweet and sacred pleasures of the night with you. I may have pried apart the velvet folds of womanhood and breathed where no man should. I may have even dipped a little of my nature into yours. But I never forced myself on you. What kind of brute do you think I am?

MARTINA: Don't you start that shit with me.

JUAN: Would I really have gone to bed with you without the consent of your ardor? Would I have spent a glorious minute of my time engulfed by you if I thought your will was not immersed in mine? I never forced myself on you. Ladies, it was the force of your beauty that had its way with me.

(LORENA swoons. ROMELIA's dress slips to the floor.)

MARTINA: *(Bravely resisting him)* It doesn't matter! In the eyes of the law, you raped us!

JUAN: The Law should keep its eyes to itself.

(The phone rings. DON DIEGO goes to answer it.)

JUAN: If it's for me, Papa, tell her I'm not here.

(DON DIEGO *remains on the phone as the others resume.*)

ROMELIA: Then what are you going to do about it?

LORENA: Are you still marrying me, Juanito?

MARTINA: Think about it, Juan. El tiempo ha cambiado, and these days, a woman assumes her rights!

JUAN: Just don't assume I respect them.

ROMELIA: (*Grabbing him*) He's mine, I called it!

LORENA: (*Grabbing his other arm*) ¡Te casas con migo, chiquito! That money's for my ring!

MARTINA: (*Shoving the others away and taking him for herself*) Get your claws off him! He's moving in with me!

LUIS: That's not fair! He raped my sister first!

ROMELIA: And he raped me before her!

MARTINA: Look, you two are still kids. You're young and strong enough to catch yourselves any guy you want. I'm a lot older. I can't go on like this much longer!

LORENA: But he told me he loved me! He wrote me passionate letters on perfumed paper telling me so! See?

(LORENA *produces a letter, which* MARTINA *unceremoniously snatches and sniffs.*)

MARTINA: Old Spice. My husband's Old Spice.

ROMELIA: ¡Quiero mi green card!

JUAN: ¡Momento! ¡Momento! I can't shack up with all of you. There's laws against that in this state. Besides, you wouldn't like it. The decent thing to do, I think, to spare everyone hassle, is to call the whole thing off and start over.

LUIS: That's not fair!

MARTINA: One of us is going to nail you!

JUAN: Then who's it going to be? You? You? Or you? I take my vows. Move in my things. Put my velvet Elvis over the bed. Make the kid respectable. What then? I guarantee you, as soon as I step off the altar, I'm going to sleep with the prettiest bridesmaid. Vows are nothing to me. I make them every day. I break them every night. ¿Que dicen? ¿Se avientan?

LUIS: He'll never change. I know him.

ROMELIA: I couldn't raise my kid like that.

LORENA: I'd be ashamed to show my face around.

MARTINA: You've got a lousy future, Juan.

JUAN: I'm only thinking of your honor. I'm a man of the flesh. Solo me casare con la mujer ideal.

LUIS: Then why can't Lorena be your ideal, if that's what you want. You told her you loved her.

MARTINA: He told us all that.

JUAN: You don't give me enough credit if you think I didn't mean it.

LORENA: Then why won't you marry us? Me!

JUAN: Biology, queridas. As much as I'm attracted, I am repelled. You're fantastic creatures, all of you, but giving in to you brings my nature back to me. You remind me that I'm only a man. Nothing special about me. No tengo magia negra en mis pantalónes. The only magical thing in my pants is usually someone else's hands. The rest is small and tender. Hardly worth the trouble. *(His tone darkens as he slowly scans each of them.)* But the mystery for me is that gazing at you draws from that soft withered skin an impossible serpent. Biology.

(They stand mesmerized for an instant. Even DON DIEGO *sets the receiver aside.)*

ROMELIA: For that you hate us?

JUAN: *(Ruefully)* Only after it's over.

LUIS: When they get pregnant.

JUAN: I'm a very lucky man and it tends to rub off. If you say your Padre Nuestros and save up your centavos, your problem could be over in a matter of days.

MARTINA: Meaning?

JUAN: I know a good abortionist.

*(*LUIS, *finally enraged, rushes toward him.)*

LUIS: I've had enough!

*(*DON DIEGO *hangs up the phone and intercedes.)*

DON DIEGO: Come on! No rough stuff in here!

(He stands against LUIS, *preventing him from attacking* JUAN.*)*

JUAN: Gotta tell you, Luis. I'm not a fair fighter.

LUIS: ¡Vamos a ver!

*(*LUIS *springs past* DON DIEGO *and grabs hold of* JUAN. *In a flash,* JUAN's *feral instincts react as he strikes* LUIS *in the face and stomach. He trips and falls to the*

floor and JUAN *plants his knee against his back. The women scream and scramble to* LUIS'*s aid.* DON DIEGO *holds them back.)*

LORENA: Luis! Let him go, Juan!

DON DIEGO: ¡NO! ¡Para tras! ¡No se muevan!

JUAN: Want me to snap your spine in half, compa?

DON DIEGO: He'll do it. He's done it before.

LORENA: Please, Juanito. Don't hurt him. He doesn't mean it.

MARTINA: *(Dashing to the phone)* I'm calling the police!

*(*JUAN *releases* LUIS *and lunges toward* MARTINA, *snapping the phone from her hand.)*

JUAN: ¡Orale, pues! Let me dial the chota. And while I'm at it, why don't I give the INS a buzz? They might like to see who's got their papers.

(He starts to dial. The others panic.)

ROMELIA: ¡No! ¡Eso no!

LORENA: ¡Basta!

MARTINA: You want to get us in trouble?

LORENA: ¡Luis! ¡Dile que no llame!

LUIS: *(Still recovering from the assault)* I dare him to do it.

LORENA: What?

LUIS: Go ahead, big man! Call them!

MARTINA: Are you crazy? *(To* JUAN*)* Juan, we won't make any trouble... we got families...jobs....Don't call them...please....

*(*JUAN *bursts into laughter as he replaces the receiver.)*

JUAN: What the hell! This is a holiday! We should be celebrating! ¿Verdad, Papa?

DON DIEGO: I think he's right about leaving these matters alone for awhile. Trust me. I know how you must feel. My honor's still more or less in one piece. I think it's only right that I offer you something for your problems.

MARTINA: In cash!

JUAN: *(Pulling out and counting his bills)* Papa, don't be such a sap!

*(*DON DIEGO *snatches the money from* JUAN *as he continues.)*

DON DIEGO: I mean every word. I'll pay for whatever expenses, medical and so forth, that you may decide on. I'll call you tomorrow. We'll make arrangements then.

LUIS: Thanks all the same, Don Diego, but I'll make my own arrangements. Save your money for your son's funeral. *(Turning to* JUAN*)* Because the next girl you try to screw will be your last. Mark my words.

MARTINA: He's right, Don Diego. One of these nights, he'll go to hell head first with a knife up his ass! *(She storms out.)*

LORENA: Una vez más. Dime que tu amor era de verdad. Just a sign that you really cared.

*(*JUAN *takes his toothbrush out and scrubs his teeth.)*

LUIS: *(Taking* LORENA *by the arm)* Don't waste your time with him. He's an animal!

*(*LUIS *and* LORENA *leave.* ROMELIA *follows them in tears.)*

ROMELIA: All I want is my green card!...

*(*JUAN *spits and laughs aloud.)*

DON DIEGO: What on earth are you thinking with? Fourteen! Sixteen! Schoolgirls and spinsters!

JUAN: It's the way of the world, jefe, and we just gotta live with it. This system of chasing down any woman in sight no longer stands the test of reason. From now on, it's only virgins for me.

DON DIEGO: But they're the most trouble!

JUAN: They're also the safest. A lot of diseases out there, Papá, and I plan on being around for a long time. I'm sticking to virgins.

DON DIEGO: And how many more of these children are you going to breed?

JUAN: Get wise, Papá. We know where those little pups will end up. Nobody really cares to see the Tenorio line extended.

DON DIEGO: How can you say that?

JUAN: Look around you, jefe. How many tiny Tenorios do you see? Eh? No woman wants her baby to have a father like me. They'd rather have it ripped from the womb than see it in my arms.

DON DIEGO: If your mother was alive, she'd be ashamed of you. ¡Y mañana va venir! I'm finishing up the decorations for her altar.

JUAN: Old man, you're going to have to get over this superstition bullshit. My old lady is dead and buried. She's history. She doesn't give a shit what I do with my free time.

DON DIEGO: She cares more for you than you think.

JUAN: Then where the hell is she? Where has she been all these years? Can you tell me that? Every year you set all this food and stuff for her like you expect her to show up for a stack of old tortillas. She's not the Downey maid anymore, jefe, she's not going to show up for the weekends to see how I'm doing in school. She's dead.

DON DIEGO: Death is not so final.

JUAN: If she ever shows up here, you know what I'm going to do?
(He removes the photograph of his mother from the altar.) I'll ask the old bitch to dance! We'll dance to the same old lullabies she sang me to sleep with!

DON DIEGO: Stop it! Put that back!

JUAN: *(Dancing with the photo pressed against his crotch)* Can you believe those songs? *(Singing)* Niña niña de mis sueños! De mi soledad!

DON DIEGO: ¡Infeliz!

(In the struggle for the photo, it falls to the floor and breaks.)

JUAN: Sorry about that, patrón.

DON DIEGO: Shut up and sit down. I'm through cleaning up after you! From now on, you're paying for your own disgraces! It so happens that was Mr Downey on the phone.

JUAN: Did you tell him we're all out of maids?

DON DIEGO: ¡Más respeto! He treated your mother with kindness.

JUAN: So?

DON DIEGO: He wants some work done on his estate tomorrow for his daughter's birthday party.

JUAN: What's it got to do with me?

DON DIEGO: You're working for Pronto Lawn and Garden now.

JUAN: Sorry. I don't do yardwork. That's for Mexicans.

DON DIEGO: You're doing it if you expect to live in this house. *(Handing him the keys and the address slip)* Here. Keys to the truck. Address. Be there at seven. *(As he retrieves the photo of his wife from the floor)* I'm sending Luis along to keep an eye on you.

JUAN: Ay, apá, he's a shit!

DON DIEGO: I don't care. He'll see to it that you work.

JUAN: Well, can I bring Fracas along just in case? At least he's good for a few laughs.

DON DIEGO: *(Examining the picture)* Take him.

(JUAN reads the address.)

JUAN: Corona Del Mar!

DON DIEGO: They're good people. Don't mess it up.

JUAN: Leave it to me, Papá!

DON DIEGO: And every dime you make is going to these women, understand? Cada centavo!

JUAN: ¡Relájate, hombre! Sabes que? Te estaba watchado, jefe. ¡Si no te relajas, te va ir mal! Your blood pressure, man. Take this for what it's worth, but maybe you need to get laid!

DON DIEGO: Out! Get out! Go!

(JUAN *runs out laughing.* DON DIEGO *gazes at the photo of his wife and speaks.*)

DON DIEGO: ¿Que voy hacer con el? No me hace caso. I can't keep an eye on him. Can you?

(*He waits for a reply. Behind him, the candles on the altar blow out, sending the scene to blackout.*)

Scene Two

(*The Day of the Dead revellers return in a whirl of dance and song. They remove the desk and bring on rakes, spades, sprinklers, and other garden tools. They also carry on a bench and whatever other accouterments are necessary to establish the Downey lawn—trellises, fake underbrush, etc. A tremendous roar is heard off, and they rush for the wings.* FRACAS *enters, operating a lawn blower across the stage. He is visibly upset. He shouts expletives over the din as he shoves the machine around. When he spies the audience, he shuts the motor off and vents his wrath on them.*)

FRACAS: As I was saying before in my frank and true manner,
I am very pissed off and partial to slander.
I was all set to party and drink myself blind
Instead of putting in some damn overtime.
My ruca was waiting with a bottle of ron,
But here I am working on the Big Downey Lawn.
Mind you, I could use the money for later tonight
When me and my girl can celebrate right,
But for now, I must deal with lawns and lawnblowers,
With Luis working faster and Juan working slower.
But Juanito's a good man to watch with the chicks.
I'll watch him closely to learn some of his tricks,
And those that don't work, I'll be sure to pass—

LUIS: (*Shouting from off*) FRACAS!

FRACAS: —to Luis, the approaching jackass.

(LUIS *angrily stalks on, dressed in muddy dungarees.*)

LUIS: All right. Where is he?

FRACAS: Who?

LUIS: Juan, that's who!

FRACAS: Oh, he's taking a break right now.

LUIS: But we just started working half an hour ago!

FRACAS: His allergies started acting up.

LUIS: Allergies? What allergies? He doesn't have no stinking allergies!

FRACAS: He's allergic to grass, Louie. It's terrible. I can't bear to look. It makes him so weak, he has to lie down or he'll fall. He had to stop to take his medicine. He's smoking it right now.

LUIS: He's smoking his medicine?

FRACAS: *(As he produces a joint of his own)* Mota, ese. See? He rolled one for me, too.

LUIS: You addicts are all the same.

FRACAS: Hold it right there, Luis! Marijuana is not addictive.

LUIS: How would you know?

FRACAS: I smoke it every day, ese.

(JUAN *rushes in, cradling something small in his hand. He is dressed in work clothes, with a bandana wrapped around his head.*)

JUAN: Fracas! Look! Check this out! See this? What's that on the leaf?

FRACAS: *(Peering closely)* Ladybugs. Two of them.

JUAN: Yeah, but can you tell me what they're doing?

FRACAS: Sure. One of them is riding the— *(He gapes at* JUAN.*)* Holy shit. Are they inseminating?

JUAN: That's right. They're fucking. Exercising the most natural of drives. Generating their own future. Getting down.

LUIS: So? They're only insects.

JUAN: They're a lot like us, Louie. A lot of these little bugs, as soon as they mate, they die. It's like doing it kills them. All life on this pinchi planet that requires sex requires death. You know what lives forever? Bacteria.

LUIS: That's why we have the sacraments. We don't need to die if we have God.

JUAN: Too bad we don't live in the Bible. We live in the real world, where even you got to do the dirty deed.

LUIS: We call it Holy Matrimony. And we treat women like ladies.

JUAN: But what's a lady to a ladybug, Louie? You're still gonna die as you multiply. Then you'll find out for sure if God is God or just a bed full of bacteria.

FRACAS: *(Still examining the bugs intently)* Pobrecítos.

LUIS: Say what you like. I'm happy with my wife. I don't need to run around like you. You may have impressed my sister, but you've got nothing I want.

JUAN: *(Producing the hundred-dollar bill)* You got change for a hundred?

LUIS: Give me that! Give it!

(The sound of voices off)

FRACAS: Hey! Look alive, ese! ¡Alguien viene!

LUIS: Shit! Straighten up and look busy! Get the rakes! Move!

(FRACAS puts the leaf in his pocket. They pretend to work very intensely, except JUAN, who gives up after a while. MR and MRS DOWNEY enter, inspecting the grounds.)

MR DOWNEY: Okay, okay. You're telling me you want the tables here and the band there? Even though you know very well we'll have to run extensions across the yard? Is that what you want?

MRS DOWNEY: I told you. I like the band there, not there. That way the tables can go up here. We can still have the nice southern exposure.

MR DOWNEY: Well, I'd rather have the band set up there and put the tables for the guests here. The hell with the southern exposure.

MRS DOWNEY: Forrest, you wanted this costume party in the first place. And you wanted to keep it outside. The least you can do is make it worth my while.

MR DOWNEY: All I want is to keep the hordes on the lawn and out of the house. I don't want this to get crazy.

MRS DOWNEY: Maybe this wasn't such a good idea after all.

MR DOWNEY: Dora, don't start with me again.

MRS DOWNEY: Do we have to discuss this in front of the help?

MR DOWNEY: Who? *(He turns to see the others.)* Oh.

(He goes to greet LUIS as MRS DOWNEY sits and watches JUAN take his shirt off to rake some leaves.)

MR DOWNEY: *(In wretched Spanish)* Loo-ees! Como ésta?

LUIS: Good morning, Mr Downey. Mrs Downey, you look very nice today.

MRS DOWNEY: Glad someone noticed.

MR DOWNEY: How long will it take you to get this ready for tonight?

LUIS: Oh, not long. A few hours at the most.

MR DOWNEY: About a quarter inch on the lawn.

LUIS: Quarter inch.

MR DOWNEY: And remember to rake up all the leaves.

LUIS: No problem—

FRACAS: "Leaf" it to us!

(FRACAS enjoys his little pun.)

MRS DOWNEY: *(Her eyes fixed on JUAN)* Are these your new helpers?

LUIS: Yes, ma'am, Fracas. And this is Juan Tenorio.

(JUAN kisses her hand.)

FRACAS: He's allergic to grass.

MR DOWNEY: Are you Diego's boy?

JUAN: Yes sir.

MR DOWNEY: I haven't seen you since you were this high. Look, Dora, it's Diego's boy!

MRS DOWNEY: He's not much of a boy now.

MR DOWNEY: I'll say. Stepping in your daddy's shoes? Eres todo un hombre!

JUAN: Something like that.

MR DOWNEY: It's a fine line of work. You're bound to go places. Don Diego's such a good man. I've always like him. You know, your mama used to work here some time ago—

(His daughter HEATHER calls from off.)

HEATHER: MOM! MOM, WAIT UP!

MRS DOWNEY: It's Heather. She must be back from the stores. Try to be nice to her, okay?

(HEATHER enters, carrying a large shopping bag—a voluptuous girl in her late teens.)

HEATHER: *(Dashing on)* Oh, Mom, wait'll you see what I got! We are talking a hit tonight! Boys will line up outside and girls will keel over and die!

MRS DOWNEY: Maybe you should let me wear it.

(HEATHER *produces her costume from the bag—a red cloak and short skirt.*)

HEATHER: Isn't it just? (*As she models it*) Doesn't it simply reek of sex? This is the kind of outfit Gamma pledges only dream of!

MRS DOWNEY: I love it! Turn around.

HEATHER: What do you think, Daddy?

MR DOWNEY: I hope you put it on your own card.

HEATHER: You haven't even looked at it.

MR DOWNEY: What else do you have in the bag?

HEATHER: Picnic basket and my mask, that's all. Why?

MR DOWNEY: Did you buy your sister a present? You didn't buy Anne a present, did you?

HEATHER: I didn't have time. Besides, she's got everything she wants.

MR DOWNEY: Go back to the mall and get your sister a nice gift.

HEATHER: Why should I? What's she ever done for me? Mom, why does he have to be such a drip?

MR DOWNEY: You watch your language around me, young lady! I won't tolerate—

MRS DOWNEY: Forrest, don't overexcite yourself. Remember what the doctor said.

(MRS DOWNEY *and* HEATHER *point to their hearts and simulate a tiny explosion.*)

MR DOWNEY: I'm not telling you again.

(*He storms off as* HEATHER *angrily shoves her costume back into the shopping bag.*)

HEATHER: God bless!

MRS DOWNEY: All right. Sit down.

(HEATHER *joins her on the bench.*)

MRS DOWNEY: What are you so testy about? Isn't your boyfriend coming?

HEATHER: No, it's too far to drive, he says.

MRS DOWNEY: There'll be other boys at the party.

HEATHER: Goobers. Sappy pinheads from down the street. I don't want anything to do with Anne's high school friends. I bought this outfit to go with the kind of guy who looks good in a red Jag. A guy like that.

(*She points at* JUAN.)

MRS DOWNEY: He doesn't have a red Jag, dear. Come on, let's see how this looks on you.

(She leads HEATHER out.)

MRS DOWNEY: And try not to call your father a drip.

HEATHER: Why not? You do.

(They are gone. JUAN drops his rake and watches them go. LUIS observes the look in his eye and sneaks behind him.)

LUIS: Pretty nice for her age, huh?

JUAN: I've seen better.

LUIS: I saw how you were looking at her.

JUAN: Looks don't mean a thing.

LUIS: Then what about the daughter? Did you like her?

JUAN: I know what you're trying to do. Forget it, Louie. You're not going to catch me so easily.

LUIS: It's a matter of time, homes. You're too weak to resist any of them for long.

JUAN: I'm stronger than you think.

LUIS: I'll believe that when I see it.

FRACAS: *(Catching sight of ANNE as she enters)* Hey, you guys! Mira no más! *(They turn to see ANNE enter—young, beautiful, serene, sunglasses. She stops to wipe mud off her shoe. In her hand, she carries a tousled bouquet of flowers.)*

ANNE: Can you guys cut me some of those orange flowers?

LUIS: No problem, Miss—

(LUIS starts to go toward the flowers with his shears. JUAN stops him. He looks at him, then at ANNE.)

JUAN: Why don't you get them yourself?

ANNE: Me?

JUAN: You're as close to them as we are.

ANNE: *(Slowly getting angry)* I don't have anything to cut them with.

(JUAN takes LUIS's shears from him and tosses them at her feet.)

JUAN: Now you do.

(ANNE regards him circumspectly for a moment, then bends down to pick up the shears. She goes to the flowers.)

JUAN: Does your father know you're doing this?

ANNE: Yes. Why should you care?

JUAN: I don't want him to blame me for destroying his garden.

ANNE: Don't worry. *(She snips a single blossom off.)* I'm only taking one.

(She tosses the shears back at him. He has to leap aside to keep them from catching his feet. She turns to LUIS.*)*

ANNE: You should teach the new help some manners, Luis.

JUAN: Like what?

ANNE: You can start by remembering who lives here, who pays your wages, and who deserves some respect.

JUAN: *(Crossing to her)* Your father, my boss, and no one in particular.

ANNE: I don't like the way you smell.

JUAN: That's a pity. You don't know what you're missing. In my line of work, these smells are everywhere. To be a landscaper is to have a long fetid love affair with the fragrances of the earth.

ANNE: You mean flowers?

JUAN: I mean everything. The stink of this fertilizer, for instance, reminds me of the orgies of grass going on right under your feet.

*(*ANNE *steps aside.)*

ANNE: Where did you learn to speak English?

JUAN: My mother.

ANNE: It's my birthday, you know.

JUAN: I know.

ANNE: I'm sixteen.

JUAN: It's a special day for all of us.

(She glares at him for a moment. Turns and goes. Everyone remains still.)

FRACAS: Wow.

LUIS: You asshole.

*(*JUAN *dips two fingers in his mouth, placing them firmly against his lower gums. Slowly he extracts them and looks down at them.)*

LUIS: What the hell is that?

JUAN: Sangre. Sangre de mi amor. This blood from my gums is a sign of real love! *(He starts to rush off in the direction* ANNE *went.)*

LUIS: Where do you think you're going?

JUAN: Get out of my way!

FRACAS: ¿Que te pasa, Juanito?

LUIS: Is this guy tripping or what?

JUAN: LOOK AT ME! My hands are shaking! I can't breathe! I feel like I'm coming alive all over again!

FRACAS: What are you talking about, ese?

JUAN: That girl! That girl! She's the one I've been waiting for! The only one!

LUIS: You've got to be kidding! You can't fall in love with her! You can't fuck with these people!

JUAN: She's the angel of the lullabies!

LUIS: Besides, I know you too well. You're going to use her like the rest.

JUAN: That's where you're wrong, ese. I'm in love with this bitch!

FRACAS: She's a rich white chick, Juanito!

JUAN: Fracas, you're looking at a new man. These hands are touching nothing but the purity of her skin. From this moment on, ese.

LUIS: You make yourself look ridiculous.

JUAN: I know this girl, Louie. She was described to me verse by verse in the songs my mother sang to me. I went to sleep dreaming of this girl.

LUIS: You're not going to change. You can't change. She's class, man. Out of your league. She wouldn't think twice about us Mexicans. You make one pass at her and you're dead. Get back to work. (*He charges off in a fury.*)

JUAN: You watch. I'm going to make her mine, Fracas. Those lips as red and tight as rosebuds. That glow in her eyes. That hair. I'll bury myself in it and call her name over and over and... (*Turning to* FRACAS) What was her name again?

FRACAS: Anna.

JUAN: ANNA! (JUAN *swoops down on the flowers and with the garden shears snips off a bunch of marigolds. He leaves in a rapture.*)

FRACAS: (*Turning to the audience*)
This is a fine situation for landscapers like me:
Cutting some grass, raking some leaves, and falling in love by three.
But that's the way things happen when a Tenorio is around,
The hearts he breaks are measured fully by the pound.
But this, I think, is different, this feels like something else.
In front of any woman, he never ever melts.
This has never happened in his many love affairs,
But she has got him firmly by the tiny little hairs.

(Pulling the frond from his pocket)
And so again, into love and death my friend has rushed...
Oh no! My bugs! They're all completely smushed!

(Blackout)

Scene Three

(Night. The same part of the garden. A slight wind. The image of a woman in black carrying a long rosary walks solemnly in. She gazes over the lawn with the eerie grace of a ghost, then with reverence pronounces:)

WOMAN: Con ésta no. Míjo, de ésta niña me encargo. We shall see how true your love, if love it is, is. Flesh is your dominion.

(She remains frozen in an attitude of pity as FRACAS emerges from another side with a hose and sprinkler attachment. He whispers fearfully to the audience.)

FRACAS: ¡Ay Dios mio¡ Man o man. Hijo de su pinchi ching!
Why does he always wait till night to do these things?
I am not one to whine, complain, or even narc,
But don't you find this a little too dark?
I'm personally more partial to midafternoons
When everyone's watching the TV cartoons
And fixing burritos by the clear light of day
Instead of standing in blackness como un pinchi guey.
(He discovers the WOMAN standing behind him.)
If it was midafternoon now, then I could see
If there was someone really there behind me
Or just an overactive shadow from the trees all about.
Well, I guess there's one way to find out....

(He turns to the WOMAN.)

FRACAS: Are you actually flesh and blood standing behind?

WOMAN: No.

FRACAS: *(Returning to the audience)*
Oh well, that's a load off my mind.
Do you see what I mean about dark nights like these?
You never know who you're going to displease!
(He slowly peeks behind him. The WOMAN is gone.) Mano!

JUAN: *(Calling from off)* Fracas!

FRACAS: That's Juanito. He and me set up these sprinklers to keep the party guests off this side of the lawn.

(JUAN *creeps in.*)

JUAN: What are you doing? Who are you talking to?

FRACAS: Juanito, you're not going to believe this, but I think I just saw a ghost! It wore a black veil over its face and held a rosary and spoke like the shadows to me!

JUAN: Probably one of the guests, you idiot! They're all decked out for the party.

FRACAS: Why don't we just go home and tell Luis to stick it where the sun don't fit?

JUAN: You don't understand, Fracas. This is love. For the first time since I knew what my organs were for. If you want to leave, go ahead and leave.

FRACAS: I can't.

JUAN: Why not?

FRACAS: You're my ride, ese.

JUAN: You're a true friend.

(*The* MAID *calls from off.*)

MAID: Who's out there!

JUAN: Oh shit!

(*They make a break for it.* FRACAS *runs and hides, but* JUAN *is caught trying to carry the hose and sprinkler off. The* MAID *enters.*)

MAID: Who is it? What is going on?

JUAN: Eh...just putting away my things. Señora.

MAID: I thought I saw you leave long ago.

JUAN: Forgot my sprinklers.

MAID: Couldn't you come back for them tomorrow?

JUAN: They're very expensive.

MAID: Are they?

JUAN: Top of the line.

MAID: Really.

JUAN: And you can never tell in this neighborhood.

MAID: Can't you? (*A red-handed pause*) Mira. No soy idiota. You're not here for the sprinklers.

JUAN: (*Humbly*) No, señora.

MAID: So why are you here?

JUAN: It's not an easy thing to explain.

MAID: Out with it. What brought you back?

(JUAN *wavers for a moment, then explodes with anguish all over her. He falls to his knees.*)

JUAN: Señora, I need your help!

MAID: My help?

JUAN: You're the only one who can!

MAID: You're crazy! Go away!

JUAN: Send me away and you send me to hell! PLEASE! You've come out of nowhere like an answer to my prayers! I'm counting on you to help me!

MAID: What can I do?

JUAN: Señora, I'm burning with love! Like a heretic trapped in the flames of his own madness, I'm consumed with the love for an angel whose name my tongue would flare in calling. When the vision fell upon my eyes, do you know what I did?

MAID: What?

JUAN: *(Breaking down)* I wept!

MAID: *(Melting)* You did?

JUAN: All my dreams came swarming back into my head, all the passions of heaven and earth rose around me. I could feel my heart gnawing on itself at the thought of such ecstacy!

MAID: My goodness!

JUAN: *(Languishing on her lap)* I threw sense off like an old coat and covered myself with this madness. I waited for a glimpse. The minutes scattered around me like pollen, impulses buzzing over like bumblebees! Visions! Oh, what visions!

MAID: Yes? Yes?

JUAN: Together. Wrapped in each other. Skin against skin. *(He runs his fingers along the bare skin of her arms.)* As soft as this. As pure. With breasts like the firm buds of spring, brimming with heat. To simply say love is to understate the fact.

(He weeps. She takes him in her arms.)

MAID: Oh my my my my my my...

JUAN: I'm sorry.

MAID: Please...You should have said something.

JUAN: All I need, señora—

MAID: I know what you need, baby. Wait here. I have a room inside. It's not much, but there's a bed. I'll make sure we're alone.

JUAN: What? *(She stamps him with a long wet kiss.)*

MAID: No-one's ever wept real tears for me before. *(She leaves.* FRACAS, *who has been spying on the exchange, springs from his hiding place.)*

FRACAS: Hijo mano, Juan. That was some act.

JUAN: That was no act. I was telling her about Anna. I was crying for Anna!

FRACAS: She thinks you were talking about her!

JUAN: Then I'll have to set her straight. I'm not going to bed with her.

FRACAS: Look at it this way, man. She's about to let you in the house. If you tell her the truth, you might as well forget it.

JUAN: She'll understand.

FRACAS: Here she comes!

(FRACAS returns to his hiding place. The MAID enters.)

MAID: The coast, mi amor, is clear.

JUAN: Señora, there's been a misunderstanding. I can't go with you.

MAID: Why not?

JUAN: I have...other commitments.

MAID: *(As she lubriciously rubs herself against him)* But what about skin against skin? The firm buds of spring? Aren't you throwing sense off like an old coat? Don't you like the way this feels?

JUAN: *(Sorely tempted)* But...I don't...even know your name.

MAID: Flor. Yours?

JUAN: Luis.

MAID: These visions you spoke of, Luis. They can be real. But we don't have much time.

JUAN: *(Resigning himself to his lust)* We don't have to take very long. Just as long as it takes.

(She leads him off. FRACAS *emerges from his hiding place.)*

FRACAS: I'll sneak inside just right behind
While their bodies intertwine.

(He follows them out. LUIS *enters and discovers the sprinklers.)*

LUIS: He's around, all right. I knew better than to underestimate that walking hard-on. Lorena, for your honor, I'll bring home that part that most dishonored you.

(LUIS *exits, taking the hose and sprinklers with him. Blackout. Eerie unearthly laughter and commotion as the costumed revelers strike the garden set and establish the next.*)

Scene Four

(*Inside the estate. A hallway with small table and vase.* FRACAS *enters, holding* JUAN's *bouquet of marigolds which he had cut for* ANNE.)

FRACAS: Let me tell you, my friends, let me make you aware,
It didn't take long to get her legs in the air.
The way he was moaning, the way she was crying,
The way he was groaning, the way she was sighing,
The way they carried on in that poor bed of hers,
You'd think they were lying on a mattress of burrs!
And yet I am distressed, the irony's cruel,
For these are the flowers he picked for his jewel.
It's hard to imagine what might be aroused
When ardor spreads like contagion all over the house.

(JUAN *straggles in, brushing his teeth.*)

JUAN: What are you looking at?

FRACAS: Man, you said nothing was coming between you and Anna. You said—

JUAN: (*Angrily*) I know what I said! You don't have to remind me.

FRACAS: Luis is not going to like this.

JUAN: How the hell am I supposed to get anywhere without pulling my shorts down? It's the only way I know to get what I want. And tonight, compa, I have a deeper resolve.

(FLOR *appears, buttoning her uniform.*)

FLOR: To get into little Anna Downey's panties?

JUAN: (*Abruptly resuming his amorous tone*) Flor, querida...

FLOR: Cut the bullshit. I know who you really are. Both of you. I've been watching you since this afternoon.

FRACAS: I think, Juanito, the jig is up.

JUAN: So you were only pulling my chain.

FLOR: Among other things. I wanted to feel firsthand, so to speak, what the big Juan Tenorio was all about. Not bad. Who knows, though, what you see in that little gavacha.

JUAN: Maybe it's what I don't see in you.

FLOR: Maybe I'm a better lover than you are a man.

JUAN: That's for me to decide.

FLOR: I can tell you right now she won't have a thing to do with you.

JUAN: We'll never know if you don't show me which room is hers.

FRACAS: I hear somebody!

FLOR: I'm going to love seeing her make a fool of you.

JUAN: Are you going to tell me or not? ·

FLOR: Upstairs. Second door on your left. But you'll have to be quiet. No one's allowed up there tonight but family.

JUAN: I'll move like a ghost.

FLOR: And if you get caught, I don't know either of you.

(MR DOWNEY's voice is heard from off.)

FRACAS: It's the old man!

JUAN: Now what?

FLOR: Over there! Inside! ¡Rapido!

(She hides them back in her room. MR DOWNEY and ANNE enter, both fully dressed in their respective costumes. MR DOWNEY is dressed as Pancho Villa, complete with wide-brimmed sombrero and munitions belt. ANNE is decked out as Cinderella, with the flowers she picked earlier sewn into her flouncy dress. FLOR nonchalantly pretends to clean the furniture nearby.)

MR DOWNEY: I don't understand it, Anne. Why are you asking me these questions? You should be out there enjoying yourself with your friends.

ANNE: I'll join them in a minute. They can take care of themselves.

MR DOWNEY: You've hardly been outside at all. We did this for you.

ANNE: I'm grateful, Daddy, and I'll go soon. But I have to know this first.

MR DOWNEY: I wish you'd tell me why.

ANNE: Daddy.

MR DOWNEY: All right. She passed away a long time ago. She went home for the weekend to be with her family and she never came back. We didn't know she had died until we got a call. It was her diabetes.

ANNE: Why didn't you tell me?

MR DOWNEY: You were a little girl. You wouldn't have understood. We thought if we'd replace her, you'd eventually forget about her. Why are you bringing this up now?

ANNE: I thought of her. I was in my room today, and I swear to you, Daddy. I felt her. I felt like she was in the house again. Watching over me like she used to. She's here.

MR DOWNEY: Anne, that's impossible. She's been gone for over ten years. There's no reason why you should be feeling this way. Can we drop this now and go back outside?

FLOR: Yes, the band is ready to play, Mr Downey.

MR DOWNEY: Flor, how do you like my costume? Can you guess who I am?

FLOR: No, señor.

MR DOWNEY: C'mon, take a guess!

(A crashing sound from off)

ANNE: What was that?

MR DOWNEY: It sounds like you have someone in your room. Are you hiding someone, Flor?

FLOR: Oh, no, señor, I would never—

MR DOWNEY: Whoever is in there, step right out this minute!

(Pause. FRACAS meekly inches out.)

ANNE: He's one of the landscapers.

MR DOWNEY: What were you doing in there?

FLOR: Mr Downey, please don't be angry. It's my fault. He's my boyfriend, you see. He was helping me with the party. He just wants to lend a hand.

MR DOWNEY: I don't care. I have enough problems with guests roaming the house. I want him off the premises.

FLOR: Yes sir.

ANNE: Are his other companions also on the grounds?

FLOR *Oh no, they went home long ago.*

ANNE: *(Approaching FRACAS)* If you see your rude friend with the shears again, tell him I think he's a total jerk.

MR DOWNEY: And don't try to fool with me, boy. Do you know who I am?

FRACAS: Pancho Villa?

MR DOWNEY: Get him out of here.

(MR DOWNEY *and* ANNE *leave.* FLOR *turns on* FRACAS, *pounding him about the head.* JUAN *re-emerges.*)

FLOR: You idiot! Are you trying to get me in trouble!

FRACAS: Ow! Wachale! Hey! Stop!

JUAN: Did you see her? She's dazzling!

FLOR: Are you deaf? She called you a total jerk!

JUAN: *(Enthralled)* I know.

FRACAS: Man, what does that tell you?

JUAN: That I'm still fresh in her mind.

FRACAS: I think you fractured my skull with your loving affection.

FLOR: Don't worry, cuz. Follow me. I'll put some ice on it.

FRACAS: *(As he follows her out)* Does that mean you'll pull my chain, too?

JUAN: Move your asses. I need you to keep that old man off my case. Now then. Upstairs. Second door on the left.

(JUAN *begins his ascent of the staircase when two of the masked revellers barrel in, one of them dressed as the Devil, the other disguised as an ass. The Devil lasciviously chases the ass around the hallway, both of them grunting and laughing with delight. They scamper about* JUAN *and then go off.* JUAN *is then distracted by the figure of the* WOMAN *in black who appears behind him. She speaks in a mournful voice.*)

WOMAN: Is there only one thing in this world you're after, my son?

JUAN: What? What do you know?

WOMAN: Can you be distracted a second time?

JUAN: Are you talking to me? The party's outside, señora.

(*The* WOMAN *turns and leaves.* JUAN *resumes his ascent just as* HEATHER *appears in her Little Red Riding Hood outfit, hooded and masked.*)

HEATHER: Where do you think you're going?

JUAN: *(Losing his patience)* Upstairs.

HEATHER: That's off-limits to you guys. You know that.

JUAN: I do?

HEATHER: You know what my Mom said.

JUAN: About what?

HEATHER: About the flowers. She wants them outside and on the first floor. Aren't you the yard man? Didn't I see you slaving outside?

JUAN: That's right.

HEATHER: Well, then, what are you waiting for? Get your butt moving. Put those marigolds where they belong.

(JUAN *is about to obey her, when he suddenly checks himself.*)

JUAN: They're not marigolds.

HEATHER: I know what they are. They're marigolds.

JUAN: I'm afraid you're wrong.

HEATHER: Look, I'm taking botany in college. I know a marigold when I see one.

JUAN: And I know cimpasuchitl when I see it.

HEATHER: Are you trying to be smart with me?

JUAN: That's what they are.

HEATHER: Well, in my house, they're marigolds.

JUAN: In the Underworld, cimpasuchitl.

HEATHER: How would you know?

JUAN: I don't know. I just know.

HEATHER: *(Turning to go on her way)* Put the marigolds where they belong.

JUAN: I'll put them where I please, you arrogant cow.

HEATHER: WHAT!

JUAN: These, miss, are the flowers which grace my dead mother's altar. My father calls them by their ancient name. Cimpasuchitl. Gaze at the center for a moment and you'll see the doorway to another world. A world where all the living are summoned to. Once a year, at this time, the altars of the dead are decked with these, and with their scent, a sensuous bond is made between this land and the one below. And every time I look into the petals, I find my mother's eyes looking back...with sadness...and pity....

(JUAN *kneels before* HEATHER, *who is drawn in by his tale.*)

HEATHER: I'm sorry. I didn't know.

JUAN: It is a kind of reckoning.

HEATHER: Who are you?

JUAN: A man with more life than he knows how to live.

HEATHER: C'mon. Your name.

JUAN: Luis.

HEATHER: What kind of sensuous bond are you talking about?

JUAN: *(Hypnotizing her with the blossom)* It is a kind of trance that you induce by meditating on the blossom. Then, closing your eyes, you think of the kind of life you might have lived before this one. It takes a while, but a feeling like sexual ecstacy lights up your brain and you have visions!

HEATHER: Of what?

JUAN: Unspeakable joy!

HEATHER: You're kidding, right?

JUAN: It's happened to me.

HEATHER: All I have to do is meditate?

JUAN: And close your eyes. *(He places his fingers over her eyelids.)* Focus all your thoughts on these flowers and let the river of passion work its way up. It should take some time. *(He starts sneaking toward the staircase.)*

HEATHER: *(With her eyes firmly shut)* Oh my god...I feel it.

JUAN: Don't say a word. You'll break the spell.

(He creeps across the stage. HEATHER cries out in ecstacy, causing JUAN to hesitate for a moment. When he resolves to continue, she moans aloud again and he wavers as he feels his arousal increasing. He takes another step away just as she belts out an even louder cry. JUAN can no longer resist it. He swerves back toward her.)

JUAN: Can you feel it?

HEATHER: Oh yes! Yes!

JUAN: Dammit. I feel it too!

(He sweeps her up in a torrid embrace.)

HEATHER: What are we supposed to do now?

JUAN: *(Caught up in the heat of the moment)* Hard to say. Cimpasuchitl is hard to resist.

HEATHER: I have a boyfriend, you know.

JUAN: And I've got a girl.

HEATHER: I can't do it with just anyone, can I?

JUAN: That's what I say!

HEATHER: Do you drive a red Jag?

JUAN: Chevy.

HEATHER: What the hell. *(She kisses him.)* Let's go.

JUAN: Where?

HEATHER: New lesson in botany. Cross-pollination.

(She leads him upstairs. FRACAS enters with an icepack on his head.)

FRACAS: Nothing becomes a legend more than a legendary urge,
And for this Juanito, that's not so easy to purge.
His celibacy's full of unavoidable sex,
The way things are going, he'll lie with me next!

(LUIS enters from behind.)

LUIS: Don't bet on it, asswipe.

FRACAS: Luis! How did you get in here?

LUIS: They all think this is a costume and I'm one of the guests.
Where's Tenorio?

FRACAS: Listen, man, you got him all wrong. He's really in love with the girl.

LUIS: Wake up and smell the chorizo. He doesn't love her. He doesn't know how. He's jacking off with himself and keeping the girls for company. His old man's cleared him before, but no one is going to save his ass this time.

FRACAS: What are you going to do?

LUIS: *(Drawing his blade)* He's going to be sorry he ever touched my sister. I'm going upstairs to look for him. Don't stop me, Fracas.

(LUIS exits. FRACAS turns to the audience.)

FRACAS: Lucky for Juan that he wasn't with Anna
But doin' the deed with her older hermana.

(He watches as HEATHER ambles in, putting on her cloak. JUAN casually follows, brushing his teeth.)

HEATHER: I don't know what got into me. There must be some awesome power in those flowers. I was reeling.

JUAN: Oh, Heather... *(He displays for her a pair of red panties.)*

HEATHER: Why don't you give them to me later?

JUAN: After the party?

HEATHER: In the greenhouse. Among the...cimpasuchitl.

JUAN: I'll be there.

(She smiles and leaves.)

JUAN: *(Tossing the panties to FRACAS)* Here. Souvenir.

FRACAS: You did it again.

JUAN: I tried, Fracas! I tried very hard not to enjoy a single minute of sex with that coed. But I couldn't help myself! Soy un hombre caído! I don't know what's happening! I don't believe in spirits or life after death, but here I am seducing this girl with the memory of my mother! Es pura grocería!

FRACAS: What about Anna?

JUAN: *(Taking his flowers)* She's mine, that's all there is to it.

FRACAS: Look, man, I should tell you. Luis is here. He's upstairs looking for you. He's got a blade.

JUAN: Baboso. He's going to ruin everything. Vamos.

(JUAN starts to leave. FRACAS is toying with the panties.)

JUAN: Are you coming or waiting for the bus?

FRACAS: *(Inhaling their fragrance)* These panties, Juanito!

JUAN: Keep them. They're mine, anyway.

(They leave. MRS DOWNEY and ANNE enter. MRS DOWNEY is dressed as Marie Antoinette, replete with powdered wig and fan.)

MRS DOWNEY: Now, was this where your father said he saw that young man?

ANNE: Right here. The maid probably already sent him home.

MRS DOWNEY: I wouldn't count on that. So many people are running around the house now, he might have snuck back in.

ANNE: I doubt it, Mom. Why would he even want to be here?

MRS DOWNEY: There's a party going on, Anne. Things disappear when the house is turned into a circus.

ANNE: You're not being fair to him. He hasn't done anything.

MRS DOWNEY: The one with Flor wasn't the good-looking one, was he?

(Suddenly, another reveller drunkenly dances on. He is disguised as the Devil, attired in the skeleton suit seen before.)

MRS DOWNEY: Excuse me. People. Hey! You're not supposed to be in here.

(The reveller dances off.)

MRS DOWNEY: They're all over the place. Now, Anne, was he or wasn't he the one with Flor?

ANNE: It was the goofy one.

MRS DOWNEY: Watch out for the other one. I know his type. He's rough, swarthy, and dark, and he has this wild animal leer. It takes my breath away.

ANNE: I'll keep it in mind, Mom.

MRS DOWNEY: I'm clearing the house of these clowns. You go upstairs and lock your door.

(MRS DOWNEY *exits.*)

ANNE: Some party.

(*She shakes her head and goes. Blackout. In the ensuing darkness, the costumed revellers once again make a set change from the hallway to* ANNE's *bedroom. Snickers and song punctuate the dark.*)

Scene Five

(ANNE's *bedroom. A single marigold lies in the center of the bed.* JUAN *and* FRACAS *enter, quietly, with awe.*)

JUAN: This is where she sleeps.

FRACAS: Smells like girl, all right.

JUAN: Like purity.

FRACAS: Who left this flower here?

JUAN: Cimpasuchitl. La flor de los muertos.

FRACAS: Do you think she left it?

JUAN: It doesn't matter. I'm here. I can't believe I finally made it.

(LUIS *springs from the shadows.*)

LUIS: Neither can I.

JUAN: Que pasó, Louie.

LUIS: I gotta give you credit, man. When you make up your mind, you go a todo huevo. You came pretty close, too. But if you think this girl is going to end up like my sister and a hundred others like her, you better think again.

JUAN: She's not like the others.

LUIS: That's what you always say. But they end up lining outside the clinic just the same.

JUAN: Not Anna.

LUIS: That makes what you did to my sister even more of a crime. You really make me sick.

JUAN: What am I supposed to do now?

LUIS: (*Flashing his knife*) Start praying, buddy.

FRACAS: ¡Watchale, Juan!

JUAN: I don't want to fight you here. Don't be a dickhead.

LUIS: I'm doing this for Lorena and the baby she's about to abort.

(JUAN kneels before him.)

JUAN: You want to cut me open? Okay. Do it here. If this is the only way I'm going to prove my good intentions. Vamanos recio.

LUIS: I mean it, Juan.

FRACAS: No, Luis, wait! I'll marry your sister!

JUAN: Just tell Anna I love her.

LUIS: *(Lowering his knife)* Mira...Juan...this goes over the line, man. Forget this girl. You're going to get yourself into deeper trouble. Go home, bro.

JUAN: No way, Louie. I'm going to see her.

LUIS: I know how to put a stop to this.

(He starts for the door.)

JUAN: What are you doing?

LUIS: You're going to get busted. Better make a run for it.

JUAN: No! Pendejo!

(JUAN fights him to prevent him from reaching the door. In the struggle, LUIS is stabbed with his own knife.)

LUIS: ¡AY! ¡MALDITO!

JUAN: Oh no! Luis, you idiot!

LUIS: *(As he dies)* Tell Lorena...I did...what I could....

(LUIS dies. FRACAS approaches.)

FRACAS: Is he dead?

JUAN: What do you think? Help me stuff him under the bed.

FRACAS: I heard you did things like this, but I never believed it. I thought you were above that. That you never meant any harm. But this...Juan, you killed the dude.

JUAN: Are you going to help me or not?

FRACAS: Man, I don't know about this. I don't want to be no accessory. I don't want his blood on my hands.

JUAN: Do you think I wanted this? Do you think I want his blood on mine? Fracas, all I want is a chance to be with Anna. Pero estos pendejos keep getting in the way. No more, ese. (FRACAS's *gaze falters as the spectre of the* WOMAN *drifts behind them unseen.*)

FRACAS: Orale pues. But after this, you're on your own.

JUAN: *(As they shove* LUIS' *body under the bed)* I want you to climb out the window and go to the truck. Back it up to the house and bring one of those large trashbags. *(He pulls the sheets down to conceal the body.)* I'm doing this for her, you know.

FRACAS: Just don't do me any favors, okay?

(FRACAS *leaps out the window.* JUAN *switches off the lights when he hears some noises and hides in the pitch blackness. The door opens and closes. A figure can faintly be made out crossing toward the light switch.*)

JUAN: I have been waiting for you. *(A gasp)* Please don't be frightened. I don't mean you any harm. Before you decide to scream or turn the light on and ruin the rest of my life, as you probably should, please hear me out. Please listen. I won't expect anything more of you. *(A pause)* Early today, when I saw you walking across the lawn, I felt like you were walking through my soul. My disbelief beat itself against me and still you were there. Beautiful. Impossibly beautiful. The embodiment of a dream. The whir of wings rose around me and for a moment I thought I was dead. I knew something glorious had forced itself on me, and that I had to see you, to tell you, that I love you. *(A pause)* You're everything. You're more than I deserve, my life and my death. I want your legs clasped around me, your lips locked on mine, your entire body draped over me like a warm wind. I want to enter your most secret dreams if you'll let me. *(A pause)* Then...you can do as you wish. *(The lights come on.* MRS DOWNEY *stands by the switch.* JUAN *is momentarily shocked. She smiles.*)

MRS DOWNEY: Muy bueno, Mr Juan.

JUAN: *(To himself, aloud)* Damn!

(She switches the light off again.)

(Blackout)

(End of Act One)

ACT TWO

Scene One

(The lights come up on eerie festivities going on in ANNE's *bedroom. Masked figures dance around the bed where* MRS DOWNEY *is lying still, as if dead.* JUAN *is standing in the shadows. The revellers scatter when* FRACAS *enters.)*

FRACAS: I believe this is where things get creepy.
What else can account for the chill in my peepee,
The taste in my mouth like bacterial jelly,
And this eerie feeling of death in my belly?
As the breath of something weird billows around us
And the fate of our actions is starting to hound us,
Even as the party fills with elation,
This night surely smacks of love and damnation.

(He snaps a trashbag to its full length and scurries off as MRS DOWNEY *finally stirs.)*

MRS DOWNEY: *(As* JUAN *brushes his teeth)* Goodness, I haven't felt this good in ages. You're quite a man. I didn't think I'd be able to keep up with you.

JUAN: *(Sullenly)* You were fine, Mrs Downey.

MRS DOWNEY: Would you call it a torrid experience?

JUAN: Torrid comes to mind.

MRS DOWNEY: It seemed to happen so fast. I was on my back before I knew it.

JUAN: No, señora. I was on my back.

MRS DOWNEY: In any case, it was a liberating workout. It's certainly not going to make things easy for me.

JUAN: What do you mean?

MRS DOWNEY: Don't take this too hard, but I don't think I want you coming around here anymore. I know how you feel about me, I'm sorry, but I think it's best that you stay off my property.

JUAN: But why?

MRS DOWNEY: Did you come in through this window?

JUAN: Yes.

MRS DOWNEY: You can go out the same way. Get your shirt on.

JUAN: Mrs Downey, did I offend you in some way? Don't you like me?

MRS DOWNEY: Of course I like you. You're fiery, passionate, very attentive, and quite capable of satisfying any woman you come near. Which is why I'm kicking you out.

JUAN: You don't want to see me again?

MRS DOWNEY: Out of the question. Please go.

JUAN: You're afraid of me.

MRS DOWNEY: Look, I have to go down and join the guests. Can I trust you to find your way out?

JUAN: Yes, but—

MRS DOWNEY: And try to keep your hands off my daughter's things, okay?

JUAN: As you wish.

MRS DOWNEY: It's nothing personal, sweetie. It's just one of those things. But if you ever come near me or my daughters again, I'll file a restraining order on you.

JUAN: Oh now I get it. You think I'm going to screw your little girls.

MRS DOWNEY: Don't be crude. I'm giving you five minutes. Then I'm sending my husband up. (She leaves.)

JUAN: Pinchi vieja!

(FRACAS returns from the window.)

FRACAS: Well, is it over? Have you made love to her?

JUAN: No.

FRACAS: Wasn't that Anna who just left?

JUAN: No. That was her mother.

FRACAS: Her mother! Dios mío! Three in one night!

JUAN: She's going to sick her old man on me, too.

FRACAS: Between you and me, Juanito, I think you're caught between a rock and a hard-on.

JUAN: I'm never going to see her.

FRACAS: Maybe we better call it a night, ese.

JUAN: I tried to hold myself back. I wanted to be frank with the old lady about Anna. But I couldn't. I just couldn't. And now I've lost her.

FRACAS: Cheer up, mano! There are lots of girls at the party back in our own block. You can pick any one you want. Not even Luis can stop you there.

JUAN: *(Taking the trashbag from him)* I wish he had. The poor fool had more balls than I did.

FRACAS: We better go! I think I hear the old man coming up now!

JUAN: I was so close...

FRACAS: So's the shit to the fan, ese! I mean it, Juanito! C'mon!

JUAN: I'm not leaving till I see her. I don't care what happens.

FRACAS: Your ass!

(FRACAS makes his getaway. JUAN hesitates, then rushes to the curtains when he hears voices. He hides as ANNE and HEATHER burst into the room.)

HEATHER: C'mon, Anne. Why don't you go down and join the party? Everyone's asking for you.

ANNE: I don't want to go. I just don't feel very festive tonight.

HEATHER: Why? What's the matter? Is it something I've done?

ANNE: No. I just want to sit here a while.

HEATHER: It's me, isn't it? Anne, I'm sorry I didn't get you anything. I was so pissed off at my boyfriend, I just didn't think.

ANNE: No, look, it's not you. It's...I don't know.

HEATHER: Oh, I bet I know what it is. You're hung up on someone, huh? Am I right? I know that feeling. I've just had someone like that give me the ride of my life.

ANNE: Really? Who?

HEATHER: I'll tell you about my guy if you tell about yours.

ANNE: Deal. Who is he?

HEATHER: I'm not supposed to say, but he's really mysterious. We fell under the spell of some weird flowers and threw caution to the winds.

ANNE: What's he like?

HEATHER: Well, he's nice and strong.—

ANNE: So is my guy.

HEATHER: He's really really handsome.—

ANNE: Same here.

HEATHER: And he's got this rough way about him!—

ANNE: Oh, this guy may seem like that, but inside he's gentle and meek.

HEATHER: He's vain and conceited.

ANNE: He's honest and courteous.

HEATHER: He's bolder than anyone I've ever known.—

ANNE: He's shy down to the root.

HEATHER: He's got so much passion in him.—

ANNE: No, he's cool and serene.

HEATHER: He's wild!

ANNE: He's a gallant!

HEATHER: Mine's a killer!

ANNE: So who is he? What's his name?

HEATHER: Luis.

ANNE: Isn't that...?

HEATHER: Not a word. We're meeting later tonight. It's your turn. Aren't you going to tell me who you're pining for?

ANNE: I can't. I don't know his name.

HEATHER: That's too bad. When you find out, let me know. I've got to go. I'm expected in the greenhouse.

(HEATHER *goes.* ANNE *lies down and sighs bitterly.* JUAN *steps out. He seems awestruck.*)

JUAN: Happy birthday...Anna...

(ANNE *springs from the bed in terror.*)

ANNE: You can't be here.

JUAN: I know.

ANNE: This is my room.

JUAN: I know. God, you're beautiful.

ANNE: You'd better go before my Mom finds you here.

JUAN: You have every right to hate me. I've been an idiot. I just wanted to see you.

ANNE: Don't look at me like that.

JUAN: It's hard not to. You are really very special. Solo eres mi preciosa. Hermosa.

ANNE: Don't come near me.

JUAN: Please. Trust me. I don't mean to scare you. See? Hand on my heart. I would never hurt you.

ANNE: Then why are you here?

JUAN: For you. My words fail me. I don't know what to say. You. You're the reason I'm even alive.

ANNE: *(Heading for the door)* I don't know about this.

JUAN: Don't go. This is the first time I have ever felt like this. It's crazy. I've never believed in the powers of Heaven before. Never. And now... I wish you would...let me...touch you.

ANNE: What for?

JUAN: *(As he reaches out and touches her)* To know what angels feel like. Angelita.

ANNE: How did you know?

JUAN: What?

ANNE: Someone used to call me that when I was a little girl. Long time ago. How did you know?

JUAN: It just had to be.

ANNE: Who are you?

JUAN: Juan. Juan Tenorio.

ANNE: Tenorio.

JUAN: You feel so right. So warm. Is something wrong?

ANNE: I knew I sensed her.

JUAN: What are you talking about?

ANNE: Did your mother work for us here a long time ago?

JUAN: Ages ago, so what?

ANNE: You're her son, aren't you? I don't believe it. I knew there was something strange. I knew I could feel her, but I never made the connection. It's you. You have your mother's eyes.

(The WOMAN *in black streams in and stands behind them, unseen.)*

JUAN: You knew her?

ANNE: She ruled this house. She cleaned it and cared for it like a living thing. She took care of Heather and me, but Conchita, as we called her, she loved to spend most of her time with me. She played with me, read me stories out of old books, sang me to sleep with songs I could barely understand because she sang them in Spanish. And she called me Angelita.

JUAN: That sounds like her, all right.

ANNE: She was so sweet.

JUAN: Too sweet. She was diabetic.

ANNE: How can you talk that way about your own mother?

JUAN: With all due respect, Anna, my mother cared a hell of a lot more for you than she did for me. All her time, all of her love, was spent here, on you. The only time I ever saw her was late at night on the weekends. She'd slip into my room and sing me the same lullabies she sang to you. And then she died. What good has the old lady been to me?

ANNE: You have her memory, don't you?

JUAN: Anna, I didn't come to discuss her. I came to see you. You're the only thing that counts now.

ANNE: Do you remember any of the songs? Can you sing one for me?

JUAN: Will you sit down beside me if I sing?

(ANNE *sits by him on the bed.*)

JUAN: There's one I know she used to like.

(*He sings it in a plaintive tone. The* WOMAN, *holding her rosary, joins in halfway.*)

JUAN: Niña niña
De mis sueños
De mi soledad
Niña niña
Duerme niña
Deje la realidad.

Niña niña
En mis brazos
Ya no llores mas
Duerme niña
De mi alma
Entre sus lagrimas.

No quiero mas que tu amor
En mi vida ya
Y tu me das todo ese amor
Hasta la eternidad.

(By the second verse, ANNE *has become lulled by* JUAN's *simple rendition. At the beginning of the third verse, unbeknownst to them, the hand of* LUIS *slowly creeps out from under the bed.)*

ANNE: That was very nice.

JUAN: I'm surprised I remembered it. So many things have come to me— *(He discovers the hand. He quickly diverts* ANNE *from seeing it.)* Oh God! Anna! Your eyes! They captivate me!

ANNE: What?

(He sweeps the hand under with his foot.)

JUAN: If I don't tell you how I feel now, I may never get the chance again.

ANNE: But you hardly know me.

JUAN: I know you well enough through these songs. The melodies acquainted me with you long ago. I've known you longer than— *(The hand emerges from another side of the bed and clutches the sheets.)* Ay, cabrón! Anna, you have to understand that I'm being absolutely sincere when I say how much I love you!

ANNE: We should get to know each other better first, don't you think? I mean, you don't strike me as a bad guy, but still—

(The hand reaches out and grabs his leg.)

JUAN: Oh god! Oh god!

ANNE: Please don't take it that way! I just need to know you better!

JUAN: *(As he struggles to free himself of its grip)* No, no, don't misunderstand me. What I want to say is....I have a past which will not let me go. I want badly to be free of myself but— *(Finally prying the hand loose and kicking it under)* Only you can help me do that.

ANNE: How?

JUAN: Kiss me. Accept me for what I am and I will be more.

ANNE: I can't do that. I just met you. You're not even supposed to be in here. You're a gardener!

JUAN: Is that what's holding you back? Are you ashamed to be seen with the Mexican landscaper? Is that it?

ANNE: No! It's not that! I don't mind what you are, it's just that I don't know who you are.

JUAN: Close your eyes, Anna. Close them!

ANNE: Okay.

JUAN: *(As he walks around the bed)* Is this the voice of someone you despise? Does this voice inspire fear and disgust in you? Or does it sound like a man who speaks from the heart?

(He stands away from the bed to see where LUIS *might appear from next.)*

ANNE: It's hard to say. *(Opening her eyes)* But I admit I like it when it sings to me. It has a power.

JUAN: *(Satisfied that he won't appear again)* If it's a power I have, it's beyond my control.

ANNE: Maybe one kiss.

JUAN: One is all I need.

(He gently kisses her. THE WOMAN, *who has been surveying the scene from behind, steps closer.* JUAN *wraps his arms around* ANNE.*)*

ANNE: What are you doing to me?

JUAN: *(Reaching for the buttons on her blouse)* This must be very warm.

ANNE: Don't do that.

JUAN: Don't be frightened.

ANNE: This is wrong.

JUAN: It can happen. Don't you want it to happen?

WOMAN: *(Speaking in ominous tones)* How long?

JUAN: Now, Anna—

WOMAN: How long will you keep her? Till the next one comes along?

JUAN: —and forever.

WOMAN: Leave her alone.

JUAN: *(As* ANNE *struggles against him)* No.

WOMAN: Solo quieres el cuerpo, mijó.

JUAN: No, I love you.

WOMAN: Then don't touch her like that.

ANNE: *(Trying to break away)* I'm not ready for this.

JUAN: Don't say a word! Not a single word!

WOMAN: She doesn't trust you.

ANNE: I can't trust you!

JUAN: Anna, please!

WOMAN: She doesn't believe you!

ANNE: I don't believe you!

JUAN: Don't turn away from me now. I've come too far.

ANNE: Let me go!

WOMAN: ¡Ésta niña no! ¡Ésta no llenarás con tu veneno! ¡Retirate!

JUAN: *(Holding her close)* No! You're mine!

WOMAN: Let her go!

ANNE: Let me go!

JUAN: I won't hurt you, Anne! Please!

WOMAN: ¡Solo vas a maldecir lo que no puedes amar!

JUAN: *(Suffocating her)* You're mine! All mine!

ANNE: Let go! Juan! I can't breathe!

WOMAN: She can't breathe!

JUAN: ¡Angelita!

ANNE: I can't breathe!

WOMAN: ¡DEJALA!

JUAN: Niña niña de mis sueños de mi soledad...

(ANNE slumps lifelessly in his arms. He kisses her.)

JUAN: You're the only girl I truly care about.

WOMAN: Pero ya esta muerta.

(JUAN turns to examine her.)

WOMAN: Infeccion. Plaga.

JUAN: Wake up. Anna, wake up.

WOMAN: Eres maligno, pero eres mio.

JUAN: Breathe, goddammit!

WOMAN: Ahora sigues tú.

(The WOMAN slips back into the darkness as JUAN tries to revive ANNE. A clamor of voices drowns out his cries. Suddenly, the door bursts open and a wild parade of revellers marches through: the Devil and other various creatures, all masked and disguised and dancing around the bed. They carouse over the body of ANNE. One of the revellers drags the body of LUIS from under the bed. JUAN is weeping over the limp body of ANNE.)

JUAN: ANNA! ANNA, WAKE UP!

(The revellers screech and echo her name as JUAN *dashes away from the bed with the knife in his hand and rushes out the window. The revellers try to restrain him as he goes. Frantic cries and screams.* MR DOWNEY *suddenly enters and everyone freezes when he sees* ANNE. *Tableau. Then blackout.* FRACAS *races out and stands in the center of what appears to be a police spotlight.)*

FRACAS: The truck was blocked in the driveway by cars
So we had to run from Corona Del Mars
Awful affair down the wealthiest street,
The night crumbling about at our feet!
We kept running, running, outrunning the lights,
I could hear the chota reading our rights!
We came to a fork and we split up right there
Juan yelled, "Correle recio si puedes correr!"
He got away, but me, Fracas Infeliz—
I ran straight to the pinchi police!

(He charges off as a blackout swallows the light.)

Scene Two

*(*DON DIEGO's *office with the altar now fully adorned with bright paper marigolds, personal trinkets and charms, candles, rosaries, pictures of various saints and presidents, and a large photograph of his wife, who is the same ghostly woman seen before. Around the shrine are platters of food, bread, and wine, and tiny urns of incense burn nearby.* DON DIEGO *is praying before the altar.)*

DON DIEGO: Concepción, if what your spirit has told me is true,
If the whispers in my soul
Have hissed the name of my son
And soaked it in the blood of innocent people,
If a black wind bearing the souls
Of Anna Downey and Luis Rosas has found its way
Into this house, this ear, this heart,
And howled their murders out,
Then I am truly shattered!
Oh, Concepción, let me have a sign
Just to confirm my foul misgivings,
Let me know that what I fear is true
And I will do that which you ask.
But I must know before I do.
(Flashes of light and thunder. He turns around to discover a single marigold upon the floor.)
This works.

(JUAN *can be heard crying from off as he dashes in.*)

JUAN: Jefe! Jefe! You've got to help me! (*He runs in and sees the blossom.*)
No. It can't be. Not here.

DON DIEGO: Cabrón. What have you done?

JUAN: What are you doing with that? What is going on?

DON DIEGO: Answer me. What have you done?

JUAN: Nothing!

DON DIEGO: That's not what I heard!

JUAN: Who the hell are your sources? The spirits?

DON DIEGO: I'm talking about Anna Downey!

JUAN: What about her?

DON DIEGO: What's the matter with you? Haven't you any honor left?
I let you get away with everything before. But I won't sit by while you
commit murder!

JUAN: (*Grabbing him by the collar*) What do you know about murder?
Who told you?

DON DIEGO: It was the voice of your mother that spoke to me.

(DON DIEGO *breaks away and prays at the altar.*)

DON DIEGO: Concepción, escuchame.
Let the ache in my heart lead you through
The caverns of Death to me—

JUAN: SHUT UP!

DON DIEGO: Visitame, Conchita, please!—

JUAN: I SAID SHUT UP!

(CONCEPCIÓN *appears amid thunder and lightning.*)

CONCEPCIÓN: ¡SILENCIO!
Make no threats to your father.
Querido, Diego.

DON DIEGO: You did come!

JUAN: So here you are.

CONCEPCIÓN: Only to feel again the shame the living feel.
Only to drag the tears again across my face.
Only to ache in places long filled with worms.
Tristesa, Diego.

DON DIEGO: Perdoname, but we both know what he's like. Even when you were with us, he was a difficult boy to rear.

CONCEPCIÓN: And now he looks so anxious. Temeroso.

JUAN: What do you expect? It's been a wicked night, crammed with whores, corpses, and now you, Mamá.

DON DIEGO: Don't forget Luis Rosas and Anna Downey.

CONCEPCIÓN: In cold blood. In the senseless pursuit of his pleasure.

JUAN: You can't blame that on me.

DON DIEGO: It's my fault.

CONCEPCIÓN: It's nothing you've done, Diego. *(Crying out)*
Ay, so many souls crying for atonement!
They trail behind me like a veil of tears!

DON DIEGO: ¡No llores! It destroys me when you cry! Tell me, what can I do?

CONCEPCIÓN: Ask them in. Show them a little courtesy. It's very cold in the halls of perdition.

JUAN: Ask who in?

DON DIEGO: They're welcome in my house any time.

CONCEPCIÓN: Prepare the altar for the others. They're here.

(DON DIEGO goes.)

JUAN: Who's here? The cops? La chota?

CONCEPCIÓN: Your guests of honor. On this night devoted to the dead, you should know who they are.

JUAN: All I know, Mamá, is that Luis got in the way and that she was mine. Anna belonged to me!

CONCEPCIÓN: I ask you this, míjo: What good is an angel steeped in your own shit? By tomorrow, she'd line up behind Lorena, Romelia, Martina, Flor, and the others you callously made love to.

JUAN: The others were matters of simple biology. Anna was something more, she was my spirit. My road to salvation.

CONCEPCIÓN: Don't worry, míjo. The road to is the road from.

(DON DIEGO returns with a tray loaded with more wine glasses and bread. He places it at the altar, then goes to CONCEPCIÓN.)

DON DIEGO: Te dejé en tu lado de mi cama una taza de tierra y plumas de paloma.

JUAN: What did he say?

CONCEPCIÓN: He's left a cup of dirt and dove feathers on my side of the bed.

DON DIEGO: *(Turning to* JUAN *as he leaves)* I'll pray for your soul. *(He goes.)*

CONCEPCIÓN: I married him when I was a girl no older than Anna Downey. That he would be so faithful only my death would prove. Are you ready to demonstrate your faith, Juan?

JUAN: Any time you want! I'm not afraid of you. I'm not afraid of anything. Bring in my guests of honor! *(With a flourish of her hand, flashes of hellish light and claps of thunder usher in the pale and deathly figures of* ANNE DOWNEY *and* LUIS ROSAS.)

JUAN: Come in! Make yourselves at home! Mi casa es su pinchi casa!

ANNE: Hello, Juan.

LUIS: Hey, homes.

JUAN: Let me extend my hospitality. There is wine at the altar and blood on my hands.

ANNE: How gracious of you.

JUAN: It's the least I can offer. Since I came to your party, it's only right that you come to mine.

LUIS: Don't we scare you just a little bit?

JUAN: Shitless, if you want me to be honest. It's not every night the dead drop in for a midnight snack.

ANNE: But we're just the figments of your lust.

JUAN: Then I shouldn't be seeing you. I never lusted after you.

ANNE: Then I shouldn't be dead.

LUIS: Me neither, compa.

JUAN: I loved you. As deeply as it was instant. I never meant to hurt you. All I wanted was one kiss. You were not a part of my excesses.

CONCEPCIÓN: Mentiras. Your lies deceive only you, mijo. I was there. Three times I put the warm flesh of a woman before you, and three times you thrust yourself in it.

JUAN: You? You set them up for me?

LUIS: And I tried to stop you, Juan. But you kept your course.

CONCEPCIÓN: Anna may have been in your heart, but it's the other organ which defines you.

JUAN: So you turned up just to fuck up my life, is that it?

ANNE: To save mine.

CONCEPCIÓN: Love is not the satisfaction of the flesh. Love is not a carnal whim.

JUAN: I loved you!

ANNE: But how quickly your fingers pried the buttons from the buttonholes. You couldn't wait. Your silver tongue and you.

JUAN: *(Turning to* CONCEPCIÓN*)* This is your fault! You fucked this up! You had no business interfering with us.

CONCEPCIÓN: You blame me for your character? You blame me for your cold-blooded act? You're a fool.

JUAN: All my life I've lived without you. I grew up with nobody's help. I didn't need you! I didn't want you! It was better for both of us that you died when you did!

LUIS: Señora, you want me to kick his ass?

CONCEPCIÓN: The dead are not accountable for the acts of the living. What you became, you became in my absence.

JUAN: And what have I become, Mama? Biology!

*(*CONCEPCIÓN *points to* ANNE.*)*

CONCEPCIÓN: You said you loved her. Do you love her still?

ANNE: I'm still your Angelita.

JUAN: I'll remember you far above the others.

ANNE: If you love me, Juan, you'll join me. *(She extends her hand to him.)* Forever, you said.

LUIS: Take her hand, ese. You want to know what real angels feel like.

CONCEPCIÓN: If you are faithful as you are vile, you'll go with her.

ANNE: Honor my memory this way or else you're damned.

JUAN: The only damnation, Anna, is giving up. This world is too rich to give up. My heaven and hell are already here.... *(With his hand over his crotch)* My bliss is now.

ANNE: Then you won't?

JUAN: *(Backing away)* Nothing personal.

LUIS: You're bogus, homes.

CONCEPCIÓN: It's just as well. She wasn't right for you. Too flimsy, too young. These gavachas are so tepid. I have your real match.

JUAN: Maybe later. ¡Ay te watcho! *(He turns to go.* CONCEPCIÓN*'s voice collars him.)*

CONCEPCIÓN: ¡MOMENTO!

(JUAN *freezes.*)

CONCEPCIÓN: Aquí tengo tu novia! (*Thunder and lightning. She ceremoniously lifts off her veil to expose the grinning countenance of a skull.*)

JUAN: What is going on? What are you doing?

ANNE: Remember what you said about a love affair with the fragrances of the earth? This is it, Juan.

CONCEPCIÓN: (*Quickly removing her dress and exposing her bones underneath*) I am your real match. La Calaca Flaca!

JUAN: This can't be happening! I'm dreaming!

CONCEPCIÓN: ¡Ay, Juanito! How long I've waited for this moment! I've been so lonely without you.

JUAN: Get away from me! I don't know what you're talking about!

CONCEPCIÓN: After all the preparations I've made, how can you say this! See, I've even brought you my dowry. (*She reaches on the altar for a large bag and from it strews bones of various sizes on the floor before him.*)

JUAN: What the hell are these?

CONCEPCIÓN: Tokens of my undying affection.

ANNE: Don't you recognize them? They're your family.

JUAN: My what?

LUIS: Tus hijos, Juan.

CONCEPCIÓN: I've been watching them for you. Just as closely as your mother cared for Anna. The generations of dust, the little babes so anxious to join me—they're here. All here. Every time the world pulls its panties down for you, this bag gets a little heavier.

JUAN: But I don't have any children.

CONCEPCIÓN: Yet here they are. It's your seed, Juan. It bursts with life it cannot support. It's a pollution that chokes the child in its own blood.

LUIS: Every one of them, Juanito. Stillborn.

JUAN: I don't believe it. These aren't my bones. You're wasting my time.

(*He tries to leave.* CONCEPCIÓN, LUIS, *and* ANNE *drive him back with the bones.*)

CONCEPCIÓN: Time is all you have left! (*As she sets the bones in a wide arc around him*) And these bones are counting down your last seconds. Cada uno. Each one. Nursed by dissolution, bred by neglect. This bone is Love.

This bone I call Virtue. And this one is Absolution. All these bones are the bones of Tenorio!

JUAN: Encarnación, flaca. That's missing. Your Love, Virtue and Absolution are nothing to me. I live for something else.

CONCEPCIÓN: Then show me. I have been anxious to feel what it is about you that drives women mad.

JUAN: Believe me, there is less to the legend than you think.

CONCEPCIÓN: Is it your caress? The look in your eye? The words you say as you slip between their thighs?

JUAN: You're getting warm.

CONCEPCIÓN: Maybe it's that little extra scrap of skin. Small and tender by your own admission. Enfolded on itself like a mystery. Cupped in a nest of dark curly hair.

JUAN: It's the cologne.

CONCEPCIÓN: You're a man of the flesh. No woman in this world or the next is safe from you. Flesh is your dominion. We were made for each other! ¡Ay lover, como me endiablas!

JUAN: But you're a calaca!

CONCEPCIÓN: (*As eerie dance music creeps in*) In the dance between the particles of procreation, yours will dance with mine.

(JUAN *tries to resist as* CONCEPCIÓN *dances and sings her song around him, but he quickly gives in and engages her in a dance of death.*)

CONCEPCIÓN: Muchacho cabrón
Mijo sinvergüenza
Barbaro inútil
Ya tu vida se inversa

Bailando con las viejas
Durmiendote con ellas
Dejandolas plantadas
Las feas y las bellas

Mijo favorito
Niño y mocoso
Creció como arbol
A ser hombre peligroso

Desde su nacimiento
Saliendo de la cueva
Él busca renacerse
con una virgen nueva!

JUAN: A bastard's what they call me
A shame to all my gender
Born to kiss and violate
A woman's flesh so tender.

All the rules we live by
The limits of my raza
Mean nothing to me, baby,
I broke into her casa!

I'll engage your bones awhile
In a lusty forward dance
I'll look you in the socket
With a twinkle of romance.

But if you got a heart
I'll break it just the same
'cause I'll walk away from you—
Tenorio is my name!

CONCEPCIÓN: Are you really so resistant
To the charms I use on you?

JUAN: Mira, mi calaca,
The dance is almost through.

CONCEPCIÓN: Are you a little hard
For my horny bones at all?

JUAN: No, no, nothing like that
But it's not exactly small.

CONCEPCIÓN: You see, you are excited—

JUAN: I'm feeling like a man—

CONCEPCIÓN: Flesh is your dominion—

JUAN: And I've gained the upper hand.

JUAN/CONCEPCIÓN: There's a power that you have
A power I command
But only one of us can win
When this dance comes to an end!

(JUAN *tears himself away from the calaca.*)

JUAN: You think that by dancing you can steal away my will to live?
You'll need more than that to win me. I've done nothing to be ashamed of!

CONCEPCIÓN: (*Ramming her hand against his crotch*) Then feel the bone that
damned you most! Feel that bone in you rising? The first one in you to rot?
I call that bone Perdition.

(He cries out in mortal agony.)

ANNE: Juan, I'm so jealous!

LUIS: Vato, you're going to be the hit of the party.

JUAN: The party's over!

CONCEPCIÓN: Oh no, mi amor! It's only just beginning!

(She waves her hand again and MR *and* MRS DOWNEY *and* HEATHER *enter amid thunder and flashes of light.)*

MR DOWNEY: So this is where the action is!

MRS DOWNEY: My, you never know when to quit, do you?

HEATHER: I waited at the greenhouse. Where were you?

JUAN: What are they doing here? Why did you bring them?

CONCEPCIÓN: They want to see the great Juan Tenorio take on his greatest conquest. So do try to die exquisitely, querido.

JUAN: Oh no you don't! Get away! I'm not dead yet!

CONCEPCIÓN: But you are! Your hereafter's already here.

JUAN: A la chingada! I'm checking out!

CONCEPCIÓN: *(Emasculating him with a gesture in the air)* Men like you don't go down easy. You don't know when to quit. I find it sexy!

*(*JUAN *falls to the ground as the calaca overpowers him.)*

JUAN: Oh god!

ANNE: But Juan, you said God was made of nothing but germs.

LUIS: And angels above are nothing but worms!

JUAN: Help me! (CONCEPCIÓN *drops him at the foot of the altar, climbs over him and straddles him.)*

CONCEPCIÓN: *(As she grinds herself against him)* Now feel what every woman is after the fragrances, the finery, and the last gasp of life. Bones foaming over with maggots! Hollow sockets where eyes, ears, and vaginas once shone like jewels! Putrefaction! ¡Huesos! ¡Cresas! And nowhere in this body is there any will to love and be loved! Nowhere in this body is there any memory of passion and fire! Is this what you wanted, Juan? Is this finally what you lust for?

JUAN: *(In great agony)* Yes!

CONCEPCIÓN: And don't you feel it rising out of you! Don't you feel it! What does it feel like, Juan? What does it feel like now! Can you tell me!

JUAN: *(Crying out)* Like hell!

CONCEPCIÓN: It is there, in every cell in your body! Biology! Stored in the signature of a single kiss!

(CONCEPCIÓN kisses JUAN. He slumps lifelessly in her arms. She raises her head and peers at the audience.)

CONCEPCIÓN: Blood on his gums. A sure sign of love.

(The others array around them the instruments of his destiny: the marigolds, the pair of undergarments, the knife, the garden shears, and the hundred-dollar bill. CONCEPCIÓN covers JUAN with her veil. While this is happening, FRACAS nimbly steps in front of the action.)

FRACAS: How do you like that? Pobre Juanito!
Lo besó la Muerte y se murió al ratito!
They found him lying on the floor of his house,
Pale as a sheet and dead as a mouse.
And though some were sorry to lose this performer,
They all agreed his next life would be a lot warmer.
It became all too clear to the parties concerned
You don't have to be raza to really get burned!
As for me, I was caught, cleared, and released
And I got to my party in time for the feast!

(As DON DIEGO returns with more victuals for the guests, who have by now turned the body of JUAN into a new Day of the Dead altar:)

FRACAS: I was never more pleased to be living, I said,
And never more wary of those who were dead,
So I said a Hail Mary and swallowed my pride,
Raised a glass of pure gold for my friend as I cried—
Tenorio, if the germs of love are ever compelled,
I'll see you screwing again or I'll see you in Hell!

ALL: *(Raising their glasses in a toast)* SALUD!

CURTAIN

END OF PLAY

PRELUDE TO A KISS

Craig Lucas

ABOUT THE AUTHOR

Craig Lucas is the author of MISSING PERSONS, RECKLESS, and BLUE WINDOW. With composer/lyricist Craig Carnelia he wrote the musical play THREE POSTCARDS. With his frequent collaborator, director Norman René, he conceived MARRY ME A LITTLE, a bookless musical fashioned from seventeen previously unpublished songs by Stephen Sondheim. He also worked with Norman René on three films—an adaptation of BLUE WINDOW which premiered on *American Playhouse* in 1987, LONGTIME COMPANION, and PRELUDE TO A KISS. Mr Lucas has written two opera texts with composer Gerald Busby, BREEDLOVE and ORPHEUS IN LOVE.

His work has been performed at Playwright's Horizons, Circle Repertory, The Production Company, Naked Angels, Ensemble Studio Theater, the Long Wharf, Berkeley Repertory, Steppenwolf, American Repertory Theater, Old Globe (San Diego), Alliance (Atlanta), and numerous other regional and resident theaters.

Mr Lucas has received the George and Elisabeth Marton Award, the L.A. Drama Critics' Award, the Drama-Logue Award, Guggenheim and Rockefeller grants, the Outer Critics Circle Award, and the Obie Award. THREE POSTCARDS was selected as Best Musical of 1986-87 by the Burns Mantle Theater Yearbook and by Time magazine as one of its ten best. LONGTIME COMPANION received the Audience Award at the 1990 Sundance U.S. Film Festival. PRELUDE TO A KISS received a Tony nomination for Best Play during the 1989-1990 Broadway season.

Craig Lucas is a cum laude graduate of Boston University, where he studied with the poets Anne Sexton and George Starbuck. He is on the Council of the Dramatists Guild. He is an associate member of South Coast Repertory and a member of Circle Repertory.

PRELUDE TO A KISS was commissioned, and premiered by South Coast Repertory on 15 January 1988. The cast and creative contributors were:

*GINNY .... Roberta Farkas
PETER .... Mark Arnott
TAYLOR .... Michael Canavan
RITA .... Lisa Zane
*NANCY .... Anni Long
TOM .... Art Koustik
MRS BOYLE .... Teri Ralston
DR BOYLE .... Hal Landon, Jr.
MINISTER .... John-David Keller
AUNT DOROTHY .... Roberta Farkas
*FAMILY FRIEND .... Anni Long
*FAMILY FRIEND'S HUSBAND .... Don Took
OLD MAN .... Frank Hamilton
LEAH .... Mary Anne McGarry
ENSEMBLE .... Lisa Black, Cynthia Blaise,
Edgar W. Chambers, Patrick Massoth,
Roberta Ornellas, Paul J. Read, Catherine Rowe

(*Roles cut from present version)

Director .... Norman René
Set design .... Loy Arcenas
Costume design .... Walker Hicklin
Lighting design .... Peter Maradudin
Sound design .... Serge Ossorguine
Stage manager .... Julie Haber
Dramaturg .... John Glore

PRELUDE TO A KISS was subsequently produced in New York at Circle Repertory.

PRELUDE TO A KISS then moved to Broadway, at the Helen Hayes Theater, opening on 1 May 1990. It was produced by Christopher Gould, Suzanne Golden, and Dodger Productions.

PRELUDE TO A KISS is dedicated
to my mother and father,
Charles and Eleanore Lucas

CHARACTERS

PETER
TAYLOR
RITA
TOM
MRS BOYLE
DR BOYLE
MINISTER
AUNT DOROTHY
UNCLE FRED
OLD MAN
JAMAICAN WAITER
LEAH

Party guests, barflies, wedding guests, vacationers

PLAYWRIGHT'S NOTE

To provide a fluidity of motion and to stress the imaginary leap required to make sense of the story, PRELUDE was originally staged with a minimum of scenery—a chair and lamp to indicate RITA's apartment, a free-standing bar for The Tin Market, a pair of chaise lounges for Jamaica—allowing the lighting to do the bulk of the work in transforming the space. We also used a great deal of underscoring with source music and sound effects (surf, traffic, popular songs, marimba bands in Jamaica), again to indicate place and create a kind of magic. PETER often changed clothes in front of our eyes, and the scenery came to him on tracks, gliding quietly. Upstage, a permanent green wall, as if in a garden, suggested that things were more than they might seem; in that wall was a large window looking out on a changing sky—night stars, distorted sunsets for Jamaica—and a twisted vine climbed up alongside the window frame. If lit from the front, the sky behind the window disappeared and a greenish, painted sky of clouds made the window once again part of the wall itself.

I would like to thank all of my collaborators in the various productions and readings of the play—the director, dramaturgs, designers, and actors. In addition, I am grateful to the Guggenheim Foundation for their generous support during rewrites, and to Kip Gould for providing enhancement money at Circle Rep.

Then the King's daughter began to weep and was afraid of the cold frog, whom nothing would satisfy but he must sleep in her pretty clean bed.
—Brothers Grimm, *The Frog Prince*

Death destroys a man, but the idea of death is what saves him.
—E.M. Forster, *Howards End*

ACT ONE

(Music. We hear a recorded vocalist as the lights go down:
"If you hear a song in blue,
Like a flower crying for the dew,
That was my heart serenading you,
My prelude to a kiss.")

(A crowded party. PETER *stands apart, then approaches* TAYLOR *and* RITA.)

PETER: I'm splitting.... Hey, Tay?

TAYLOR: Hey, Pete, did you meet Rita?

PETER: No. Hi.

RITA: Hi.

TAYLOR: *(Overlapping)* Rita, Peter, Peter, Rita.

PETER: Actually, I...

TAYLOR: *(Overlapping)* What's everybody drinking? Reet? Can I fill you up there?

RITA: Oh, I'll have another Dewar's, thanks.

TAYLOR: Pete?

PETER: No, nothing, thank—

TAYLOR: Don't worry, I've got it taken care of. You two just relax. One Dewar's, one beer...

(He moves off. Pause.)

PETER: How do you know the Sokols?

RITA: I don't. I mean, except from the hall.

PETER: Oh, you're a neighbor.

RITA: I couldn't sleep.

PETER: Oh, really? Why?... How long have you lived here?

RITA: I haven't slept since I was fourteen. A year and a half.

(Beat)

PETER: Did you say you hadn't slept since you were fourteen?

RITA: Pretty much.

PETER: You look great!

RITA: Thank you.

PETER: Considering. Rita what?

RITA: Boyle.

PETER: Peter Hoskins.

RITA: Hoskins?

PETER: As in Hoskins disease?

RITA: Oh, Hodgkins.

PETER: No, no, it was just a...nonhumorous...flail.

RITA: What? *(He shakes his head.)* I like your shirt!

*(*TAYLOR *returns with drinks.)*

TAYLOR: Dewar's, Madame?

RITA: Thank you.

TAYLOR: No beer, sorry.

PETER: Wine's fine. Thanks... Rita has insomnia.

TAYLOR: Oh yeah? Listen, I've got to pee, I'm sorry, excuse me. Forgive me...

(He is gone again.)

PETER: What do you do when you're not *not* sleeping?

RITA: Oh, I usually, you know...write in my journal or—...Oh, for a living, you mean? I'm a bartender.

PETER: Oh. Where?

RITA: *(Overlapping)* Yeah. At the Tin Market.

PETER: Oh, I know where that is. One for Pete.

RITA: Yeah.

PETER: I guess it's a good place for an insomniac to work. You work Saturdays? *(She nods.)* Well, you must make good money. Well, so you hate it, I'm sorry, I can't help that. What are your aspirations, in that case?

RITA: I'm like a graphic designer.

PETER: Oh, great.

RITA: I studied at Parsons.

PETER: This is good.

RITA: What do you do?

PETER: I make little tiny, transparent photographs of scientific articles
which are rolled on film like microfilm only smaller. You'd like it.
It's really interesting.

RITA: What are your aspirations in that case?

PETER: I should have some, shouldn't I? No, I I I I I I, uh, can't think of the
answer, I'm sorry.

RITA: That's okay!

PETER: So why can't you sleep? You know what's good? I forget what it's
called, it's an herb.

RITA: I tried it.

PETER: It didn't work?

RITA: I can't remember what it's called either. My memory is terrible!

PETER: Maybe that's why you can't sleep. You forget how tired you are.
Well... If you ever need any help getting to sleep. *(Beat)* Sorry. *(Beat)*
It was nice talking to you.

RITA: You, too.

PETER: Get some sleep.

RITA: I'll try.

(PETER addresses the audience)

PETER: I stood outside for a while, just listening to the silence. Then I tried to
figure out which window was hers and what her life might be like and why
she couldn't sleep. Like that. *(Beat)* The spell was cast.

(The Tin Market)

PETER: Hi.

RITA: Oh, hi.

PETER: Is this all right?

RITA: No, I'm sorry, you can never come in here.... What's new?

PETER: Since yesterday? Well, let's see, so much has happened.
You look great.

RITA: What'll you drink?

PETER: Do you have Molson?... *(She nods.)* So, did you get some sleep?

RITA: Eventually.

(She sets down his Molson.)

PETER: Thank you.

RITA: You?

PETER: Sleep? Oh, I don't have any trouble. But...let's see, I read *The White Hotel* today.

RITA: Oh.

PETER: That was pretty much it.

RITA: Yeah.

PETER: You?

RITA: Oh, I slept, mostly.... How was *The White Hotel*?

PETER: Did you read it?

RITA: No, but I've read some of the case histories it's based on.

PETER: You have? Freud's? Case histories? You've read Freud.

RITA: Have you?

PETER: No, but... This book?

RITA: Uh-huh?

PETER: Starts with this very high-falutin' sexual dream thing, you know?

RITA: Yeah, I've heard everybody beats off when they read it.

(Beat)

PETER: Uh-huh.

RITA: I'm sorry.

PETER: You heard that?

RITA: Go on.

PETER: ...It's very depressing, the book.

RITA: Uh-huh.

PETER: This lovely, very neurotic woman goes into therapy with Freud himself—

RITA: Right.

PETER: And he sort of cures her so that she can go on to live for a few years before being killed by the Nazis in a lime pit. Happy. Happy stuff.

RITA: So why were you in Europe for ten years?

PETER: How did you know I was in Europe?

RITA: Word gets around.

PETER: You asked Taylor about me? You were asking around about me? Let's get married.

RITA: Okay.

PETER: I just went, you know.

RITA: He said there was a story and you would have to tell me.

PETER: He did?... Okay, this is the story and I'm not making this up.

RITA: Okay.

PETER: And it's not as sad as it sounds.

RITA: Shoot.

PETER: My parents?

RITA: Uh-huh?

PETER: Separated when I was four. And I went to live with my grandparents who are unfortunately deceased now. I'm going to make this as brief as possible.

RITA: Take your time.

PETER: And—

RITA: We can go up to my place if you want. When you're done.

PETER: And-everything-worked-out-great-for-everybody-it-was-amazing.

RITA: No, go on.

PETER: Were you serious about that?

RITA: I'm off in about seven minutes. Your parents.

PETER: My parents. I'm four years old. I go to live with my grandparents. My grandfather had to go into a nursing home when I was nine, then my grandmother had to go when I was eleven; they were both sick, so I go to live with my mother who by this time is remarried to Hank.

RITA: Uh-huh.

PETER: Very unhappy person, ridicules me in front of the other two children they have created from their unsavory loins, so I go to live with my father, who is also remarried, *three* other children, Sophie, the new wife, hates me even more than Hank.

RITA: This is like Dickens.

PETER: The only nice thing Sophie ever did for me was make the same food twice when I had made the mistake of saying I liked it. Usually she would stop cooking whatever it was I said I liked.

RITA: What was it?

PETER: What I liked? Spaetzles?

RITA: Oh, god.

PETER: You've had spaetzles?

RITA: Oh, sure.

PETER: You like them?

RITA: I love them.

PETER: You do?

RITA: Uh-huh. Anyway.

PETER: You love spaetzles. Anyway, everyone is unhappy now.

RITA: Uh-huh.

PETER: Sophie really can't stand the sight of me, because I remind her that my father was married to someone else and....

RITA: Right.

PETER: And my father does not seem too fond of me, either. I don't know if he ever was, but so one night I say I'm going to go to the movies and instead I go to Europe.

RITA: What movie?

PETER: *The Wild Bunch,* I think, why?

RITA: Did you call them first?

PETER: Not until I got there.

RITA: Europe?

PETER: And I called collect.

RITA: That is....

PETER: Yeah.

RITA: Good for you.

PETER: Yeah. So. Why'd you ask which movie?

RITA: That is fabulous.

PETER: That's the story.

RITA: How did you eat? I mean....

PETER: Oh, I had about three thousand dollars saved up from my paper route. But that's a whole other kettle of....

RITA: Spaetzles.

PETER: Yeah. So...

RITA: You lived in Amsterdam?

PETER: You're a spy, aren't you?

(TOM *enters, behind the bar.*)

TOM: Hey, kiddo.

RITA: Hi. Tom, this is Peter.

TOM: Hi.

PETER: Good to meet you.

RITA: *(To* PETER*)* You want to go?

PETER: Now? Naaaaaaaa. *(To us)* I love the little sign when you buy your ticket to the roller coaster: "Ride at your own risk." As if the management is not at all concerned with your safety, the entire contraption is about to collapse, and to top it off, there are supernatural powers out there just waiting to pull you off the tracks and out into, you know, your worst, cruelest nightmare—the wild blue. They want you to believe that anything can happen. *(Beat)* And they're right.

(Outside. They walk.)

PETER: Uh-huh.

RITA: So.

PETER: So they disowned you?

RITA: No. I never told them.

PETER: Oh.

RITA: It was like...I mean, they didn't need to know what I was involved with. I don't tell them everything.

PETER: I've never known a Communist.

RITA: Socialist.

PETER: Socialist.

RITA: But...I mean, I was only in the Party for about two months.

PETER: What happened?

RITA: Oh, I just...I felt like they were basically not interested in anything except being right.

PETER: Right.

RITA: And they didn't support the Soviet Union, not that they should—

PETER: Uh-huh.

RITA: —and they didn't support Mao, and they didn't support the United States. It's like where are you going to live?

PETER: Right.

RITA: But...I started by doing leaflets for them and then posters. I still did that after I left. What?

PETER: Nothing.

RITA: It was such a strange time.... You're a good listener.

PETER: So now you're....

RITA: Oh, I guess I'm a Democrat.

PETER: Me too.

RITA: But...they're such Republicans.

PETER: Your parents?

RITA: No, the Democrats. Beneath the skin.

PETER: Oh, uh-huh?

RITA: But...I don't know. I guess it's like the U.S. It isn't perfect.

PETER: Right. *(Pause)* Where do they live?

RITA: My parents? Englewood Cliffs. It's right across the bridge. It's nice, actually.

PETER: What do they do?

RITA: My dad's a dentist.

PETER: Oh, really?

RITA: Uh-huh.

PETER: Wow.

RITA: Why?

PETER: No, I just think that's...interesting.

RITA: It is?

PETER: I think so. I don't know.

RITA: My mother's a mother.

PETER: Do you have brothers and sisters? *(She shakes her head.)* They must dote on you.

RITA: What's Amsterdam like? D'you speak Dutch?

PETER: Ja.

RITA: Say something in Dutch.

PETER: Uh... Je hebt erg witte tanden.

RITA: What's that?

PETER: You have very white teeth.

RITA: Oh. Thank you.

PETER: Now you say, Om je better mee op te eten.

RITA: What is it?

PETER: Om je better mee op te eten.

RITA: Om je metter—

PETER: Better...

RITA: Better...

PETER: ...mee op te eten.

RITA: ...mee op te eten.

PETER: Om je better mee op te eten.

RITA: Om je better mee op te eten.

PETER: Great. You've got a good ear.

RITA: Oh. Good ear, clean teeth.

PETER: You do.

RITA: What did I say?

PETER: I can't tell you.

RITA: *(Overlapping)* I knew you were gonna say that, I knew it!

PETER: No, it's untranslatable.

RITA: I'm sure it is. No, come on.

PETER: I'll tell you someday....

RITA: So what did you do there?

PETER: In Amsterdam? I will, I promise.

RITA: How old were you when you went?

PETER: Sixteen.

RITA: Oh, wow.

PETER: I catered for the first couple of years and made sandwiches during the day; then I tutored rich little cutie-pies on their English and went to school at night. Finally I came back when my dad died.

(Pause)

RITA: Do you see your mom or your family at all? *(He shakes his head.)* Never?

PETER: Nope.

RITA: Do you call them? *(He shakes his head.)* You miss them?

(Headshake. Pause.)

(RITA's apartment)

PETER: This is great.

RITA: You want a Molson?

PETER: You drink Molson—

RITA: Uh-huh.

PETER: —in your own home?

RITA: I've been known to.

PETER: That's really....

RITA: A coincidence.

PETER: A coincidence. So why can't you sleep? I want to solve this.

RITA: I really wasn't exaggerating. It's been since I was fourteen.

PETER: That's a lot of journal keeping.... Have you seen doctors?

RITA: I've seen all the doctors.

PETER: Uh-huh.

RITA: Of every known...

PETER: Right.

RITA: *(Overlapping)* Persuasion. I've ingested countless...

(She hands him a Molson.)

PETER: Thanks.

RITA: Pills, liquids, I've seen an acupuncturist.

PETER: You did? What did it feel like?

RITA: Little needles in your back.

PETER: It hurt?

RITA: Sometimes.

PETER: They always lie.

RITA: I know.

PETER: You're really beautiful. *(She laughs.)* You are.

RITA: Thank you. That's.... No, thank you.

(They kiss. She laughs.)

PETER: This is not supposed to be the funny part.

RITA: No, I know, I'm sorry.... I'm, I guess I'm nervous.

PETER: Why are you nervous? Don't be nervous.

RITA: All right.

(He approaches to kiss her.)

PETER: Don't laugh... All right, you can laugh. *(They kiss.)* Am I going too fast? *(She shakes her head.)* Is this tacky of me? *(Headshake)* Oh good. *(They kiss.)* This is definitely the highlight of my weekend. *(She smiles.)* So maybe we should just, you know, watch some TV, have happy memories of this and anticipate the future— *(She is shaking her head.)* —We shouldn't? *(They kiss.)* I would really, really like to see you with all of your clothes off and stuff like that.

RITA: I would really, really like to see you with all of your clothes off and....

PETER: Stuff like that? *(To us)* When you're first getting to know someone and in that blissful, psychotic first flush of love, it seems like every aspect of their personality, their whole demeanor, the simple, lovely twist of their earlobes and their marvelous phone voice and their soft, dark wet whatever is somehow imbued with an extra push of color, an intensity heretofore... you know. *Unknown.*

(RITA's apartment. Later.)

PETER: Christ!

RITA: What?

PETER: Happiness!... Are you?

RITA: Uh-huh.

PETER: You are? It's like a drug.

RITA: It is a drug.

PETER: Sex?

RITA: To snare us into mating.

PETER: I must be peaking then.

RITA: No, the body manufactures it.

PETER: Uh-huh.

RITA: Like epinephrine or something.

PETER: Maybe that's where they got the word "crack".

RITA: Shut up. I prefer hole. Frankly.

PETER: Hole?

RITA: And dick.

PETER: Slit.

RITA: Ugh.

PETER: This is sick.

RITA: Tool, I like.

PETER: Uh-huh.

RITA: It's practical.

PETER: Wait a minute, did I detect an earlier note of cynicism in your comment about mating?

RITA: Oh. No.

PETER: You don't like kids?

RITA: No, I love them.

PETER: But you don't want to have them?

RITA: No, I don't, but....

PETER: Why not?

RITA: I just don't.

PETER: Your career?

RITA: What career? No, I think kids are great, I just don't think it's fair to raise them in the world. The way it is now.

PETER: Where else are you going to raise them? We're here.

RITA: I know, but....

PETER: It's like what you were saying about the socialists. (RITA *hesitates.*) Say.

RITA: Like...the woman in *The White Hotel.* People really do struggle their whole lives just to die in lime pits, and not just in books. Women go blind from watching their children being murdered.

PETER: Not in this country they don't.

RITA: No, they get shot on the sidewalk in front of their houses in some drug war. I mean, just what you went through being passed from one parent to another who didn't even—

PETER: I survived....

(Pause)

RITA: I'll be lying in bed late at night and I'll look at the light in the room and suddenly see it all just go up in a blinding flash, in flames, and I'm the only one left alive.... I can't look at you sitting there without imagining you...dying...bursting into flames....

PETER: No wonder you can't sleep.

RITA: The world's a really terrible place. It's too precarious. *(Pause)* You want kids, obviously. I wish I could say I did.

PETER: It's okay.

RITA: What's your dirtiest fantasy?

PETER: Excuse me? No, I thought you just said what's my dirtiest fantasy.

RITA: What?

PETER: No, I can't—

RITA: Yes, you can. Please?

PETER: I'm sorry, I can't. What's yours, though? I'd be curious.

RITA: *(Overlapping)* I asked you first. Come on.

PETER: Oh god.

RITA: Please.

PETER: Well, they change.

RITA: Sure. What's one?

PETER: One?

RITA: Uh-huh.

PETER: Well... One?

RITA: Uh-huh.

PETER: Might be that someone...you know....

RITA: Uh-huh.

PETER: —who might just happen to be around the apartment—

RITA: Uh-huh.

PETER: *(Mimicking her)* Uh-huh, uh-huh. Might...sort of just, you know, spontaneously start crawling across the floor—

RITA: Uh-huh.

PETER: —on their hands and knees and...more or less unzip me with their, uh...teeth.

RITA: I'd do that.

PETER: You would?

RITA: Uh-huh.

PETER: Right now? *(She nods; to us:)* We saw each other every night for the next six weeks. And it wasn't just the knees and the teeth, despite what you think. I would stop by my apartment now and then to see if the view out onto the airshaft had improved any, but my clothes had all found their way over to Rita's, and my books. And then...

*(*RITA's *apartment. Six weeks later.* PETER *is serving dinner.)*

PETER: That was the Communist?

RITA: Socialist.

PETER: Socialist.

RITA: No. That was the one who liked to dress up, go out.

PETER: Oh, right. But you don't like to go dancing, do you?

RITA: Sometimes. I change.

PETER: Uh-huh.

RITA: People do.

PETER: So before that was the Communist?

RITA: Socialist.

PETER: *(Overlapping)* Socialist. And before that...?

RITA: Oh, it was just high school, you know. This looks great.
No, wait, there was someone else, who was it?

PETER: Is that what's going to happen to me?

RITA: Oh no, John, I told you about John.

PETER: The one who wanted to run away with you? Is that what's going to happen to me?

RITA: You're gonna want to run away?

PETER: You're going to forget my name over dinner with someone else equally enamored of you and just attribute it to your lousy memory? "Oh, yes, that's right, Peter. Peter—"

RITA: Probably.

PETER: "What did he look like?" And then you'll tell them my dirtiest fantasy and how you degraded yourself just for a home-cooked meal.

RITA: Mmmm. *(They are eating.)* I told my parents about you.

PETER: What did you tell them?

RITA: I said that you were very considerate.

PETER: In what way?

RITA: I said— Well, I mean, we talk very frankly about sex.

PETER: You and your parents?

RITA: And I said that you always brought protection....

PETER: You did not.

RITA: And that you were very attentive to whether or not I had an orgasm.

PETER: This is such bullshit.

RITA: No, I said they should meet you, what do you think?

PETER: Protection.

RITA: They're nice.

PETER: I'm sure.

RITA: So are you free this weekend?

PETER: Sure.

RITA: Don't be nervous.

PETER: All right. Did you tell them about my family and everything?

RITA: My mother.

PETER: She knows the story?

RITA: Uh-huh.

PETER: All about me?

RITA: Uh-huh.

PETER: Will you marry me?

RITA: Uh-huh.

PETER: You will?

RITA: Uh-huh.

(Beat)

PETER: I just wanted to see how it sounds.

RITA: It sounds great.

PETER: This is too fast. Isn't it?

RITA: Is it?

PETER: I don't think so.

RITA: Neither do I.

PETER: You'll marry me?

RITA: Uh-huh.

PETER: You will?

RITA: Uh-huh.

(The BOYLE home. Doorbell.)

RITA: Mom?

MRS BOYLE: Nice to meet you.

RITA: Dad.

PETER: Dr Boyle.

RITA: These are my parents....

MRS BOYLE: So I understand you're a manager in a publishing firm.

PETER: That's correct. Yes.

DR BOYLE: That must be, uh.... What kind of firm is it?

MRS BOYLE: Publishing.

DR BOYLE: What kind— Don't belittle me in front of new people.

MRS BOYLE: Belittle?

RITA: Dad, please.

DR BOYLE: What kind of publishing firm is it? I was asking.

PETER: It's, uh, scientific publishing. They publish, you know, scientific publishing—things—journals! I knew I knew that.

RITA: *(To* PETER*)* You want a beer?

PETER: Sure.

MRS BOYLE: In the morning, Rita?

RITA: Yes, Mother, we have been drinking nonstop for weeks, it's time you knew this about us.

MRS BOYLE: I'll have one too, then.

RITA: You will?

DR BOYLE: Me, too.

PETER: A bunch of lushes here, Rita, you didn't tell me.

DR BOYLE: Oh, I can pull out four wisdom teeth on a fifth of Stoli.

PETER: You can?

MRS BOYLE: He's teasing you.

DR BOYLE: Scien— What kind of scientific?

PETER: Abstracting and indexing. It's a service.

DR BOYLE: Like a database.

PETER: It is a database.

DR BOYLE: It is a database. Covering...?

PETER: All kinds of fields.

DR BOYLE: All kinds.

PETER: Pretty much, you know, everything from energy to robotics to medical articles. I've memorized our marketing material.

DR BOYLE: I've seen this.

*(*RITA *hands everyone his/her beer.)*

PETER: Thank you.

(They clink bottles.)

DR BOYLE: I've seen this sort of thing.

PETER: Yeah.

DR BOYLE: So you're the manager...?

PETER: The manager of the fiche department.

DR BOYLE: Microfiche.

PETER: Right.

MRS BOYLE: The what is it?

DR BOYLE: Microfiche.

PETER: It's like microfilm only smaller.

MRS BOYLE: Uh-huh.

PETER: Little film.

DR BOYLE: Why do you do that?

PETER: Microfiche?

DR BOYLE: No, why does the company do microfiche?

PETER: Oh, I see. Because if you want to call up and—

DR BOYLE: Oh, I—yes, yes, yes, yes, yes.

PETER: *(Overlapping)* —ask for like—

DR BOYLE: Right, a certain article.

PETER: Right. We can retrieve it for you. And we also film the abstract journals we actually publish so....

DR BOYLE: To save space.

PETER: Right. Yes, in libraries, it saves space.

DR BOYLE: All right. We approve.

RITA: Daddy.

MRS BOYLE: Marshall.

DR BOYLE: Maybe now she'll get some sleep.

MRS BOYLE: Now how long have you two been going out?

RITA: Over a year now.

(PETER *looks at* RITA; *beat.*)

PETER: About that. Yeah.

MRS BOYLE: Rita says you've been abroad.

PETER: Yes, I have.

MRS BOYLE: Where?

PETER: Amsterdam, for the most part, but...

MRS BOYLE: Marshall was in Korea.

PETER: Oh, was it nice? Oh, no, no, I see—

MRS BOYLE: Nice!

DR BOYLE: Some people might have been able to relax, I don't know, bullets flying.

PETER: *(Overlapping)* Right. Right.

MRS BOYLE: We're playing with you.

DR BOYLE: Okay, here you go.

(DR BOYLE starts to untuck his shirttail.)

RITA: Oh no, Daddy, please, god, please—

DR BOYLE: *(Overlapping)* This is the only scar you'll ever see in the shape of a saxophone.

MRS BOYLE: It really is, people think he's kidding.

PETER: Really?

DR BOYLE: If he's going to be in the family, he's got to see these things.

(The BOYLE home. A month later.)

PETER: *(To us, as he changes into his wedding garb)* I stood in front of the full-length mirror in their upstairs guestroom, looking out over the yard at the little tent and the band and the food which had been catered; I felt a certain kinship with these people, the caterers.

(RITA sneaks up, covers his eyes.)

RITA: Don't look, it's bad luck.

PETER: All right, but— Wait, wait— You don't believe that, do you?

RITA: *(Overlapping)* You looked.

PETER: I didn't look.

RITA: You're looking.

PETER: Wait, I won't look. I won't.

RITA: *(Overlapping)* No, you've already cursed the first fourteen years of our marriage.

PETER: I love you.

RITA: What about when I'm a hundred years old with a moustache and yellow teeth?

PETER: I'll still love you.

RITA: And I'm sagging down to here and I'm bald?

PETER: I'll love you all the more.

RITA: Are you sure?

PETER: Yes, I promise.

RITA: And I won't ever want to make love and I can never remember anything?

PETER: You can never remember anything now.

RITA: That's true. Okay.

(She leaves; PETER's eyes remain closed.)

PETER: What about me?

(TAYLOR comes in with two beers; he is wearing sunglasses.)

TAYLOR: What about you?... You okay?

PETER: Great, Taylor.

TAYLOR: They're holding for the musicians.

PETER: Okay.

(TAYLOR helps PETER dress.)

TAYLOR: Now listen. There's nothing at all to worry about here.

PETER: I know that.

TAYLOR: This is a natural step in life's plan. Like sliding down a bannister.

PETER: Right.

TAYLOR: That turns into a razor blade. No, I don't want you to think of this as anything more than one of the little skirmishes we all wage, each and every day of our lives, in the eternal struggle against mediocrity and decay. Straighten your tie.

PETER: I straightened my tie.

TAYLOR: Fix your face. You're not compromising yourself.

PETER: Thank you.

TAYLOR: Not at all. You see all those middle-aged guys down there in their checked pants and their wives in the flouncy dresses?

PETER: Mm-hm.

TAYLOR: They were all very hip once. But... There's the music. You okay?

PETER: Just go.

TAYLOR: Relax. I've got the ring.

PETER: Great. Go.

(TAYLOR *kisses* PETER *on the cheek, mouths "I love you".*)

(*The* BOYLE *home. Outside.*)

MINISTER: ...to keep the solemn vows you are about to make. Live with tender consideration for each other. Conduct your lives in honesty and in truth. And your marriage will last. This should be remembered as you now declare your desire to be wed.

PETER: I, Peter, take thee, Rita, to be my wedded wife, to have and to hold from this day forward, for better or for worse, for richer or for poorer, in sickness and in health, to love and to cherish, till death us do part, according to God's holy ordinance; and thereto, I pledge thee my troth.

RITA: I, Rita, take thee, Peter, to be my wedded husband, to have and to hold from this day forward, for better or for worse, for richer or for poorer, (*Halting*) in sickness and in health, to love and to cherish, till death us do part, according to God's holy ordinance; and thereto, I pledge thee my troth.

MINISTER: For as much as Rita and Peter have consented together in holy matrimony and have witnessed the same before God and this company, pledging their faith and declaring the same, I pronounce, by the authority committed unto me as a Minister of God, that they are Husband and Wife, according to the ordinance of God and the law of this State, in the Name of the Father, and of the Son, and of the Holy Spirit.... (PETER *and* RITA *kiss.*) I think a little applause would be in order.

PETER: (*To us*) And there was some polite applause as if we'd made a good putt or something, and we all made a beeline for the champagne with the strawberries in it.

(*The* BOYLE *home; outside. Later.*)

RITA: Peter, you remember my Aunt Dorothy and Uncle Fred.

PETER: Yes, good to see you.

UNCLE FRED: Peter and Rita, that's very euphonious.

PETER: Yes.

AUNT DOROTHY: Isn't it?

RITA: Sometimes we get Peter and Reeter.

AUNT DOROTHY: Oh.

RITA: Or Pita and Rita.

PETER: Excuse me, Rita, who's the guy in the green coat? Over by the food?

RITA: Oh... (RITA *sees the* OLD MAN.) Oh, yeah. I don't know.

MRS BOYLE: Everybody shmush together, come on! Marshall!... *(People crowd together around* PETER *and* RITA.) *Marshall!*

DR BOYLE: What?

MRS BOYLE: Get in the picture, come on!

DR BOYLE: Jesus Christ, I thought you were on fire.

MRS BOYLE: Get in, everybody! All right. Say "bullshit"! Smile!

("Bullshit". "Cheese". Flash.)

DR BOYLE: Don't tell her—

MRS BOYLE: Wait, I want to get another one. Don't move. Ohhhhh.

DR BOYLE: *(Overlapping, continuous from earlier line)* —you don't need a flashbulb in the middle of the day.

UNCLE FRED: My face hurts, hurry up!

MRS BOYLE: All right, say "Bullshit".

(Again)

AUNT DOROTHY: Oh, I had my face in a funny position.

UNCLE FRED: Whose fault is that?

AUNT DOROTHY: And don't say it's always that way.

PETER: Mom, who's the guy over by the bar?

MRS BOYLE: Who?

PETER: See who I mean?

MRS BOYLE: Oh...

*(*RITA *and the* OLD MAN *toast one another with their champagne.)*

RITA: Isn't he great?

MRS BOYLE: No, I thought he was with your firm.

PETER: *(Shaking his head)* Unh-uh.

(The OLD MAN *starts toward them.)*

MRS BOYLE: Marsh? Right behind me, don't look now, he's very peculiar.

DR BOYLE: Never seen him before in my life.

MRS BOYLE: He's not with the club, is he?

(The OLD MAN *comes up to them.)*

OLD MAN: Congratulations. Both of you.

RITA: Thank you.

PETER: Thank you very much.

TAYLOR: *(Extending his hand)* I'm Taylor McGowan.

OLD MAN: You make a lovely couple.

TAYLOR: Your name, I'm sorry?

OLD MAN: And what a wonderful day for it.

RITA: *(Mesmerized by him)* Yes.

(TAYLOR shakes hands with the empty air.)

TAYLOR: Good to meet you.

OLD MAN: How precious the time is.... How little we realize 'til it's almost gone.

DR BOYLE: You'll have to forgive us, but none of us seems to remember who you are.

RITA: It's all right, Daddy.

OLD MAN: I only wanted to wish the two young people well. And perhaps to kiss the bride. Before I'm on my way.

DR BOYLE: Well—

RITA: I'd be flattered. Thank you.

TAYLOR: Some angle this guy's got.

RITA: My blessings to you.

(The OLD MAN takes RITA's face in his hands. There is a low rumble which grows in volume as they begin to kiss. Wind rushes through the trees, leaves fall, no one moves except for RITA, whose bridal bouquet slips to the ground. The OLD MAN and RITA separate and the wind and rumble die down.)

RITA: And you.

(The OLD MAN seems off balance; DR BOYLE steadies him.)

DR BOYLE: Do you want to sit down?

AUNT DOROTHY: Get him a chair, Fred.

TAYLOR: Too much blood rushing to the wrong place, I guess.

(The OLD MAN stares at PETER and RITA.)

DR BOYLE: Are you dizzy?

OLD MAN: Peter?...

(UNCLE FRED brings a chair.)

DR BOYLE: Here you go now.

(He eases the OLD MAN *into the chair, takes his pulse.* PETER *remains fixated on the* OLD MAN. RITA *has withdrawn from the crowd; she examines her dress, her hands, the air around her, as if it were all new, miraculous.)*

MRS BOYLE: I thought you said you didn't know him. *(*PETER *is mystified.)* Peter?

DR BOYLE: Take it easy now.

OLD MAN: DR BOYLE:
(To PETER*)*
Honey? Honey?... It's me.
What's happening?...
Why is...? Why is   You're okay now, just
everybody...?   breathe for me, nice
                                         and easy.

OLD MAN: *(Staring at* DR BOYLE*)* Daddy, it's me.

AUNT DOROTHY: Ohhhh, he thinks Marshall's his father.

TAYLOR: Where do you live, can you tell us?

DR BOYLE: Okay. He's doing fine. Everybody relax.

AUNT DOROTHY: Get him a glass of water, Fred.

DR BOYLE: He's had too much to drink, I suspect. Am I right? A little too much champagne?

(The OLD MAN *begins to nod, strangely.)*

MRS BOYLE: Should I call an ambulance? Marshall?

DR BOYLE: No, no. He's going to be fine.

OLD MAN: I've had too much to drink.

DR BOYLE: That's right. Somebody get him a cup of coffee.

*(*UNCLE FRED *arrives with water.)*

AUNT DOROTHY: Coffee, make it coffee.

MRS BOYLE: Where do you live, can you tell us?

OLD MAN: Please...

MRS BOYLE: Is there someone we can call?

OLD MAN: I'm sorry for any trouble I've caused.

(The OLD MAN *starts to stand.)*

DR BOYLE: There's no trouble.

MRS BOYLE: Don't let him, honey—

DR BOYLE: *(Overlapping)* We just want to see you don't hurt yourself.

UNCLE FRED: *(Returning with coffee)* Here you go.

OLD MAN: No, thank you.

(The OLD MAN *is backing away.)*

UNCLE FRED: Don't burn yourself.

OLD MAN: No.

AUNT DOROTHY: He doesn't want it, Fred.

MRS BOYLE: Don't just let him wander off is all I'm saying.

DR BOYLE: All right, Marion—

MRS BOYLE: He could fall and he could hurt himself, that's all—

DR BOYLE: He's not going to sue us, trust me.

(DR BOYLE and TAYLOR *follow the* OLD MAN *off.)*

MRS BOYLE: And find out where he lives!

UNCLE FRED: He'll be fine.

AUNT DOROTHY: I'm sure he's a neighbor or someone's gardener.

MRS BOYLE: Whose?

UNCLE FRED: *(Same time)* That's right.

MRS BOYLE: *(Starting to exit)* I know everyone in a five-mile radius.

AUNT DOROTHY: Marion, stay here.

UNCLE FRED: Marion—

AUNT DOROTHY: Go with her.

MRS BOYLE: He's not going to bite me, now stop it, Frederick, if you want to come, come.

(UNCLE FRED follows MRS BOYLE off.)

PETER: *(To* RITA*)* Are you all right? *(She nods.)* Are you sure?

AUNT DOROTHY: Oh, what a fuss. Forget all about it, pretend it never even happened.

PETER: We're okay, thanks.

AUNT DOROTHY: Don't you both look so wonderful, and you notice who he wanted to kiss, not me. Oh, you're going to have such a good time, where is it you're going again now? Marion told me.

(PETER waits for RITA *to answer before:)*

PETER: Jamaica.

AUNT DOROTHY: That's right. For how long?

PETER: Two weeks.

AUNT DOROTHY: Oh, they loved it there last year.... Your mom and dad... Well, I'm going to leave you two alone. Do you want another glass of champagne while I'm at the bar?

PETER: No, thanks.

AUNT DOROTHY: No?...

(AUNT DOROTHY *moves off.*)

PETER: That was so weird, wasn't it? Calling me honey? He just seemed so vulnerable. I swear I've never seen him before.... You're okay? (RITA *nods.*) You sure? You seem...kind of.... Okay.

(*The others begin to filter back on.*)

TAYLOR: *(Overlapping)* Unbelievable.

AUNT DOROTHY: What happened?

TAYLOR: Just took off down the street, kept going.

DR BOYLE: *(Overlapping)* Everything's fine now, it's all under control.

TAYLOR: *(To* PETER*)* Guess he thought you were both kind of cute, huh?...

MRS BOYLE: Oh, my poor babies, to spoil your whole wedding.

AUNT DOROTHY: Have some champagne, Marion.

MRS BOYLE: No, my god, I'll throw up all those strawberries. *(To* RITA*)* Your father thinks that's the Evans' gardener, but I don't think it is, do you?...

DR BOYLE: *(Overlapping)* Enough, Marion.

MRS BOYLE: That's not the Evans' gardener, is it?... Rita?

(*All eyes on* RITA; *she turns to look over her shoulder before turning back and smiling.*)

RITA: Must have been my kiss is all.

AUNT DOROTHY: That's right.

DR BOYLE: *(Overlapping)*   UNCLE FRED:
That's right.   There you go.

RITA: Drives the men wild.

UNCLE FRED: Hear, hear!

TAYLOR:
This is a party, come on!

MINISTER: A toast!

AUNT DOROTHY:
Here's to the lucky
couple!

UNCLE FRED:
Hear, hear!

DR BOYLE: *(To* MRS BOYLE*)*
Come on, give me a kiss.

TAYLOR: *(Singing)*
 "Celebrate, celebrate!
Dance to the music!"

MINISTER:
To the lucky couple!

(Someone starts to sing "For they're a jolly good couple!" *Everyone joins in, then singing fades.)*

PETER: *(To us, as he strips down to bathing trunks.)* And there was a toast to us and to love and to Jamaica and to our plane flight and to airline safety and to the old drunk whoever he was. Whoever he was. I was completely trashed by the time the limo pulled up to take us to the airport. Dr Boyle told us to sign anything we wanted onto the hotel bill, his treat, and off we went.... The whole way down on the plane and straight through that first night in the hotel, Rita slept like a baby. I couldn't. For some reason. I kept hearing that poor old guy calling me "Honey". "Honey, it's me." Who's "me"? And I'd wanted to protect him. *(Pause)* In the morning we headed down to the pool, husband and wife.

(Jamaica. Poolside. The WAITER *stands beside* PETER *and* RITA, *both in chaise lounges.* PETER *holds a drink in a coconut shell, decorated with a paper umbrella.)*

PETER: *(To* RITA*)* Don't you want to try one?

RITA: *(To the* WAITER*)* Just a seltzer water.

PETER: Okay. *(To the* WAITER*)* I'll take another, thanks. *(The* WAITER *retreats. Beat.* PETER *notices something on* RITA*'s wrist.)* What's that?

RITA: You like?

PETER: Well...sure, where'd you get it?

RITA: Just now.

PETER: In the shop? Here? It's not gold, is it?

RITA: Fourteen carat.

PETER: You're kidding. How much was it?

RITA: Fifteen hundred or so.

PETER: Dollars?

RITA: Why? He said to charge anything.

PETER: You charged fifteen hundred dollars on your dad's bill?

RITA: I like it.

PETER: Well... You do? It's sort of like a...it's like a charm bracelet, isn't it?

RITA: It is a charm bracelet.

PETER: Like old women wear? I'm sorry. Look, if you like it, I think it's great. And he did say.... You're right, he's your dad.

RITA: Relax, we're on vacation.

PETER: I know.

RITA: And you're my puppy puppy.

PETER: Your puppy puppy?

RITA: And the world is a wonderful place to live, admit it!... Do my back?

(He takes the sunscreen, looks at it before applying it.)

PETER: Twenty-five?... I keep thinking about that crazy old schmuck from the wedding.

RITA: Mmmm, that feels good, darling!

PETER: Who do you suppose he was?

RITA: Hm?

PETER: The old guy.

RITA: Oh, I don't know.... My fairy godfather come to sprinkle the fairy dust on us.

PETER: Aren't you curious?

RITA: Nope. Come for a swim.

PETER: You just put the stuff on.

RITA: I know. Come on, I'll race you!

(She runs off.)

PETER: *(To us)* Our first full day being married and she seemed like a different Rita. I told myself, It's the excitement. And, come on, it's the rest of your life, you want it to be wonderful. It's natural to ask, "Is this the right person for me? Am I the right person for her?... Who the hell is she, anyway?"

(RITA returns, dripping wet.)

RITA: Oh, I love it here, don't you? *(Singing as she dries herself)* "Yellow bird, so high in banana tree..."

PETER: Are you sorry you married me?... Rita, you were supposed to laugh.

RITA: Oh, shut up.

PETER: Okay.

RITA: I want to go jet-skiing and I want to go scuba-diving and I want to go up into the mountains and see the monkeys, okay? And maybe go to a soccer game? *(She plants a noisy kiss on him.)* With you on my arm.

(Beat)

PETER: Do you ever think how we're each a whole, separate being beside one another. Each with a heart pumping inside and a soul and all our memories. How I can never, no matter how close we ever become, share your past, be with you as a nine-year-old, as a baby.

RITA: Don't worry about it, all right?

PETER: I wasn't.

RITA: Just take things as they come and enjoy them. That's what life's for.

PETER: You're right. You're absolutely right.

(Pause. RITA catches PETER staring at her.)

RITA: Feast away!

PETER: All right, I wasn't going to bring this up, but.... Now just hear me out first; I know what you're going to say, but.... Okay. You know how you never get any time to work on your portfolio and— Well, now that we have just the one rent, what if—just for a while, not forever—you quit tending bar and let me support you.

RITA: Sure.

PETER: What? You'd consider it?

RITA: Why not?

PETER: Really?

RITA: Let you bring home the bacon for a while. Right?

PETER: Right.

RITA: If it'd make you happy.

PETER: Baby, I'm sorry, I'm freaking out. Are you sorry you married me?

RITA: No. *(Remembering)* Oh. Ha-ha-ha.

PETER: I'm serious this time.

RITA: Don't be a silly.

PETER: Okay. Okay. *(To us)* Not okay. The days went by. We went to the soccer game, we windsurfed, or windfell, we ate, we snorkeled, we walked on the beach, always under a ton of sunscreen. And Rita was tireless. Fearless. And sleeping, not that there was anything wrong with that. No, no. Nothing was wrong—exactly. But nothing felt...nothing *felt*. *(Pause)* About a week into the vacation...

(The pool. The WAITER *stands beside them.)*

WAITER: Something from the bar?

RITA: Another seltzer, please, and clean this up, would you, it's drawing flies.

PETER: Oh, I'll have a Long Island Ice Tea this time, thanks. *(The* WAITER *moves off.)* Doesn't it ever bother you sometimes, though? The black/white thing? I mean, it's so obviously a class issue here, not that it isn't in New York. But you'd think they'd all just rise up and kill us all poolside.

RITA: Why is that?

PETER: Because. We have the money and they don't.

RITA: We worked for it, didn't we?

PETER: Well, your father worked for it, in this case. But, I mean, you talk about the world being so precarious, everything ending in a blinding flash; it would seem a little less likely if things were a little more egalitarian, wouldn't it? If there were a slightly more equal distribution of the wealth, that's all.

RITA: You want to give 'em your money, go ahead.

PETER: No, I... Why would you—?

RITA: Peter, you're doing it again.

PETER: I know.

RITA: You take a perfect situation and you pee all over it. Be happy.

PETER: Okay, I was just referring to the people we saw living in abandoned cars and refrigerators out by the airport.

RITA: That was terrible. But you don't have to look at it, do you?

PETER: Oh, good attitude... Look, I'm just trying to make conversation, Rita, you're the Commie in the woodpile, not me.

(Beat)

RITA: Whatcha reading?

PETER: The case histories? Freud.

RITA: Oh. Sounds interesting. Can I read it when you're through?

(PETER *stares at her. The* WAITER *returns.*)

WAITER: I'm sorry, Sir, the bartender say he don't know what that is.

PETER: A Long Island Ice Tea? (*To* RITA) What goes into one?... Rita? An Ice Tea? How do you make it?

RITA: I'm sorry, darling, I've forgotten.

PETER: What, do you have it all written down behind the bar or something?

RITA: I'm on vacation.

PETER: So you can't remember a drink recipe for something I'd like to order?

RITA: (*Overlapping*) Yes. That's right. On the money. Bingo! It's a real busman's holiday with you around, you know? You could fuck up a wet dream!

(*She walks off. Beat.*)

PETER: (*To the* WAITER) Nothing right now, thanks. (*To us*) It's one thing to forget a drink recipe or a book you read a long time ago, maybe, *maybe*, but your *ideals*? It was as if she had switched channels, switched...*something*. (*Pause*) Our last night we walked out on the beach in a light mist...like cloth being pulled across your skin.

(*The beach. They walk.*)

RITA: Oh, it's so beautiful, isn't it? It's great to be alive. And young. There will never be a more perfect night. Or a better chance for two people to love each other. If they don't try so hard. (*Beat*) I remembered the recipe for Long Island Ice Tea. White rum, vodka—

PETER: You don't have to prove anything to me, Rita. (*Pause*) You know... I was thinking about you growing up. What— Like, what was it like having a surgeon for a father?

RITA: Oh...well, it was nice. I always thought, "He helps people."

PETER: What about your brothers and sisters? How did they feel about it?

RITA: You'd have to ask them.

PETER: (*To us*) Nobody's memory is that bad! Or was she toying with me? That wasn't like her at all. Unless something was terribly, terribly wrong.

RITA: Peter? Make love to me.

PETER: Here?

RITA: No one'll see. I want to have your baby.... I want your baby inside me.

PETER: You don't know how that makes me feel.

RITA: Yes I do.

PETER: You don't want babies, don't you remember? You've read Freud's case histories and your father's a dentist, not a surgeon. You don't have brothers and sisters.

RITA: Why are you telling me all this?...

PETER: What, you were teasing me?

RITA: Of course I was teasing you. Did you think I didn't know those things?... Sweetie?

PETER: You never call me that or "Puppy puppy", you never say "Don't be a silly" or "Bring home the bacon" or pull the skin off your chicken. You're not drinking, you're not using salt, Rita, you're suddenly—

RITA: I want to have your baby. I'm taking better care of myself. Now, please, darling, relax. You're having some kind of a—

PETER: No. No! You're a Communist, Rita, or Socialist, Democrat, whatever you are, you don't defend the social order in Jamaica or anywhere, you have.... You're just not.... You're not...*you*. It's like you don't even need me anymore.

RITA: You need to take a hot bath and look at the moon and breathe life in.

PETER: Rita is afraid of life, she doesn't drink it in.

RITA: I'm going to insist that you see someone as soon as we get back to New York.

PETER: Je hebt erg witte tanden.

RITA: Thanks.

PETER: What did I say?

RITA: You said my teeth are white, you know what you said.

PETER: *(Embracing her)* Yes! Thank you. My baby. What do you say?

RITA: What do you mean?

PETER: What's your line? What do you say? Your line, you memorized it.

RITA: I'm sorry, Peter—

PETER: *(Overlapping)* In Dutch! Rita, what do you say?

RITA: I say goodnight.

(She turns, starts to walk off; he grabs her.)

PETER: No, please! Rita!

RITA: *(Overlapping)* Hey! Watch it, pal!

PETER: I want you to be you, Rita, I want you!

RITA: I am me. This is all I am. I'm sorry I can't be whatever you want me to be. This is me. And maybe what you saw wasn't here at all.

(She walks off. Pause. PETER *looks at us. The sound of surf breaking. Lights fade.)*

(End of Act One)

ACT TWO

(The BOYLE *home.)*

MRS BOYLE: Peter!

DR BOYLE: There they are.

MRS BOYLE: Don't you both look wonderful.

DR BOYLE: Not much of a tan here.

PETER: Well, we decided not to age on this trip.

MRS BOYLE: Well, you both look wonderful.

DR BOYLE: Rested.

PETER: That's right.

MRS BOYLE: *(To* RITA*)* Did you sleep? *(*RITA *nods.)* Ohhhh.

PETER: Like a baby. Every night straight through.

DR BOYLE: Well, you're having a good effect on her.

RITA: It's so good to see you both.

MRS BOYLE: What'll you drink? Beer?

RITA: Nothing for me, thank you, Mom.

DR BOYLE: Peter?

PETER: Sure, thanks. Rita's quit drinking.

MRS BOYLE: Ohhh. Really?

DR BOYLE: Wonderful.

MRS BOYLE: So now tell us everything.

RITA: It was terrific.

PETER: It was just great and we can't thank you enough.

MRS BOYLE: How was the weather?

RITA: Perfect.

PETER: Oh, yeah. Really.

DR BOYLE: Did you get any golf in there?

RITA: That was the one thing we didn't quite get to, I'm afraid.

MRS BOYLE: *(To* PETER*)* He's teasing her.

DR BOYLE: We took Rita for golf lessons every year for I don't know how many years—

MRS BOYLE: Three.

DR BOYLE: Or four.

MRS BOYLE: Three.

DR BOYLE: Three. Okay.

RITA: Well—

DR BOYLE: *(Overlapping)* She never got with it.

RITA: Maybe I'll try it again. I'm serious, I might like to.

(Beat)

MRS BOYLE: Did you go snorkeling?

RITA: Oh, sure.

PETER: You name it, we tried it. Rita even wanted to go up on one of those kites—that they haul from behind the boats?

MRS BOYLE: Oh, you're kidding. No!

RITA: Peter was upset by all the poverty, wanted to give them all our money.

*(*DR *and* MRS BOYLE *turn and stare at* PETER.*)*

PETER: Oh, show them the bracelet you bought, Rita.

*(*RITA *shakes her head.)*

RITA: I didn't bring it.

PETER: Ohhh, too bad.

MRS BOYLE: I want to see.

PETER: It's gold. It's incredible. All these big things hanging down from it, must weigh about a ton....

MRS BOYLE: Sounds expen—

DR BOYLE: *(Overlapping)* But you know, that's the reality— Excuse me— You can't escape it, wherever you go. *(Pause)* Poverty.

MRS BOYLE: No.

RITA: That's what I told him.

DR BOYLE: It's reality.

(Pause)

MRS BOYLE: Oh, speaking of which, that man from the wedding, Rita—
Your father told me not to bring it up, but—was not the Evans' gardener.
I called up over there after you left for the airport.

DR BOYLE: All right, enough.

PETER: Who do you think he was, though?

RITA: I told you, I thought he was my fairy godfather.

DR BOYLE: That's right.

(Pause)

PETER: Strange.

MRS BOYLE: *(To* RITA*)* Well... Why don't we let the men talk about whatever
it is men talk about and you can help me set the table?

RITA: Great. Fun.

MRS BOYLE: And I can show you the sketch I did of your father in class.
We'll be ready to eat in about fifteen minutes, gents.

PETER: Terrific.

*(*RITA *follows* MRS BOYLE *off.)*

DR BOYLE: When do you start work?

PETER: Tomorrow.

DR BOYLE: You folks gonna have enough room in that apartment of Rita's?

PETER: Oh sure.

DR BOYLE: Another beer there?

*(*PETER *shakes his head. Beat.)*

PETER: Does Rita...? She seem okay to you?

DR BOYLE: Why, something the matter?

PETER: No. No.

DR BOYLE: Tell me, for godsake.

PETER: No. She seems changed a little bit.

DR BOYLE: Well, you're married now. And you're dealing with a slippery
entity there.

PETER: Uh-huh.

DR BOYLE: She's always had the highest expectations of everybody. Especially herself. But... I don't know, in some way she's always been...uncertain. Drove her mother and me crazy for a while.

PETER: Yeah, she told me a little bit. Her politics and stuff.

DR BOYLE: Politics?

PETER: Oh...n—

DR BOYLE: *(Overlapping)* What politics?

PETER: No, no, I was mixing it up with something else....

DR BOYLE: You'll get used to her. She's young. You're both young.

PETER: She gets, you know, really forgetful sometimes.

DR BOYLE: I know.

PETER: Forgets whole...

DR BOYLE: Years. I'm aware.

PETER: She's given up salt, too.

DR BOYLE: Oh, she has. I've got to do that.

PETER: And she pulls the skin off her chicken.

DR BOYLE: Oh. Well, she's way ahead of me. Watching out for her old age already...

(Pause)

PETER: She's thinking of maybe quitting her job at the bar, too, so....

DR BOYLE: She is.

PETER: Yeah. So I can support us.

DR BOYLE: Outstanding. You must be making her very happy. Congratulations...

PETER: Thanks.

(PETER's office)

TAYLOR: Hey!

PETER: Hey!

TAYLOR: No tan.

PETER: No tan.

TAYLOR: We missed you.

PETER: Thanks.

TAYLOR: Welcome back. Listen, Kollegger wants to know what happened to April.

PETER: Oh. The N.I.H. never sent the documents.

TAYLOR: Oh. What do I tell him?

PETER: Tell him the N.I.H. never sent the documents.

TAYLOR: *(Overlapping)* —never sent the documents. I like the angle.

(TAYLOR starts to leave.)

PETER: Listen, Tay?

TAYLOR: Yeah.

PETER: If you could switch souls with somebody?... Like go inside their body and they go inside yours?... You know? Switch?

TAYLOR: ...Yeeaaaaah?

PETER: Do you think it would be possible, if you didn't know someone, to impersonate them, by just being inside them and...looking like them?

TAYLOR: Where are they?

PETER: Inside you.

TAYLOR: And you're inside them?

PETER: Right.

TAYLOR: Why would you go inside another person's body if you didn't know them?

PETER: It's conjecture.

TAYLOR: I think I know that, Peter. But wouldn't you do better to pick someone you knew, a particular person you envied—

PETER: Right.

TAYLOR: —or admired so that you could do or be or have the things this other person did or bee'd or had?

PETER: Maybe. Yes.

TAYLOR: Are you Rita now? Is that what you're telling me? You two have merged?

PETER: All right, here's another question. Have you ever... This is sort of a bizarre question. Have you ever been having sex with somebody...?

TAYLOR: Nope.

PETER: And they're doing everything, you know, right, more or less.

TAYLOR: Oh, right, sex, I remember, go ahead.

PETER: And you just get the feeling that...something is wrong? I mean, they pretty much stop doing some of the things they used to do—

TAYLOR: Ohhhh.

PETER: —and only do certain other things now, more...

TAYLOR: Right.

PETER: ...traditional sorts of things.

TAYLOR: Blow jobs, you mean.

PETER: No, I'm not talking about anything specific.

TAYLOR: No one likes to do that.

PETER: Well, that happens not to be strictly the case, but....

TAYLOR: No woman has ever enjoyed doing that, I'm just telling you. It's common knowledge.

PETER: You haven't had sex, but you know all about it.

TAYLOR: Hey, you asked me.

PETER: Yes, I know I did.

TAYLOR: I'm just trying to help.

PETER: Thank you. A lot.

TAYLOR: Welcome back.

PETER: Great talking to ya. *(To us)* That night everything was miraculously restored....

(RITA and PETER's apartment.)

RITA: Hi.

PETER: Hi.

RITA: How was work?

PETER: Okay.

RITA: It was?... Making you a surprise.

PETER: What?

RITA: Guess.

PETER: I can't. What's this?

RITA: Dewar's.

PETER: What, you're back on the sauce? What's the surprise?
(She sniffs the air; he does too.) Spaetzles?

(RITA *smiles.)*

PETER: You're kidding.

RITA: I'm sure they won't be anywhere near as good as Sophie's,
but then I'm not such a cruel mama, either. You want a Molson?

PETER: Sure.

(She goes off; he picks up a book.)

RITA: *(From off)* So, I don't know, I made some calls about taking my
portfolio around today, but the whole thing terrifies me.... *(She returns
with his Molson.)* And I started reading that, finally.

PETER: *The White Hotel?*

RITA: Cheers.

PETER: Cheers.

RITA: You didn't call the doctor, did you?

PETER: No, I will.

RITA: No, I don't want you to.... I know things were hard in Jamaica. Maybe
it's taken me this time to get used to being married, but...I love you, Peter.

(They kiss. He pulls away, holding on to her.)

PETER: You read her journal, didn't you? You figured out how to fix your
hair from the pictures in the albums and what to wear, what she drinks....
Where is she? Please. I won't be angry. You can go back wherever you came
from and I won't tell a soul, you don't have to tell me who you are. Just tell
me where Rita is and we'll pretend this never took place. *(Pause)* Okay. Play
it your way. But I'm on to you.

(PETER *walks out.)*

(The Tin Market. The OLD MAN *is seated as* PETER *enters.)*

TOM: Hey, Pete, you're back. How was your honeymoon?

PETER: Good, thanks.

TOM: How's Reet?

PETER: Great.

TOM: Where is she?

PETER: Oh, not feeling too well, actually. Let me have a double vodka on the rocks....

TOM: Got your postcard.

PETER: Yeah?

(PETER *sees the* OLD MAN.)

TOM: There you go. It's on the house. (PETER *does not respond.*) Don't mention it. *(To the* OLD MAN*)* Dewar's?

(The OLD MAN *nods.)*

PETER: Is he a regular?

TOM: Oh, yeah, last couple of weeks or so, I guess. Why? You know him?

(PETER *downs his drink as* TOM *takes the* OLD MAN *his.* PETER *crosses to the* OLD MAN*'s table.*)

PETER: Have we... Have we met? *(The* OLD MAN *nods.)* Mind if I sit? *(He does.)* You were at my wedding, weren't you? *(The* OLD MAN *nods. Beat.)* Do I know you? *(The* OLD MAN *nods.)* What's my stepmother's name?...

OLD MAN: *(Unable to remember)* Uhhh...

PETER: What's the movie I said I was going to see the night I left for Europe?...

OLD MAN: *The Wild Bunch!*

PETER: Je hebt erg witte tanden.

OLD MAN: Not anymore.

(He shows PETER *his teeth.)*

PETER: What shape's your father's shrapnel scar?

OLD MAN: He thinks it's shaped like a saxophone, but it's not.

PETER: I knew it wasn't you! I *knew* it. Oh, I knew it! Oh my god, Rita.

(They embrace.)

OLD MAN: Baby.

PETER: Oh... *(Beat.* PETER *pulls back.)* ...god... Maybe we shouldn't.... Maybe... How much do we owe you here, Tom?

TOM: No, man, it's on the house.

PETER: Oh, okay, great. Great. *(To the* OLD MAN*)* Okay? *(To* TOM*)* I'm just gonna walk the old guy down to the subway.

TOM: Okay.

PETER: Good to see you, Tom.

TOM: You, too. Tell Rita I hope she feels better.

PETER: I will. I will. *(To the* OLD MAN*)* Come on, let's get out of here.

(Outside. They walk.)

PETER: How are you?

OLD MAN: I've missed you.

PETER: Where have you been?

OLD MAN: Brooklyn. In Borough Park. I stayed with his family. Julius Becker. He had his wallet on him. I didn't know what else to do, where to go; I couldn't call my mother or go to the police. Who would believe me, right?

PETER: Let's head back toward the apartment. Okay?

OLD MAN: They could throw me into an institution or an old folks' home; I didn't even have our keys. I had to pretend to be him until you figured it out. And I knew you would.

PETER: I think this is like one of those dreams where you tell yourself, Just hang on, and we're all gonna wake up. We'll walk in and she'll be there and it's gonna be okay, Rita.

OLD MAN: I just keep thinking there's something I'm forgetting.... When he leaned in to kiss me I saw this look in his eye, you know? And something.... I've got to slow down, I'm sorry.

PETER: That's okay.

(They slow their pace.)

OLD MAN: I get short of breath.

PETER: Better?

OLD MAN: What was I saying?

PETER: You get short of breath.

OLD MAN: Before that. Peter, I'm not senile.

PETER: I know, I know.

OLD MAN: I was holding your hand and then I wasn't. I was turned all around. You were over there and I was over there. I thought it was a mirror, that's why I reached out—to steady myself, and instead I saw his hand...this hand...on me.... And then everybody was staring at me and my dad was saying I'd had too much to drink and I don't know, I thought I had salmonella.

PETER: Really? That's great.

OLD MAN: I thought if I went along with it, then you'd all come running out after me and say, "It's a joke, come on, Rita, you're going on your honeymoon." And we'd laugh.... I just kept walking, past all the cars parked for the wedding. I was afraid to look down at my shadow to see if it was true—my reflection in the windows.... I found this card in his wallet. *(He shows* PETER *the card.)* "In case of emergency, please notify Mr and Mrs Jerome Blier." His daughter and her husband. They came and picked me up.... *(Beat)* So how was our honeymoon? (PETER *does not laugh.)* Oh, come on!

PETER: I'm fine.

OLD MAN: Does he know you know?

PETER: HE? Yeah. He does.

OLD MAN: She. Whatever. He does?

PETER: Yes, I think so.

(They have stopped walking. They look up at the apartment.)

OLD MAN: Is he there now?

PETER: *(Nodding)* I think maybe you should wait outside in the hall in case he tries to bolt. All right?

OLD MAN: Peter?

PETER: What?... I know, come on.

(The apartment. PETER *enters. The* OLD MAN *stands outside the open door.)*

PETER: Rita?

*(*DR BOYLE *emerges from the bedroom with a suitcase; the* OLD MAN *recedes out of sight.)*

DR BOYLE: Peter.

PETER: What's the matter? Where's Rita?

DR BOYLE: I'm sorry about all this, Peter.

PETER: Did something happen?

DR BOYLE: You know I am. You know I like you.

PETER: What do you mean you're sorry?

DR BOYLE: Rita's gone back to New Jersey with her mother, Peter.

PETER: Why?

DR BOYLE: I think it would be best if you didn't come out to the house or call for a while until she calms down.

PETER: I went for a walk. Calms down?

DR BOYLE: We brought both cars so I could pick up some of her things. And I'll be out of your way momentarily.

PETER: Wait a minute, Dr Boyle, I'm....

DR BOYLE: I'm sorry for whatever personal turmoil you're going through, Peter.

PETER: Turmoil? What did she tell you?

DR BOYLE: If you want me to refer you to somebody.... Rita says you're suffering from delusions, Peter. And I should tell you she's talking about filing for a divorce or an annulment, whichever would be—

PETER: What? Wait.

DR BOYLE: *(Overlapping, continuous)* —most appropriate under the circumstances. I'm awfully sorry.

PETER: What circumstances? What sort of delusions did she say I was suffering from?

DR BOYLE: Rita...

PETER: Go on. I want to hear this.

DR BOYLE: She was hysterical, Peter, when she called us.

PETER: What did she say?

DR BOYLE: Rita says you're convinced that she's someone else.

PETER: Someone—? What, and you believe that? What does that mean? Dr Boyle, I went for a walk. We had a— Okay, we had a fight. I went out. You and Mrs Boyle never have fights? We had a difference of opinion.

DR BOYLE: I practically had to carry her to the car. Are you telling me that nothing else has happened between the two of you? Nothing at all?

PETER: Seriously, Marshall, think about what you're saying. Rita... You're—

DR BOYLE: *(Overlapping)* If you'd seen that girl's face—I'm sorry, I'm just—I'm going to have to defer to my daughter's wishes.

PETER: I can't believe this. You're just going to take her word?

DR BOYLE: It's a little difficult to believe...knowing Rita as I do, Son, that this—

PETER: You don't know her.

DR BOYLE: *(Overlapping, continuous)* —is all about a squabble, a tiff as you say.

PETER: *(Overlapping)* You don't know anything about her, that's the absurd part. You don't know your own flesh and blood.

DR BOYLE: Well, I'm sure you're right.

(DR BOYLE starts to leave; PETER halts him.)

PETER: Rita was a Communist, did you know that? That she was in a Communist—Socialist party? And, all right, here's something else you don't know: We didn't go out for a year. We didn't go out for anything like a year; we went out for two months—at that point, six weeks. We haven't known each other six months now! You wouldn't know if she was lying to you, because you don't know her; you only see what you want to see. And she's lying to you now, Dr Boyle, she may know certain facts—

DR BOYLE: Let go of my sleeve, please.

PETER: *(Under, continuous)* —but that's from reading Rita's journals! She doesn't— Watch her! Watch the way she sits! Her eyes!

DR BOYLE: See a doctor, Boy, all—

PETER: *(Overlapping)* Rita— Watch the way she listens to everything we say, the way she *chews* for godsake, it isn't her! Open your eyes!

DR BOYLE: I'd like to leave now, Peter. *(Beat)* Thank you.

(He goes out.)

PETER: This isn't happening.

(The OLD MAN returns.)

OLD MAN: He didn't see me.

PETER: Look...I like you very much. I'm not equipped for this. I'm sorry. I still like you.

OLD MAN: *Like* me?

PETER: I'm not...I don't feel the same way about you, I'm sorry. I'm not attracted to you.

OLD MAN: What, are you nuts? I don't think that's the issue, Peter, have a seat, come on, you're—

PETER: If I thought that you were really here, Rita... What's the name of the guy you went out with in high school? Wait. You told me once—Rita did—but I've forgotten. And if I can't remember, then you can't. The one who wanted to run away.

OLD MAN: John.

PETER: Oh Rita. *(Beat)* It could have been in my unconscious. You know that. You've read Freud. Haven't you?

OLD MAN: You're not imagining me. Or we're both insane....

PETER: All right, *think*. We've got to try to figure out how.... This just does not happen.

OLD MAN: Tell me about it.

PETER: All right...let me see his wallet, please. May I? *(The* OLD MAN *hands over the wallet.)* Thank you. Becker? Is he Dutch, do you know?

OLD MAN: Is it a Dutch name?

PETER: You're the one who says you live there, Rita, Jesus!

OLD MAN: Well, they don't speak Dutch. I mean, I can't exactly ask. I'm trying to keep a low profile in case they find out I'm really a girl, okay?

*(*PETER *has rifled through the wallet's contents, found the card.)*

PETER: How do you say the daughter's name?

OLD MAN: Blier. Leah and Jerry. Why?

*(*PETER *picks up the phone, starts to dial.)*

PETER: How old?

OLD MAN: Old, I don't know, you know. Forty?... What are you doing?

(Phone rings. LEAH *enters, carrying receiver.)*

LEAH: Hello?

PETER: Hello, Mrs Jerome Blier?

LEAH: Yes?

PETER: Hi, my name is Larry...White from the Delancey Street Human Resource and Crisis Intervention Center. Is your father a Mr Julius Becker?

LEAH: Is something wrong?

PETER: No, no, he's right here, Mrs Blier.

LEAH: He is?

PETER: Yes, he's fine, he's in good hands.

LEAH: *(Overlapping)* What happened, please? Where—?

PETER: *(Overlapping)* Nothing's happened, Mrs Blier. He apparently walked up to a couple of young gentlemen and, uh, asked them if they knew what city he was in and they were kind enough to call us here at the hotline.

LEAH: I see.

PETER: But your father's here now and he seems to be fine.

LEAH: Where are you, let me write it down. My husband's—

PETER: *(Overlapping)* I'd like to ask you a few questions first if that's all right.

LEAH: My husband's gone to move the car. I'm sorry.

PETER: Where was your father born, Mrs Blier?

LEAH: Oh, in Amsterdam. Nobody seems to know the exact year.

PETER: And is he on any medications?

LEAH: He's done this before, you know.

PETER: He has.

LEAH: Two weeks ago he disappeared. We had to go and pick him up in New Jersey.

PETER: Was there some reason? Did he know someone there?

LEAH: Not that I'm aware of, no.

PETER: Are you sure?

LEAH: No.

PETER: Is your father suffering from any mental or neurologic disorders, Mrs Blier?

LEAH: He's been.... He hasn't been himself since my mother died last fall.

PETER: I see.

LEAH: Then he had to move in with us.... I'm sorry, is he there now?

PETER: Yes.

LEAH: Could I speak to him, please?

PETER: Well, I'd like to finish filling out my form—

LEAH: *(Overlapping)* I won't be a moment.... Please.

PETER: All right. Hang on. *(To the OLD MAN)* Mr Becker, it's your daughter.

(The OLD MAN shakes his head vigorously.)

OLD MAN: *(Loud, for LEAH's benefit:)* Who?

PETER: She'd like to talk to you. Your daughter!

(The OLD MAN takes the receiver.)

LEAH: Daddy?... Daddy?

OLD MAN: Yes?

LEAH: It's Leah. Are you all right?

OLD MAN: I'm fine.

LEAH: Where are you?

OLD MAN: I'm here.

LEAH: Where did you go?

OLD MAN: I didn't go anywhere.

LEAH: Now you stay there.

OLD MAN: I'm not going anywhere.

LEAH: And you do what the man says.

OLD MAN: Oh, stop worrying about it.

LEAH: All right. I love you.

OLD MAN: Don't worry about it.

LEAH: All right, let me talk to the...

OLD MAN: *(Under, to* PETER*)* Here, you talk to her.

(The OLD MAN *hands* PETER *the phone.)*

PETER: *(Into the receiver)* Mrs Blier?

LEAH: Yes?

PETER: Is there anything about your father's condition, is there any reason why he might—

LEAH: I can't put him in a home!...

PETER: No one's suggesting that you put your father in a home, Mrs Blier, not at all.

LEAH: I'm sorry. I didn't mean to burden you with any of this.

PETER: You're not burdening anyone.

LEAH: We found out he has lung cancer three months ago. And cirrhosis he's had for years. I can't put him away. He doesn't even have a year to live. You know?... If you knew the man he used to be. He ran his own stationery store for forty-seven years. *(Beat)* Let me have your address, please.

PETER: I'm going to have to call you back, Mrs Blier.

LEAH: Well, wait, my husband's just gone to park the car.

PETER: *(Overlapping)* No, I'm sorry, I'm— I will, I'll call you back.

(He hangs up.)

LEAH: Hello?

*(*LEAH *disappears.)*

OLD MAN: What? What's the matter?... What did she say?

PETER: Nothing.

OLD MAN: Am I sick?

PETER: No.

OLD MAN: This is me, Peter, remember?

(Pause)

PETER: You have lung cancer. And cirrhosis. She said she thought you had a year to live.

(Pause)

OLD MAN: Well... Am I Dutch, anyway?... Okay, first thing, we need a plan. What does he think happened to me? Where does he think I am? Maybe he doesn't think. Maybe it wasn't intentional. Is that possible?

PETER: It was intentional.

OLD MAN: Maybe it's some form of hypnosis. *(Pause)* All right, here's what we know: He wouldn't have called my parents if he was going to disappear. Obviously he wants to be me. Why?... Well, who wouldn't? He doesn't know I've found you, so I probably shouldn't go outside in case he's spying on us and Leah will definitely go to the police anyway, so.... My dad isn't going to leave me alone with you for a while, I know that. Mom's the one who's going to want us back together; she's crazy about you, and she isn't going to want me around the house, and she certainly won't believe what I'm telling her, she never does, so.... I say that our best bet is try and get her to bring him here. Don't you?

PETER: He'll scream.

OLD MAN: Let him. The last time somebody broke into one of these apartments, they used a blowtorch and nobody even called—I mean, I had a fire in the kitchen once and went screaming out into the hall. Nobody even opened their doors.... We'll think of something. *(Pause)* Okay?...

(Pause)

PETER: *(To us)* The next six days were the worst, the strangest of my life. I called in sick. We moved back and forth from room to room. We played cards, I cooked, we watched TV. It was as if we'd been married forever, suddenly, without the sex. At night I could feel the loneliness coming off of both of us like heat. The third day I called her parents; no answer. I tried again later—the same. The next day, same. After dark we went out to the house; not a sign. We used the spare key to get in; a few suitcases missing, according to Rita, that was all. The next night, still nothing. I called Rita's

Aunt Dorothy in Cincinnati. She had no idea where they were and wanted
to know why I didn't know. I told her Rita and I had split up. She was sorry
to hear it. Rita and I, meanwhile, kept up the pleasantries, the old married
couple we'd become.

(The apartment. PETER *stares at the TV.)*

OLD MAN: Something to eat?... Maybe I should teach myself to cook now
that I've got the time. What do you think?

PETER: Great.

OLD MAN: Who's winning? *(*PETER *shrugs.)* Who's playing? *(*PETER *shrugs
again.)* Well...

PETER: Rita?

OLD MAN: What?

PETER: What if they never come back?... What if they're gone forever?

OLD MAN: Well...

PETER: I miss your face.

OLD MAN: Don't think about it.

PETER: How soft it was.

(Pause)

OLD MAN: I miss it, too.

PETER: Your hair was so great.

OLD MAN: Oh, come on.

PETER: And your little white feet.

OLD MAN: What, you don't like these? *(Pause)* You know...if you think how
we're born and we go through all the struggle of growing up and learning
the multiplication tables and the name for everything, the rules, how not
to get run over, braid your hair, pig-Latin. Figuring out how to sneak out
of the house late at night. Just all the ins and outs, the *effort*, and learning
to accept all the flaws in everybody and everything. And then getting a job,
probably something you don't even like doing for not enough money, like
bartending, and that's if you're lucky. That's if you're not born in Calcutta
or Ecuador or the U.S. without money. Then there's your marriage and
raising your own kids if...you know. And they're going through the same
struggle all over again, only worse, because somebody's trying to sell them
crack in the first grade by now. And all this time you're paying taxes and
your hair starts to fall out and you're wearing six pairs of glasses which
you can never find and you can't recognize yourself in the mirror and your

parents die and your friends, again, if you're lucky, and it's not you first. And if you live long enough, you finally get to watch everybody die: all your loved ones, your wife, your husband and your kids, maybe, and you're totally alone. And as a final reward for all this...you disappear. *(Pause)* No one knows where. *(Pause)* So we might as well have a good time while we're here, don't you think?

PETER: I don't want you to die, Rita.

OLD MAN: I don't want me to die, either. And I'm going to. So are you. Hopefully later and not sooner. But we got to have this. I mean, what a trip! Meeting you and being in love. Falling. It was bitchin' for a while. And okay, so this isn't such a turn on, I admit. But...

PETER: I adore you.

OLD MAN: What? My hearing. No, I'm serious.

PETER: I said *I adore you!*

OLD MAN: That's what I thought.

PETER: For better or for worse.

OLD MAN: Huh?

PETER: I said: You would have hated Jamaica. Trust me.

(The OLD MAN *rises, crosses to* PETER. PETER *stands. They face one another for a moment.* PETER *can't bring himself to kiss the* OLD MAN. *The* OLD MAN *hands* PETER *the phone.)*

OLD MAN: Try again.

*(*PETER *dials. Phone rings.* MRS BOYLE *enters with receiver.)*

MRS BOYLE: Hello?

PETER: Oh, Marion, it's Peter.

MRS BOYLE: I thought it might be you.

PETER: Where've you been? I've been worried. How's Rita?

MRS BOYLE: They've just run down to the store; I may have to get off. She's terrible, Peter. We took her to London. She was so shook up, Marshall thought she needed a rest. I don't know, I was tempted to call you from over there, but I didn't, I'm sorry.

PETER: Is she okay?

MRS BOYLE: What happened between the two of you, Peter? If you don't want to tell me you don't have to.

PETER: No, I do, I just am not sure I know. I said—I guess I must have said something about her not being the same person. And then I lost my temper with Dr Boyle; I said some things I didn't mean. I was just so surprised to see him here. You know? Did he tell you?

MRS BOYLE: No, Peter.

PETER: But I would do anything to get Rita back. *(Looking at the* OLD MAN*)* I love her with all my heart and soul...

MRS BOYLE: Well, she says that you're unstable and she's sorry she ever met you. I don't know, you don't seem so unstable to me.

PETER: No.

MRS BOYLE: Maybe I'm being naive.

PETER: No, you're not.

MRS BOYLE: That's what all unstable people say, Peter...I'm teasing you.

PETER: If I could just see her....

MRS BOYLE: You can't come here, Peter. If either of them knew I was talking to you, they'd have me shot at sunrise.

PETER: How's she been? Is she okay?

MRS BOYLE: Oh, I don't know what her problem is.

PETER: If she wants me to see a psychiatrist....

MRS BOYLE: Well...

(The OLD MAN *scribbles something on a pad and hands it to* PETER, *who reads as he talks.)*

PETER: Marion, what if...it's just a thought, but what if you told her I was going away on business for a couple of weeks—

MRS BOYLE: Are you?

PETER: No, wait.

MRS BOYLE: Oh.

PETER: And you said she could stop by to pick up the rest of her things from storage in the basement, you know, all her old letters and journals from her childhood and all that stuff she's left here, and then when you came by with her I'd be here. And we could talk.

MRS BOYLE: Oh, I don't know, Peter.

PETER: I have to see her. Even if she won't even speak to me... Please.

(Pause)

MRS BOYLE: When would you want us?

PETER: Anytime.

MRS BOYLE: I'm not promising anything.

PETER: I understand....

MRS BOYLE: Monday?

PETER: Monday's great.

MRS BOYLE: All right, I'll try. That's all I can do.

PETER: I understand. Thank you.

MRS BOYLE: What time?

PETER: Anytime.

MRS BOYLE: Noon, say?

PETER: Noon's great. Fine.

MRS BOYLE: High noon.

PETER: High noon.

MRS BOYLE: All right.

PETER: Thank you very much...

MRS BOYLE: Peter?

PETER: Yes?

MRS BOYLE: What you said before about Rita not being the same person?

PETER: Uh-huh?...

MRS BOYLE: They never are, Peter. They're never Rita. They're never Dr Marshall Boyle, not the way that you think they should be. They're always someone else. They're always changing.

PETER: Uh-huh.

MRS BOYLE: That's life. That's marriage. They're always growing and shifting and so are you.

PETER: Right.

MRS BOYLE: She may not be the picture of the woman you thought she was, but that's an image, Peter. That's just a picture. Words.

PETER: I know.

MRS BOYLE: I'm sure you're not always the prize either.

PETER: No.

MRS BOYLE: Nobody is. But I know she loves you and misses you.

PETER: I miss her too.

MRS BOYLE: All right. We'll see you Monday then.

PETER: Thank you, Mom.

MRS BOYLE: All right.

PETER: Bye.

MRS BOYLE: Bye now.

(They both hang up. MRS BOYLE *disappears.)*

PETER: She'll try.

(Long pause. PETER *slowly kneels and kisses the* OLD MAN *tenderly on the mouth.)*

(The apartment. Darkness. RITA *and* MRS BOYLE *enter, switching on the lights.)*

MRS BOYLE: I don't want you to be angry with me.

RITA: I'm not. Relax.

MRS BOYLE: *(Looking around)* He keeps it clean.

*(*PETER *enters.* RITA *does not see him at first.)*

RITA: Yeah. He likes things in their proper— *(She sees* PETER.*)* —places.

MRS BOYLE: Now I want you to talk, Rita, I want you both to talk, that's all. Peter has something he wants to tell you. If after you've heard him out you don't want to stay, then I'll be downstairs in the car. You can do that much, since you took the trouble to marry him. You might actually thank me someday.

PETER: Mom, are you sure I can't get you something to drink?

MRS BOYLE: No, thank you, Peter. *(To* RITA*)* This was my idea, by the way.

*(*MRS BOYLE *goes out. Pause.)*

PETER: How've you been?

RITA: I'm sorry.

PETER: Why? You're here now.

RITA: I wanted to come, I just....

PETER: You did? Really? Well... It's been real lonely here without you, Rita. *(*PETER *has maneuvered into a position between* RITA *and the exit. The* OLD MAN *appears behind* RITA*; he carries a kitchen knife and a length of rope. She does not see him immediately.)* You went to London, your mom says. *(*RITA *turns, sees the* OLD MAN *as* PETER *grabs* RITA *from behind.)* Okay. Tie his feet. *(*RITA *and the* OLD MAN *are holding each other's gaze, unable to move.)* Rita! Come on!

RITA: You don't have to do this.

PETER: Tie him!

(PETER *takes the rope as* RITA *and the* OLD MAN *continue to stare at one another.*)

RITA: This is not necessary, kids.

PETER: Give me the knife. (PETER *still holds on to* RITA *from behind.*) Give it to me! (PETER *takes the knife in one hand, holds* RITA'*s arm behind her back with the other.*) Now kiss him. (*The* OLD MAN *kisses* RITA *on the mouth. They separate.* PETER *releases* RITA *and wields the knife, particularly wary of the* OLD MAN.) Rita?

OLD MAN: No. It didn't work.

PETER: (*To* RITA) Is it you?

(RITA *is shaking her head.*)

OLD MAN: No!

PETER: Rita?

RITA: I don't know how it happened. I don't know what I did.

PETER: (*To* RITA) I'll kill you, I swear to god.

OLD MAN: Peter.

PETER: (*Threatening her with the knife*) How did you do this? How the hell did you do this?

OLD MAN: Put the knife down, please.

PETER: (*To the* OLD MAN) I'll take care of this, Rita! It's a trick, don't you know that much?

OLD MAN: (*Overlapping*) He doesn't know. Give it to me. (*The* OLD MAN *is holding out his hand.*) Please. Peter.

(PETER *is looking from one to the other, paralyzed with doubt.*)

PETER: Are you here? Rita?

OLD MAN: I'm right here.

PETER: Talk to me if you're here.

OLD MAN: Give me the knife.

PETER: I can't. I'm sorry.

OLD MAN: Then just put it down. (*Slowly* PETER *lowers the knife.*) Thank you.

(*Beat*)

RITA: (*To the* OLD MAN) Where'd you go?

PETER: Watch him.

RITA: I couldn't imagine what happened to you.

OLD MAN: Twelve twenty-two Ocean Avenue.

RITA: How is Leah?

OLD MAN: I think she misses you.... She keeps putting on professional wrestling on the TV and I just sorta sit there, trying to look interested.

RITA: Interested? It's a joke. We laugh at it together.

OLD MAN: She keeps making soup and offering me another cup and another cup.

RITA: Oh, it's full of fat, she doesn't know how else to make it....
Your mother...she isn't serious about the peanut butter and mayonnaise?

OLD MAN: Oh, she made you one? A sandwich?

PETER: Stop this.

OLD MAN: I haven't had one of those since grade school, I forgot all about— Did you try it?

PETER: Rita!

OLD MAN: Oh, they're really good....

(Beat)

RITA: I wanted it, that's all. That's all I know. I'm not hiding anything from you; I don't know any more than that. I started out to take a walk. To just try and get as far away from me as I possibly could, I didn't care. I took the first bus I saw at Port Authority: "Englewood Cliffs". It sounded romantic enough.

OLD MAN: Englewood?

RITA: Yeah. I got off the first street corner; dogs came up to play. And what's this? A *wedding*. Young people starting a life. I had some champagne, nobody bothered me. What did it matter what I did? I wished to god I were that young bridegroom starting out. Or the bride, for that matter. Look at the shine in those eyes.

OLD MAN: You're kidding. I was freaked from the moment I woke up.

RITA: Yeah?

OLD MAN: I was terrified.

RITA: No, I thought to myself, If I could shine like the light of that girl over there, I'd never take another drink, I'd let my liver hang on another decade, stay out of the sun, eat right. This time I would floss.

OLD MAN: I remember now. It was you. Oh god, it was your eyes shining back. And you kissed me and, let me be over there, please, let me skip to the end of all this hard part. I wanted to be you. For one second of one day, what would it be like to just be. And—

RITA: Yes.

OLD MAN: —not be afraid.

(They begin to overlap one another ever so slightly.)

RITA: If I could just get inside.

OLD MAN: If I could get inside.

RITA: I'll kiss the bride. I'll be the bride.

OLD MAN: My whole life would be behind me.

RITA: My whole life would be ahead of me again. Look at her. The soft arms. The white teeth—

OLD MAN: That smell.

RITA: The sweet smell on her breath.

OLD MAN: A man.

RITA: Not like something rotting coming up from your insides, but soft—

OLD MAN: Like a father.

RITA: Like a baby. And white.

OLD MAN: An old man... With nothing—

(Together:)

OLD MAN/RITA: Nothing to lose. All you've got to do is want it. Bad enough.

(Their eyes are locked. The light in the room dims as if the sun outside were obscured by a cloud—a low rumble. RITA is now standing; the OLD MAN is now seated.)

RITA: My god.

OLD MAN: Like an old suit...

PETER: Rita?

OLD MAN: Don't you see? My wife and daughter had a bond. I loved them both so much I wanted to eat them alive.

RITA: I saw their photographs. Your mom. You just wanted them back, the way they were.

OLD MAN: And women cry, you think. It feels good.

RITA: Yes, it does.

OLD MAN: Women make a life inside their body and that life comes out and holds on to them—

RITA: Yes.

OLD MAN: Clings to them, calls them up from school and says, "I'm sick, Ma, come pick me up." That baby is theirs for life. Where are they now? My wife. My mother.

RITA: They're right here.

OLD MAN: To be able to look back from their side of the bed with their eyes. At last. *(To* PETER*)* And you, my boy. I tried to be patient, I tried to be interested. I called every hotel in Kingston, "What the hell is a Long Island Ice Tea?" You're a sweet kid, no hard feelings, but you're not my type....

PETER: Please.

OLD MAN: I don't know.... The idea of living forever... It's not so good. *(Beat)* And those parents of yours you can keep.

RITA: Thank you.

(The OLD MAN *walks to the door, turns back.)*

OLD MAN: Do yourselves a favor: Floss.

(He goes out.)

PETER: Rita?... Oh, Rita... Oh my beautiful...

RITA: My body. My body.

(He unties her feet.)

PETER: There they are. Look at those. Yes! Your hair.

RITA: I'm here. I'm not afraid.

PETER: I know.

RITA: I'm not afraid.

PETER: Oh, I love you.... Give me a smile. *(She does.)* Je hebt erg witte tanden. Je hebt erg witte tanden.

RITA: Ohhhhhh, I don't remember what I'm supposed to say, Peter, I know I memorized it.

PETER: Om je better mee op to eten.

RITA: You promised you'd tell me. What does it mean?

PETER: The better to eat you with. Oh, Rita. Never to be squandered... the miracle of another human being.

RITA: You're the miracle.

PETER: No, you are.

RITA: You.

PETER: You.

(They clasp one another. Music plays. PETER lifts RITA and carries her, finally, across the threshold as the Vocalist sings: "How my lovesong gently cries/ For the tenderness within your eyes./My love is a prelude that never dies:/ My prelude to a kiss." Lights fade.)

END OF PLAY

SEARCH AND DESTROY

Howard Korder

ABOUT THE AUTHOR

Howard Korder was born in New York City and graduated with a BA in Theater from the State University of New York at Binghamton. His play BOY'S LIFE was presented by Lincoln Center Theater in 1988, directed by W H Macy and featured the Atlantic Theater Company. It was nominated for the Pulitzer Prize. His play LIP SERVICE was adapted for broadcast by HBO in 1989, winning cable television's Ace Award for best theatrical presentation. His other plays include FUN, NOBODY, and NIGHT MANEUVER.

SEARCH AND DESTROY received the Los Angeles Theater Critics' Award for Best New Play, and the Joseph Kesselring Prize from the National Arts Club. Korder's latest play is entitled THE LIGHTS. Currently, he is writing a screenplay for Errol Morris, director of THE THIN BLUE LINE and A BRIEF HISTORY OF TIME.

SEARCH AND DESTROY was commissioned, and originally produced by South Coast Repertory on January 12, 1990. The cast and creative contributors were:

MARTIN MIRKHEIM . . . . Mark Harelik
ACCOUNTANT, DR WAXLING, CARLING . . . . Jarion Monroe
LAUREN, JACKIE, VOICE OF FLIGHT ATTENDANT, VOICE OF
RADIO ANNOUNCER . . . . Anni Long
ROBERT, RON . . . . Anthony Forkush
KIM . . . . Philip Anglim
MARIE, TERRY . . . . Dendrie Taylor
ROGER, STATE TROOPER . . . . Hubert Baron Kelly
HOTEL CLERK, LEE . . . . Dom Magwili
SECURITY GUARD, NUÑEZ . . . . Art Koustik
BUS DRIVER, PAMFILO . . . . Vic Trevino

Director . . . . David Chambers
Set design . . . . Chris Barreca
Costume design . . . . Dunya Ramicova
Lighting design . . . . .Chris Parry
Sound design . . . . David Budries
Stage manager . . . . Julie Haber
Assistant stage manager . . . . Jaime Vasquez

SEARCH AND DESTROY was later presented by the Yale Repertory Theatre (Lloyd Richards, Artistic Director), in New Haven, Connecticut, on November 27, 1990.

SEARCH AND DESTROY was produced on Broadway by the Circle in the Square Theatre (Ted Mann, Artistic Director), in New York City, on February 26, 1992.

SEARCH AND DESTROY was also produced in London at the Royal Court.

CHARACTERS

MARTIN MIRKHEIM
ACCOUNTANT
LAUREN
ROBERT
JACKIE
KIM
MARIE
ROGER
HOTEL CLERK
SECURITY GUARD
DR WAXLING
BUS DRIVER
RON
PAMFILO
NUÑEZ
LEE
TERRY
STATE TROOPER
RADIO ANNOUNCER
CARLING

TIME

The present

PLACE

The United States of America

(As the house lights dim)

MAN'S VOICE: *(Over speakers)* I get letters. Yes I do. People with problems. "Dr Waxling, I see you on television...Dr Waxling I am *confused*, Dr Waxling I'm in *trouble*, I turn to *you*...as a last resort." To me. A message for these viewers. I hope they're watching. I'm only saying it once. "I'm trapped by my limitations," there *are* no limitations, ANYTHING IS POSSIBLE. "I can't escape the past," the past is *dead*, THROW IT AWAY. "I'm *worried*. I don't feel *safe*. I *want* to change but I'm *frightened* by my OWN WEAKNESS." Is that *you*? Is that your "problem?" Then I tell you *what*. You better be strong. It's that simple. *You...better...be...strong.*

ACT ONE

Scene One

(An office. MARTIN *in a chair,* ACCOUNTANT *seated behind desk.)*

MARTIN: Okay. This... *(Pause)* Here is my plan. I see myself as, uh, I feel, I think my *abilities*.... I hate fear. Hate it. Fear that makes you...that *stops* you. From realizing your...yourself. *Your...self.* What you *are*. What you know you could *be*. Because of that fear? No. *(Pause.* ACCOUNTANT *shifts his papers.)* And this is not, "Hey, make me king," or, um, "Why can't *I* sleep with cover girls," because people who, that's not an *ambition*. That's...they don't know anything. The world, themselves...they waste their energies. On...what? It's foolish. Have a purpose. A *serious* purpose. Because...okay. Here we are, Planet Earth, boom. What's important? A neat desk? "He was kind to children"? No. "I will *die* one day so let me leave something behind." Something *good*. Something *lasting*. Something of myself. Let them know I was here. Let them *know* I was here. Let them know. *(He looks at the* ACCOUNTANT. *Pause.)*

ACCOUNTANT: You owe the state of Florida forty-seven thousand, nine hundred and fifty-six dollars.

MARTIN: Uh-huh. Okay.

ACCOUNTANT: Exclusive of interest and penalties.

MARTIN: I understand *your* position—

ACCOUNTANT: You failed to file or substantially underpaid corporate taxes for the last fiscal quarter of 1990, the first fiscal quarter of 1991, the second fiscal quarter of 1991, and the fourth fiscal quarter of 1991. That is as Mirkheim Enterprises, Incorporated, doing business variously as Startime Booking, Big Top Tours, and The Southern Skating Spectacular. You are listed as sole proprietor of Mirkheim Enterprises, is that correct?

MARTIN: I'm trying to explain, my intentions—

ACCOUNTANT: I need to know if that's correct, Mr Mirkheim. *(Pause)*

MARTIN: Yes.

ACCOUNTANT: In the last quarter you filed, you claimed—

MARTIN: My corporation—

ACCOUNTANT: *Corporation* claimed as operating expenses the mortgage and maintenance on a condominium apartment in Boca Raton. This apartment is also listed as your place of residence.

MARTIN: Okay, *first*, I work at home so—

ACCOUNTANT: You claim payment of twenty-two thousand dollars to a Ms Lauren Mirkheim as a nonexclusive consultant to your firm. We are interested in the nature of her services.

MARTIN: She happens to hold a business degree from—

ACCOUNTANT: We are interested in seeing your records. We are interested in your *corporation's* income during the last year. We are very interested in determining—

MARTIN: What's your point. *(Pause)* Please.

ACCOUNTANT: You owe the state of Florida forty-seven thousand, nine hundred fifty-six dollars. Exclusive of interest and penalties. *(Pause)*

MARTIN: What if I don't have it?

ACCOUNTANT: The state of Florida is legally empowered to place a lien upon your holdings, both real and intangible, and initiate criminal proceedings. We do not like to be taken advantage of, Mr Mirkheim.

MARTIN: I was not taking advantage, sir, I—

ACCOUNTANT: How would you describe it? *(Pause)*

MARTIN: It's outside my main focus.

ACCOUNTANT: Your *main* focus.

MARTIN: The area of my concern.

ACCOUNTANT: Which is.

MARTIN: I've been *telling* you.

ACCOUNTANT: You're frightened of dying, was that it?

MARTIN: No, please *listen*. I *know* how this looks. I *know* why I'm here.

ACCOUNTANT: Why are you here.

MARTIN: I am here...because I haven't paid as much attention recently to—

ACCOUNTANT: That's not exactly—

MARTIN: Attention as I should have to something you seem to...something important. It's important. I've let it go too long, that's a bad mistake. Now whatever my debts are I'll honor them. I give you my word. All I ask, simple request, not to be bullied, not to be threatened. I'm speaking to you openly because I believe there's a better way to be. So when I say I'm trying to achieve something, and haven't had time to attend to every—

ACCOUNTANT: You're a young man, Mr Mirkheim.

MARTIN: Can I just—

ACCOUNTANT: You're a very young man with a healthy income and a bad attitude towards reporting it. I suggest you make time for matters of more pressing import.

MARTIN: Such as?

ACCOUNTANT: Forty-seven thousand, nine hundred—

MARTIN: No, now you're— Is that supposed to *scare* me? I owe *money*? Some *numbers*? You think that's what *counts*?

ACCOUNTANT: It might warrant *my* respect.

MARTIN: I bet it would.

ACCOUNTANT: Excuse me?

MARTIN: You'd be down on your knees shaking. You'd be sobbing to Jesus. *(Pause)*

ACCOUNTANT: You owe us, Mr Mirkheim. It's time to pay. This office will be in touch with you shortly. You might find the services of a lawyer useful.

MARTIN: I don't need one.

ACCOUNTANT: Your expertise is vast.

MARTIN: Are we done?

ACCOUNTANT: For now.

MARTIN: Let me tell you something.

ACCOUNTANT: Mmm-hmm.

MARTIN: This country... *(The* ACCOUNTANT *looks away.)* Excuse me... *(The* ACCOUNTANT *looks at him.)*

ACCOUNTANT: Yes?

MARTIN: ...Is about *possibilities.*

ACCOUNTANT: I'll keep that in mind, Mr Mirkheim. Have a nice day.

Scene Two

(A sun deck. LAUREN *on chaise lounge in bathing suit;* MARTIN, *in suit and tie, on top of her.)*

LAUREN: *(After a moment)* Marty. *(Pause)* Marty.

MARTIN: Yes.

LAUREN: Please.

MARTIN: What.

LAUREN: Don't fuck me on the sun deck. *(Pause)*

MARTIN: Why not?

LAUREN: I don't *want* you to. *(Pause)*

MARTIN: Let's go inside.

LAUREN: No.

MARTIN: Come on.

LAUREN: The cleaning lady's there.

MARTIN: She won't see us.

LAUREN: Marty. *Marty. (Pause)* We're not doing any more of this. It's *over.* Okay? *(Pause.* MARTIN *stands up.)* I thought you were trying celibacy.

MARTIN: I am.

LAUREN: You should try harder.

MARTIN: I should. I'm going to. I *will. (Pause. He picks up a book lying by the chaise.)* Still on the same chapter.

LAUREN: It's a long book.

MARTIN: He says some very important things in here.

LAUREN: Well.

MARTIN: About the world. How to live.

LAUREN: Since when do you read?

MARTIN: Since now.

LAUREN: I just can't get into it.

MARTIN: He's on TV every week. You could watch with me.

LAUREN: Let's not start.

MARTIN: We could be together.

LAUREN: Marty, make up your mind.

MARTIN: I *want* us together. I wanted us to *change* together.

LAUREN: I'm happy the way I am.

MARTIN: Everyone says that.

LAUREN: I know it. I know how *I* feel.

MARTIN: You shouldn't do coke.

LAUREN: Well thank God I never saw you trying to suck your face off a mirror.

MARTIN: I'm done with all that.

LAUREN: I forgot, you're a new man.

MARTIN: I'm trying to be.

LAUREN: We're not kids now, Marty.

MARTIN: That's exactly *why*.

LAUREN: So walk out on me, give up a good business—

MARTIN: No, no, I didn't "give it up," I—

LAUREN: Running around the country five years, finally I think I get to stay in one—

MARTIN: Lauren, Lauren, *listen* to me, the business was nothing. Circus tours. Booking wrestlers. Polka bands. It proved nothing. What is *that*. What have I *done*.

LAUREN: What've you done, you have a condo, you have—

MARTIN: No. Not things. Deeds. I'm talking about deeds. *(Pause)*

LAUREN: My lawyer thinks you shouldn't be here.

MARTIN: I'm going.

LAUREN: I'm sorry I have to say that.

MARTIN: I have an appointment anyway.

LAUREN: And you'll take care of that check.

MARTIN: Yeah, I just forgot to transfer the money. It'll clear this time. *(Pause)* Can you wait a week, ten days?

LAUREN: Again?

MARTIN: Last time. I promise. There's a project I'm working on. Something I care about. When it's done everything'll be different.

LAUREN: Will it.

MARTIN: Yes. I wish you could understand that. *(Pause)*

LAUREN: Alright.

MARTIN: Thank you. *(He offers her the book.)* Here.

LAUREN: It's okay.

MARTIN: I can get another copy.

LAUREN: I'm done with the book, Marty. *(Pause)* What is it?

MARTIN: Hmm?

LAUREN: What's your project? (MARTIN *looks out front. Pause.)*

MARTIN: You can see clear to the horizon from here.

Scene Three

(A terrace. Evening. MARTIN *in his suit.* ROBERT *in casual wear. Sounds of a party from inside.)*

ROBERT: Where'd it go, Marty.

MARTIN: I don't know, Rob.

ROBERT: Where'd all that money *go,* you know. I mean Jesus. Six hundred points they're saying, "No cause for alarm." Fuck me. *(Pause)*

MARTIN: How much did you lose?

ROBERT: A lot. Boodles. Great entire boodles. Fuck fuck why didn't I see this coming. Why am I throwing this *party.*

MARTIN: You'll make it back.

ROBERT: Will I. *(Pause)* How'd you come out.

MARTIN: I'm not too worried.

ROBERT: You're not.

MARTIN: It's just, you know, the economy.

ROBERT: Just that, huh?

MARTIN: Yeah.

ROBERT: God bless you, Marty. (JACKIE, ROBERT'S *wife, enters. She sees* MARTIN.*)*

JACKIE: Oh. *(To* ROBERT*)* Are you spending the whole evening out here?

ROBERT: I'd like to enjoy my terrace before I jump off it.

JACKIE: It's your friends in there, not mine.

ROBERT: Honey, I kinda lost several hundred thousand dollars today. Be nice to me.

MARTIN: Hello, Jackie.

JACKIE: Yes. *(She exits. Pause.)*

MARTIN: She's mad at me.

ROBERT: Well, you know, Lauren's calling her.

MARTIN: Yah.

ROBERT: What do you want, they're sisters. *(Pause)* Tell you what my broker says.

MARTIN: What.

ROBERT: Fear.

MARTIN: What about it?

ROBERT: He thinks it's going to be big. He thinks we're gonna be hearing a lot from fear in the nineties. It's going to be the fear decade. And he says... *(A man, KIM, walks onto the terrace. ROBERT drops his voice.)* He says now's the time to ground-floor it.

MARTIN: Fear?

ROBERT: Fear-related industries. Blood analyzers. Viral filters. UV screens. Toteable security systems. Impact-proof leisure-wear, I've seen that. I mean this is you walk into K-Mart, you go buy something make you feel safe. Very cutting edge, very hot. Which sounds great except here I am stuck with my pants around my ankles three hundred k in the hole. Majorly sucks. *(Pause. Party noise from inside.)*

MARTIN: *(Producing book)* You read this, Rob?

ROBERT: *(Not looking at it)* Wish I had time, Marty.

MARTIN: You should.

ROBERT: What's it, the Trump thing? Dead meat, kid, dead meat.

MARTIN: No, he talks about all this stuff. And what it means.

ROBERT: Who does.

MARTIN: Doctor Waxling.

ROBERT: I'm sorry?

MARTIN: Luther Waxling. Who wrote the book. *(Pause)*

ROBERT: Guy on cable three in the morning?

MARTIN: Yes.

ROBERT: Staying up late, buddy boy. *(He looks at the book.) Daniel Strong.*

MARTIN: Right.

ROBERT: Looks interesting.

MARTIN: No, you're only saying, but it is.

ROBERT: I'm sure.

MARTIN: He, what he does, it's the story of this young, Daniel, Strong, it starts, he's born—

ROBERT: Uh-huh.

MARTIN: And he grows up in this, the world, where the system, the schools and everything, it, it *crushes* him, inside, they teach to him to be worthless—

ROBERT: Yeah, right.

MARTIN: And then, as a man, he goes on a jour— an *adventure*, which, he discovers within *himself* the power—

(JACKIE enters.)

JACKIE: Your business partner's doing lines in the playroom.

ROBERT: Shit.

JACKIE: We agreed no drugs tonight.

ROBERT: He was clean at the door.

JACKIE: Well he scored off somebody.

ROBERT: Yeah, I'll, okay. *(JACKIE exits.)* Marty, excuse me.

MARTIN: I just want to tell you about this.

ROBERT: Sounds great, really—

MARTIN: Yeah, so, I want to *do* something with it.

ROBERT: Huh?

MARTIN: I want to buy the book, the rights to the book, and do something with it.

ROBERT: You want to...

MARTIN: Buy the rights. Make a movie. *(Pause. ROBERT laughs.)* What's funny?

ROBERT: "Mirkheim Studios Presents..."

MARTIN: So? *(ROBERT keeps laughing.)* Why not?

ROBERT: No, good luck.

MARTIN: You think I can't do it?

ROBERT: I.... It's not like booking Smurfs On Ice, Mart.

MARTIN: I'm aware of that.

ROBERT: You see good money, Mart. What do you want, respect?

MARTIN: I want to *achieve* something—

ROBERT: Bad time for that, boyo. Trust me. *Good* time for sticking to what you know and holding on to what you got, yes?

MARTIN: No, 'cause by applying my *abilities*—

ROBERT: Mart. Honestly. Honestly now. Let's not...*overestimate*, huh? Who we are?

MARTIN: What are you saying?

ROBERT: I'm saying...what am I saying, you've been lucky. It was easy pickings these last few years and we've *all* been very lucky. But top of the food chain you're not. *(Pause)* And I *speak* this out of love.

MARTIN: I thought you could help me.

ROBERT: What I'm doing.

MARTIN: Not like this.

ROBERT: You want money? I can't *give* you money. I set you up once, I can't do that now.

MARTIN: I don't want money. I want contacts. You know people.

ROBERT: I know *some* people.

MARTIN: So put me in touch with them. *(Pause)*

ROBERT: Did you *talk* to the guy?

MARTIN: Which.

ROBERT: The book guy.

MARTIN: Not yet.

ROBERT: So if you can buy the thing you don't even know. *(Pause)* Marty? Right?

MARTIN: It's not a problem.

ROBERT: Why's that.

MARTIN: Because when I meet him he'll see.

ROBERT: What, that you floss nightly?

MARTIN: That I understand what he's talking about. We have to change, Rob. Can't you feel that? We all have to *change*. (ROBERT *looks at him. Pause.* JACKIE *enters and stands there.*)

ROBERT: Okay. (*He turns and starts off with her. To* MARTIN:) Call me later.

MARTIN: Does that mean you'll help?

ROBERT: It means call me later. (*They exit.* MARTIN *looks out. Silence.*)

KIM: People waste their time.

MARTIN: Pardon?

KIM: They waste their time. They make excuses, they consider the fine points, they start arguments. Factors arise. Moments pass. Directions are mislaid. We sit in the car. We wonder where we were going, and why we had to get there. You smoke?

MARTIN: No.

KIM: I do. Helps me think. You mind? (MARTIN *shakes his head.* KIM *lights a cigarette.*) Get evenings like this in the Mediterranean.

MARTIN: Do you.

KIM: Oh yes. (*Pause*)

MARTIN: (*Offering his hand*) Martin Mirkheim.

KIM: Kim Feston.

MARTIN: You're not a friend of Rob's?

KIM: No.

MARTIN: I didn't think so. (*Pause*)

KIM: And are you in business, Martin?

MARTIN: Well, I...yes.

KIM: I say this: God bless the businessmen.

MARTIN: Why's that.

KIM: They are the...*agents* of our hope.

MARTIN: Huh. (*Pause*) That's a lovely phrase.

KIM: You appreciate language.

MARTIN: I'm not good at it myself....

KIM: But you're keen to the possibilities.

MARTIN: It just strikes me a certain way.

KIM: You are not a modern man. (*Pause*)

MARTIN: And yourself?

KIM: Yes?

MARTIN: Are you in business?

KIM: On occasion.

MARTIN: Ah.

KIM: In a freelance capacity. With an overseas consultancy firm. Mostly based in New York.

MARTIN: What brings you here?

KIM: Doing some work. For your friend's partner I *think*.

MARTIN: Sounds interesting.

KIM: Well. *(Pause. They look at each other.)* I've read that, you know.

MARTIN: *Daniel Strong*?

KIM: Uh-huh.

MARTIN: You're kidding.

KIM: No. It had a...powerful effect on me.

MARTIN: Really.

KIM: Oh yes. That scene on the mountaintop.

MARTIN: Hmm, he's all alone, he's lost, starving...

KIM: The sun begins to rise, the city stretched out far below...

MARTIN: He remembers the day he killed his father.

KIM: He hears a voice—

MARTIN: His *own* voice saying what?

KIM: "There was nothing to be forgiven. And anything was possible."

MARTIN: Right. Right.

KIM: The best book when you're nineteen. *(Pause)*

MARTIN: I'm going to make a movie of it.

KIM: Yes. I overheard. What a superb idea.

MARTIN: You're not in the...film—

KIM: No.

MARTIN: Sorry.

KIM: Oh, don't apologize. We don't have to do that. *(He smiles.* ROBERT *enters with* JACKIE *behind him. Pause.)*

ROBERT: Uh...yeah. Um... *(Pause)* Look. I'm really sorry about this. I'm gonna...I'm afraid gonna have to ask you to, ah, to leave my house. I'm sorry. *(Pause)*

KIM: Are you speaking to me?

ROBERT: Yah. *(Pause)*

KIM: Why?

JACKIE: You know why. *(KIM and JACKIE look at each other. Pause.)*

KIM: Thank you for having me. You spread a lovely buffet.

JACKIE: You're welcome.

KIM: *(To MARTIN)* We should talk more. If you're ever in New York...give me a call. I mean that. *(He hands MARTIN a business card and exits. MARTIN watches him go, then turns to ROBERT and JACKIE.)*

MARTIN: What... *(ROBERT gestures " don't ask" and starts walking away. MARTIN stops him.)* Rob. I'll do it myself.

ROBERT: Huh?

MARTIN: I'm going to do it myself. *(ROBERT looks at him. Pause.)*

ROBERT: This fucking *day*...

Scene Four

(Another office. A receptionist, MARIE, behind desk. MARTIN stands before her with a small bandage on his temple.)

MARTIN: I'd like to see Dr Waxling.

MARIE: Is he expecting you?

MARTIN: Oh yes.

MARIE: Your name, please?

MARTIN: Martin Mirkheim.

MARIE: Thank you. *(She picks up phone.)* Mr Mirkheim to see Dr Waxling. *(Pause)* He says so, yes. *(Pause. To MARTIN.)* May I ask what this is in reference to?

MARTIN: It's a personal matter.

MARIE: *(Into phone.)* He's says it's personal. *(Pause. To MARTIN:)* He'll be right with you.

MARTIN: He will. Thank you. *(Pause)* Is the show taped here in Dallas?

MARIE: Huh?

MARTIN: Dr Waxling's show, taped in the building?

MARIE: No. The station.

MARTIN: Of course.

MARIE: These are the Waxling Institute's International Headquarters.

MARTIN: Ah. *(Silence.* ROGER *enters in business suit.)*

ROGER: Hello.

MARTIN: Hi.

ROGER: I'm Roger.

MARTIN: Yes. Alright.

ROGER: You wanted to see Dr Waxling.

MARTIN: Correct.

ROGER: That's not possible right now.

MARTIN: Why?

ROGER: He's busy.

MARTIN: I see.

ROGER: Perhaps I can help you.

MARTIN: It's a personal matter.

ROGER: Of what nature?

MARTIN: A personal nature. *(Pause)*

ROGER: Well, we're very happy you've walked in, sir. Getting personal is what we're about.

MARTIN: Thank you.

ROGER: You should know that Dr Waxling requests applicants first complete the Mastery Sessions before individual consultation. A lot of what he says is based on exposure to the introductory material. Now I'd be happy to set up an appointment with one of our—

MARTIN: Who *are* you?

ROGER: Excuse me?

MARTIN: Who are you?

ROGER: I'm Roger. I'm Doctor Waxling's assistant.

MARTIN: Roger. Okay. I'm not here for that. Would you please tell him that Martin Mirkheim wants to see him. I am president of Mirkheim Enterprises,

Incorporated. I have flown here directly from Florida and I have something very important to discuss with him.

ROGER: What would that company be, sir?

MARTIN: Mirkheim Enterprises is a diversified organization focused primarily in the field of entertainment.

ROGER: I'm not familiar with it.

MARTIN: We're a prominent presence in the southeastern states.

ROGER: Ah.

MARTIN: I own, my company owns, several television stations in Florida and, *Georgia*, WKRG there, we also have interests, are *active in*, the, area, of motion picture production, which, maybe you've heard, it's primed for very very explosive growth on the Peninsula with heavy involvement from the major studios.

ROGER: I wasn't aware of that.

MARTIN: Yes, very exciting. We're about to enter into an agreement with Twentieth Cent— legally I shouldn't say, and, ah, unfortunately I have a busy schedule in Dallas, leaving tomorrow, I'm meeting very shortly with some petroleum people, if Doctor Waxling wishes to talk I'm afraid it's going to have to be in the next half-hour. *(Pause)*

ROGER: And that would be in reference to....

MARTIN: The matter I've mentioned.

ROGER: The personal matter.

MARTIN: Yes. *(Pause)*

ROGER: I'm sorry sir, you're out of luck. Doctor Waxling is taping all day.

MARTIN: Ah, Roger. Yes. That's very good. I realize you're just doing your job, but—

ROGER: Sir, I've told you—

MARTIN: I don't think you quite understand what—

ROGER: No. No, I do understand, sir. I do. You want to see the Doctor. You can't. I will certainly tell him you stopped *in*...and I hope you enjoy your stay in Dallas.

MARTIN: Listen, your behavior—

ROGER: Mr Mirkheim. This building has an excellent security staff.

MARTIN: It does.

ROGER: Yes. *(Pause)* Goodbye. *(He shakes* MARTIN's *hand and exits. Pause.* MARTIN *rises and turns to* MARIE.*)*

MARTIN: How come no one here has an accent?

MARIE: You mean like a Texas accent?

MARTIN: Yah.

MARIE: Well, you know. Everybody's from everywhere.

MARTIN: Hum. *(Pause)* Was he someone important?

MARIE: He thinks so. *(Pause)* You're a producer?

MARTIN: Pardon?

MARIE: A movie producer?

MARTIN: Yes. That *is* what I am.

MARIE: Huh, what kind movies?

MARTIN: Various...kinds.

MARIE: Like slasher stuff?

MARTIN: No.

MARIE: People talking ones.

MARTIN: I suppose.

MARIE: Those are okay.

MARTIN: Well.

MARIE: Anything I would know? *(Pause)*

MARTIN: Did you see *Field of Dreams*?

MARIE: Yuh.

MARTIN: I was involved on that.

MARIE: Huh. *(Pause)* Bang your head?

MARTIN: Sorry?

MARIE: Your head.

MARTIN: Oh. No. *(Pause)* Well. *(He starts out.)*

MARIE: Could I send you one?

MARTIN: Send me what?

MARIE: One I wrote. A script.

MARTIN: Ah.

MARIE: Yeah, I took a class, I mean, why not, right? 'Cause I *have* ideas.

MARTIN: Right.

MARIE: Could, would you mind if I did? *(Pause)*

MARTIN: What's your name?

MARIE: Marie.

MARTIN: Marie. Hi. Listen—

MARIE: I know, send it to your whatever.

MARTIN: No. No, I don't work that way, Marie. I don't treat people like that. I would like to hear about your script.

MARIE: Really.

MARTIN: I *can't* right now.

MARIE: Sure, thanks.

MARTIN: I'm leaving tomorrow. I could—no, I'm sorry.

MARIE: What?

MARTIN: No, it wouldn't sound right. Send me your script.

MARIE: What wouldn't?

MARTIN: I'm free tonight, but to—

MARIE: You want me to come to your hotel. *(Pause)* Right?

MARTIN: *My* hotel. Ah. *(Pause)* Yah, sure. Why don't you do that. I'm at the Omni Atrium. It's over by—

MARIE: It's right by the airport.

MARTIN: Yes. Exactly.

MARIE: There's a restaurant there. If you want to eat.

MARTIN: The hotel? Of course. I hope you'll be my guest.

MARIE: I mean in the airport. *(Pause)*

MARTIN: Well, that's fine too.

MARIE: Okay. *(Pause)* I know something you don't.

MARTIN: What?

MARIE: There's blood on you.

MARTIN: Where? *(She points at his tie. MARTIN lifts it up to reveal a half-dollar sized spot of blood. MARIE touches it with her finger.)* It's still wet. *(She holds up her finger. MARTIN looks at it. The phone rings twice.)*

Scene Five

(An airport snack bar. MARTIN *holding bound script,* MARIE.)

MARIE: Everybody's dead all over. Okay. She's caught. The spinesucker has her pinned against the wall. With his other hand he cracks open her boyfriend's head and smears his brains all over her tits. Okay. The elevator's stuck between floors. This thing comes out of him like a gangrene penis with a lobster claw and starts burrowing into her. The pain's unbearable. Okay. Finally she manages to reach the switch on the radial saw and rips it into him. But he just smiles, okay, his stomach opens up and he absorbs it, like he does and goes on pumping her up. She's gonna die, that's all. *Except* inside him the saw's still going, spinning around, he starts shaking and there's a, what do you, close shot, yeah, and the saw rips out of his chest, there's this explosion of meat and pus pouring out like from a fire hose, he climbs on her and tries to shove the penis claw down her throat, okay, but she hacks it off with the saw okay he goes shooting back against the glass door okay they break he falls five floors, onto the metal spike in the fountain it goes straight through his face, his brains spurt out and slide into the water like fresh cum okay. He's dead, he's dead, he's finally fucking dead. She walks away that's the end. *(Pause)*

MARTIN: And this is your *first* script.

MARIE: No. I wrote one in class.

MARTIN: Ah. *(Pause)* The same sort of— ?

MARIE: Horror, yeah, I like the horror.

MARTIN: Mmm.

MARIE: Makes you feel something.

MARTIN: Yes. *(Pause)* It's very violent.

MARIE: You wouldn't do that?

MARTIN: I might.

MARIE: How much would you pay me for it?

MARTIN: That depends.

MARIE: Half a million dollars?

MARTIN: I have to read it first.

MARIE: Sure. *(Pause)*

MARTIN: How's the burger?

MARIE: Okay.

MARTIN: They just leave them sitting under heat lamps all day.

MARIE: I don't come here for the food. *(Pause)*

MARTIN: You from Dallas, Marie?

MARIE: Cincinnati.

MARTIN: What's that like?

MARIE: This. Basically like this.

MARTIN: How long you been working for the Doctor.

MARIE: Few months.

MARTIN: Have much to do with him?

MARIE: Sometimes. Sometimes much.

MARTIN: Tough man to get to.

MARIE: You shoulda made an appointment first.

MARTIN: There was a little mixup.

MARIE: I would of let you in, but Roger...

MARTIN: He seems very dedicated.

MARIE: Two tabs Dexadrine he thinks he's Mighty Mouse. You told him you know the Doctor?

MARTIN: Well, I don't like to throw names around. We'll get it all straightened out tomorrow.

MARIE: You're seeing the Doctor tomorrow?

MARTIN: I do have other business, but possibly I could squeeze—

MARIE: 'Cause I think he's starting a lecture tour tomorrow.

MARTIN: What?

MARIE: Yeah, he's gonna be in Minneapolis.

MARTIN: Minneapolis.

MARIE: Right. In Minnesota. *(Pause)* Are you alright?

MARTIN: Oh yes. I'm fine. He told me, of course. I forgot. Minneapolis.

MARIE: Big trip for nothing, huh.

MARTIN: For nothing, no, I met you, I have, there's your *script*, ah, *Dead World*....

MARIE: My teacher says it's not a good title.

MARTIN: Oh no, very eye-catching.

MARIE: Thanks. *(Silence. Jet takes off.* MARIE *follows it with her eyes. Pause.)* That's the last plane for two hours.

MARTIN: They'll probably want to close up.

MARIE: You can sit here all night, they don't care.

MARTIN: Is that what you're going to do?

MARIE: I don't know.

MARTIN: Well, I better get back. I'm up early tomorrow, some big meetings in town before I fly out.

MARIE: Okay. *(Pause)* Kye ask you a question?

MARTIN: Of course.

MARIE: How come you lie so much?

MARTIN: What?

MARIE: You lie a lot. *(Pause)*

MARTIN: How do you mean?

MARIE: Um...the office this afternoon you lied you had an appointment, you said some stuff to Roger I don't know sounded kinda stupid you told me the Doctor knows you maybe he does I don't think so. And the other stuff about the movies and everything, I kinda wonder about, 'cause the movies, that's California, you're in Dallas, you're sitting in the airport snack bar and you're talking to *me.* And I'm not anybody.

MARTIN: Uh-huh.

MARIE: So that's a lot of lying in the time I know you, which isn't very long. *(Pause)*

MARTIN: Does that bother you?

MARIE: It might. I lie. I don't do it right. I lie at the end when I'm scared and I don't get anything. You're lying at the beginning. What do you want to get? *(Pause)*

MARTIN: Marie.

MARIE: Yah.

MARTIN: I need your help.

MARIE: What for?

MARTIN: I *have* to get to Doctor Waxling. I flew here from Florida. I'll fly to Minneapolis, I don't care. I have to reach him.

MARIE: Why?

MARTIN: Because...alright. Yes. I lied, I lied, I did. I'm a liar. I don't want to be. I *want* to be true. To make myself *become* true. But it's so hard, Marie. You know what I'm saying?

MARIE: You're not a movie producer.

MARTIN: That's not the point—

MARIE: Are you?

MARTIN: No I'm not. Yes I *am*. I *am* a producer. No, I *haven't* made a movie. So what. So *what*, right? I am what I say I am because what...what you say you *are*, that's what you'll be.

MARIE: Just by saying it.

MARTIN: Okay. Okay. I understand. You're thinking, what is he, he lures me here, no, lures me, he's promising things, my script, get me into *bed*...alright. I *admit* it. There it is. But...but...listen to me. Do you believe in anything?

MARIE: Do I...

MARTIN: Believe. In anything. *(Pause)*

MARIE: Not especially.

MARTIN: I do. Now this is true. I *do* believe. I believe in myself. I believe in my power to affect things. And if you help me, you will have that power too. I need to meet the Doctor. I *need* to get his book. The rights to his book *Daniel Strong.* That means something to me. It *means* something. I know you feel that. I know you *understand* what I'm saying. I know it. *(Pause)*

MARIE: If you went to Minneapolis....

MARTIN: I will do that. Yes. Then what?

MARIE: What I could do is get you a pass. For backstage. You just walk through.

MARTIN: And then I would....

MARIE: Talk to him.

MARTIN: The Doctor.

MARIE: Yeah.

MARTIN: Can I mention your name?

MARIE: Um...

MARTIN: Or is not a good idea.

MARIE: Not a good idea.

MARTIN: I completely understand. *(Pause)* Marie.

MARIE: I know, you're welcome.

MARTIN: No, that's not what I was going to say. I... *(Pause)*

MARIE: Yeah?

MARTIN: I want to tell you that I feel very...*connected* to you right now. And in this world...at this *time*...that matters.

MARIE: Thank you. *(Pause. She takes his hand, rests it on the table, and spreads the fingers.)* You seem tense.

MARTIN: I am. I'm tense. *(Pause)* My plane...

MARIE: Sorry?

MARTIN: I, my plane today, it's, we had a non-standard touchdown.

MARIE: A crash?

MARTIN: No. Not a crash. It's not called a crash. Landing gear wouldn't open. They had to spray the runway with foam so we could slide in. *(Pause)*

MARIE: Did anyone die?

MARTIN: No. Actually. I cut my forehead.

MARIE: Were you afraid?

MARTIN: I tried not to be. I tried to *make* myself not...I couldn't. Um. Couldn't get away from it. That fear. Of...yeah. *(Pause)* At this moment I'm finding myself very attracted to you.

MARIE: Uh-huh.

MARTIN: I've taken a vow of *celibacy*...

MARIE: You have.

MARTIN: I just wanted to tell you that.

MARIE: Okay. *(Pause)* I'm gonna tell *you* a secret, Mr Mirkheim. That nobody knows.

MARTIN: Yes.

MARIE: Why this place is good.

MARTIN: Why.

MARIE: Be quiet. Be very quiet inside yourself. Don't think. Don't look at me. What do you hear. *(Pause)*

MARTIN: Nothing. I... *(Pause)* Nothing.

MARIE: That's right. *(She puts his hand against her forehead.)* If you you close your eyes? You can feel the strip lights humming. *(She closes her eyes.* MARTIN *looks at her. Faint humming sound.)*

Scene Six

(Hotel desk. MARTIN, CLERK.*)*

CLERK: Did you enjoy your stay at the Omni Atrium, sir?

MARTIN: Oh yes indeed.

CLERK: Make sure the bill is right, that was the Cattleman Suite one night, three twenty eight sixty-five for a double....

MARTIN: Single.

CLERK: Pardon?

MARTIN: Single. Just me.

CLERK: Oh. I see. *(Pause)* I understood you had a guest.

MARTIN: A guest.

CLERK: In the suite. Staying. *(Pause)*

MARTIN: Right. Very good. Just, ah, put it on the card.

CLERK: Yes sir.

MARTIN: She—

CLERK: I understand completely. *(He puts card through phone link.)*

MARTIN: Great. *(Pause)* So they watch that lobby, huh.

CLERK: Well, our security's pretty state of the art. We don't want the guests to have any cause for alarm or— *(Loud beep)* Okay. Ah. We're not getting clearance here, sir.

MARTIN: We're not.

CLERK: Uh-uh. *(Pause)*

MARTIN: What's that, the—?

CLERK: VISA.

MARTIN: Right. Right, that's the *company's*— here, put it on my personal— *(He takes out another card.)*— Tell you what, make it easy, we'll do cash. Not gonna tell me you don't take cash, are you.

CLERK: Course we do, sir.

MARTIN: *(As he counts out bills.)* Glad to hear it.

CLERK: Sorry about this.

MARTIN: Hey, that's your job. Take it seriously.

CLERK: I do, sir.

MARTIN: I see that. I think it's terrific. I really do.

CLERK: Just trying to get somewhere.

MARTIN: You will, believe me. This is yours. *(He holds out a twenty-dollar bill.)* No, come on. Really.

CLERK: *(Taking it.)* Thank you sir. Have a *very* good trip.

MARTIN: Oh, I'm going to. I know I'm going to. This just absolutely has to be the most incredibly fine day. (CLERK *turns to register.* MARTIN *looks at credit card.)*

Scene Seven

(Meeting room. Overhead projector standing next to podium with "Rodeway Inn" plaque.)

(Transparency on wall reading:
THE FOUR RULES OF SUCCESS
1. STRENGTH NEEDS NO EXCUSE.
2. THE PAST IS POINTLESS.
3. JUST BECAUSE IT HAPPENED TO YOU DOESN'T MAKE IT INTERESTING.
4. THE THINGS YOU APOLOGIZE FOR ARE THE THINGS YOU WANT.*)

*(*MARTIN *handcuffed to chair.* SECURITY GUARD, *in suit and tie, sitting opposite. Silence.)*

MARTIN: Indian name, isn't it?

GUARD: What.

MARTIN: Minneapolis?

GUARD: American.

MARTIN: One last question.

GUARD: Mmm.

MARTIN: *Are* these necessary?

GUARD: Your behavior made them necessary.

MARTIN: Because you grabbed me. Sir. *You* grabbed *me*. Would you like that? Would you want that *done* to you? Sir? *(Pause)* You're *employed* by Dr Waxling?

GUARD: I'm employed to protect the security of this motel.

MARTIN: I had a pass.

GUARD: You were asked to leave.

MARTIN: A *pass*, sir.

GUARD: Function was ended.

MARTIN: My flight was late, that's not a crime.

GUARD: Function ends, room's closed.

MARTIN: And that's a law.

GUARD: It's policy.

MARTIN: It's policy, why are you *keeping* me here?

GUARD: By request.

MARTIN: From whom?

GUARD: Couldn't say.

MARTIN: Sir. (GUARD *looks at him.*) We *make* the world. However we choose to act, that's what this world will be. Just consider it. (GUARD *looks away. Silence.* ROGER *enters.*)

ROGER: Hello.

MARTIN: Hi.

ROGER: Mr Mirkheim, isn't it?

MARTIN: Roger. Good to see you.

ROGER: You like to travel, Mr Mirkheim.

MARTIN: Yes, I do.

ROGER: How did you enjoy Dallas?

MARTIN: *Loved* it. Great city, great people.

ROGER: Took care of your business there?

MARTIN: Mmm-*hmm*.

ROGER: And here you are in Minneapolis.

MARTIN: I am indeed. *(Pause)*

ROGER: Now this pass, Mr Mirkheim.

MARTIN: Yes.

ROGER: Obviously I'm *curious*...how'd you get it?

MARTIN: Ha.

ROGER: No, but really.

MARTIN: I don't think that matters.

ROGER: You don't.

MARTIN: No.

ROGER: Fair enough. *(Pause)* You're from where'd you say *Florida*?

MARTIN: That's right.

ROGER: Live in Boca Raton down there, nice town.

MARTIN: Oh yes.

ROGER: Run a booking agency is it? Various names. You're legally separated from your wife. You were born in Rigdewood New Jersey. You're not in the film business. You're not talking to any studios. You're not making deals, huh?

MARTIN: Where'd you get this?

ROGER: Just, basically, we can agree on these facts, right?

MARTIN: Who *told* you this?

ROGER: These are just facts, Mr Mirkheim. Very basic facts about a person's life, very easily obtained. Now I bet there are other facts, maybe not quite so easy to find, but nonetheless worthwhile, especially when heard in a court of law.

MARTIN: Okay. We need to stop right here 'cause what you're doing, you're threatening me, that doesn't work.

ROGER: It doesn't.

MARTIN: No, 'cause that's the *past*. You're talking about the past and whatever happened to whoever it was, it's not me. I'm here right now and *that's* me and what is at this moment, *that* is what I will deal with. Talk to me about that.

ROGER: I see.

MARTIN: No you don't. You think I'm like you, and the things you're scared of, your reputation, your good *name* or being punished, that's worthless. I know you. I know what you do. You're still worried mommy'll find the tissues under the bed. *(Pause. ROGER takes out a small memo book.)*

ROGER: *(Reading)* 305 673-5400.

MARTIN: What?

ROGER: Florida Bureau of Taxation. *(Pause)*

MARTIN: Yes?

ROGER: I think *they* might like to hear about your recent adventures.

MARTIN: What'd you speak to my wife? I have to tell you my wife and I, not to cast, the thing about her, she's, a little bitter, basically she's wasting her life—

ROGER: *(Starting out)* Mirkheim Enterprises, wasn't it?

MARTIN: Okay.

ROGER: Excuse me?

MARTIN: Okay. What. What. *(Pause)*

ROGER: Who gave you the pass, Mr Mirkheim. *(Pause)*

MARTIN: The receptionist.

ROGER: Who is that.

MARTIN: In Dallas. Marie.

ROGER: How did that happen, Mr Mirkheim.

MARTIN: It just did.

ROGER: It just *came* upon her to give you this pass.

MARTIN: That is correct.

ROGER: Did you know her? Before?

MARTIN: No.

ROGER: But you know her now.

MARTIN: Yes. *(Pause)*

ROGER: Would you excuse me, please?

MARTIN: Right. *(*ROGER *exits. Pause. To* GUARD:*)* Nice place, Minnesota?

GUARD: I like it.

MARTIN: Bet you're a native, huh.

GUARD: I'm from Baltimore.

MARTIN: What brought you here.

GUARD: Work.

MARTIN: Good. Good for you. *(*ROGER *re-enters, followed by* DR WAXLING.*)*

ROGER: Mr Mirkheim? This is Dr Waxling.

MARTIN: Yes, yes—

ROGER: He'd like to talk to you. (ROGER *whispers briefly to* GUARD, *who nods and exits.*)

MARTIN: Yes. Dr Waxling. I...what an honor, sir, what a *great* honor, you have been...I wish I could shake your hand, as you can see I'm... First *impressions*, huh? Let me organize my thoughts, I'm not here to bore you with my problems. The first thing I want, I *need* to tell you, is what a tremendous influence your work has— I mean drifting through my, my *life*, all the time afraid to say I don't know *anything*. I DON'T KNOW ANYTHING. Than a baby. And for you in your work to say "Yes it's true and don't pretend, *yes* it's true and *that* will set you free," has made me strong. In myself. I *believe* in myself. And for this I just would like to say...thank you. (*Pause*)

WAXLING: Did you fuck my woman?

MARTIN: Huh?

WAXLING: That girl, you're fucking her?

MARTIN: I'm sorry, I don't...

WAXLING: Roger.

ROGER: Dr Waxling would like to know if you've had sexual congress with Marie.

MARTIN: No. (*Pause*)

WAXLING: Has he been frisked?

ROGER: Yes sir. (WAXLING *reaches over, grabs* MARTIN *by the lapels and slams his head against a chair.*)

WAXLING: Hey. *Hey.* Do I have your attention? (MARTIN *nods.*) Two things people do really rub me the wrong way. One is *lie*, the other is fuck my women.

MARTIN: Not lying—

WAXLING: What?

MARTIN: I'm not lying, sir—

WAXLING: No no. No. You're fucking with my things, my things, *mine*, I own them you don't *touch* them I don't care who you are. I *know* that girl, she has a *low* self image, *easily* manipulated, don't think she won't tell me, huh? Everything. (*Pause*)

MARTIN: I slept with her.

WAXLING: You did.

MARTIN: Yes.

WAXLING: *(Grabbing him again)* You greasy little fuck—

MARTIN: That's it. Dr Waxling. That's *all.*

WAXLING: He *just* screwed her, that's all, guys in fucking *suits*—

MARTIN: I *slept* with her. Just, in the same bed. We slept. *(*WAXLING *holds him. Pause.)* Like Daniel Strong does. To test himself.

WAXLING: Who?

MARTIN: Daniel Strong. Daniel *Strong. (Pause)*

WAXLING: You read that, huh. *(*MARTIN *nods.)* You read my little offering. You had to come see me. Over great distances through hardship to gaze upon my face.

MARTIN: Yes. *(Pause)*

WAXLING: Roger.

ROGER: Yes, Doctor.

WAXLING: How many.

ROGER: Well as I explained the print ad mixup—

WAXLING: How many.

ROGER: Ninety-eight.

WAXLING: How many takers.

ROGER: Now some reason here a lot of Shriners—

WAXLING: How many.

ROGER: Two for the seminar.

WAXLING: Two.

ROGER: Yes. *(Pause)*

WAXLING: Where you from?

MARTIN: Boca Raton, it's in Flo—

WAXLING: What time I'm on there.

MARTIN: Three a.m. Sundays.

WAXLING: Oh that's fine. Really splendid. Three a.m., Rodeway Inn ninety fucking Shriners. I'm doing well. I'm making a *big* noise.

ROGER: The marketing strategy—

WAXLING: They're not *buying* me. I'm not being *perceived.* As a *threat.* I'm not being taken as a threat.

ROGER: I think, when people get scared enough our message—

WAXLING: When's *that* happening, Roger. When are they gonna get *scared*?

ROGER: In *USA Today* a poll showed....

WAXLING: Fucking TV my *room* doesn't work....

ROGER:...Homeowners' fear of— I'll have it checked—

WAXLING: Get me something *chocolate.* (ROGER *looks at* MARTIN, *then exits. Pause.)*

MARTIN: Very often the people who advise us—

WAXLING: No. Don't.

MARTIN: Pardon?

WAXLING: Don't try to impress me with your "thoughts." Please. *(Pause)* What *is* it with you people, huh?

MARTIN: Who do you mean, Dr Waxling?

WAXLING: I mean *you people*. Holed up in your ratty little rooms scribbling on shopping bags. "Now my destiny seems clear.... It will all happen today." Not here, buddy. You're not plugging me in some hotel lobby. I'm not your double. I'm not sending messages through your schnauzer. You stay away from *me* and you stay away from my *things*. What are you, crossing guard or something? Hospital orderly?

MARTIN: I'm a movie producer.

WAXLING: Are you now.

MARTIN: Yes.

WAXLING: And *not* some obsessional lunatic chasing me around the country convinced I hold the key to your life.

MARTIN: No.

WAXLING: Good. 'Cause I catch you fucking with my things again we don't mess with trespassing harassment thirty days of fun. I'll make you disappear. Produce that. *(He starts out.)*

MARTIN: I— Could we discuss business?

WAXLING: What?

MARTIN: I came here to discuss business. A business proposition. For you. *(Pause)*

WAXLING: Yes?

MARTIN: I believe your book *Daniel Strong* has great commercial potential and I wish to offer you a substantial sum of money in exchange for the worldwide motion picture rights.

WAXLING: Uh-*huh*.

MARTIN: Would you be interested in, in such an arrangement?

WAXLING: With you?

MARTIN: Dr Waxling, I don't blame you for, for— This is not how I wanted to approach you. This is not according to my *plan*. Now you protect yourself. I see that and I think it's wise. Because, I hope you will allow me to say this, people aren't listening, they are twisting what you have to say, they are pushing you down. You of all people. I know how it is not to be heard. I don't want to see this happen to you. I would like to bring your message to millions of people in a simple way they can understand. And yes I would like to profit by it. I would like people to know my name. To see my name and know that I have done what they could not. That will live on when I am gone. *(Pause.* WAXLING *takes a bottle of No-Doz and swallows three or four tablets. He looks at* MARTIN.*)*

WAXLING: It's basically an adventure story.

MARTIN: And what a story.

WAXLING: It has certain other...*elements*....

MARTIN: Which affected *me* so—

WAXLING: They trashed it of course.

MARTIN: They didn't understand.

WAXLING: The intel*lec*tuals.

MARTIN: They were scared.

WAXLING: Join their little club.

MARTIN: You were ahead of your time.

WAXLING: The *guardians*. Of *culture*. Our *heritage*. Our precious *heritage*. You know what heritage is?

MARTIN: What?

WAXLING: It's a Theme Park. With two hundred million personnel managers looking for a salad bar and some fake Elvis in skintights.

MARTIN: Huh.

WAXLING: And me. I'm a voice crying in the Rodeway Inn.

MARTIN: Dr Waxling. I am here to help you change all that. If you would only let me. *(Pause)*

WAXLING: How much are we talking about?

MARTIN: How much...

WAXLING: Money.

MARTIN: Well...the potential, once we get—

WAXLING: No, no. How much will you pay me?

MARTIN: Ah...well...I wasn't really prepared to get into numbers right—

WAXLING: But just for instance.

MARTIN: How much would you need?

WAXLING: I would need at this moment to live and work in the area of five hundred thousand dollars.

MARTIN: Uh-huh...

WAXLING: Half a million the book is yours. You own it you do what you want. *(Pause)*

MARTIN: That could be arranged.

WAXLING: How soon.

MARTIN: Ah, certainly I could advance you a few thousand up front, then when I—

WAXLING: A few thousand.

MARTIN: Yes, of course once it was all in place you'd be seeing—

WAXLING: Where is it now?

MARTIN: Dr Waxling...ah...the kind of money you're—

WAXLING: What do you have now? Right now? Quarter of a million? Let's talk. Hundred thousand? Convince me. How much, come on. *(Pause)*

MARTIN: I have...access to financing.

WAXLING: You have...*access.*

MARTIN: Yes, there are certain interested parties—

WAXLING: Give me your wallet.

MARTIN: Huh?

WAXLING: I want your wallet.

MARTIN: I—

WAXLING: Wallet. *(Pause. MARTIN manages to get out wallet with cuffed hands and offers it to WAXLING. WAXLING looks through it, finding only two or three bills inside.)*

MARTIN: Dr Waxling...if you tell me what you're looking for, I would...I'd be happy to...um... (WAXLING *looks at* MARTIN. *Pause.*) What? (WAXLING *keeps staring at him.*) What is it?

WAXLING: This is over.

MARTIN: Dr Waxling, I am *committed* to—

WAXLING: No, it's alright, really. My fault. I almost took you seriously. You're a nice little tadpole, you shagged my receptionist that's okay.

MARTIN: If you give me some time to, to *structure*—

WAXLING: Oh please. Go *away*. I'm too old for this. There's nothing to talk about.

MARTIN: Please, Dr Waxling, I *beg* you—

WAXLING: YOU HAVE NOTHING IN YOUR POCKET. You're no kind of threat here. You're no threat at all. Get yourself some money, young man. Go...get...*money*. (*He throws the wallet at* MARTIN.)

Scene Eight

(*A bus.* Day. MARTIN, *asleep. Paperback on seat next to him.* BUS DRIVER, *with plastic trash sack, shaking him.*)

DRIVER: Up and at 'em, Johnny. Let's go.

MARTIN: Huh?

DRIVER: All out. Come on. Thank you for choosing Trailways. (*Pause*)

MARTIN: What time is it?

DRIVER: Six a.m.

MARTIN: Are we in Miami?

DRIVER: Huh?

MARTIN: This is Miami?

DRIVER: This is Provo.

MARTIN: Can you tell me when we reach Miami?

DRIVER: Lemme see your ticket. (*Pause*) You were supposed to change at K.C.

MARTIN: What?

DRIVER: Miami you had to change at K.C. (*Pause*)

MARTIN: I'm where?

DRIVER: Provo. Utah. (MARTIN *puts his face in hands and starts rocking back and forth.*) Johnny. Hey Johnny. You okay there. Johnny.

MARTIN: Sorry.

DRIVER: You sick or something?

MARTIN: No.

DRIVER: Somebody you can call?

MARTIN: I don't think so. (*He stands. Pause.*) Is it cold in Provo?

DRIVER: Gets cold, yeah. It's cold now.

MARTIN: You're from Utah?

DRIVER: Seattle.

MARTIN: I'm from Florida.

DRIVER: How about that.

MARTIN: I grew up in New Jersey.

DRIVER: It's a big country.

MARTIN: Yes. (*Pause*)

DRIVER: (*Picking up paperback*) This yours? (MARTIN *doesn't answer.* DRIVER *drops book in sack.*) Good coffee over the 76 there.

MARTIN: Thank you. Thank you very much.

DRIVER: So you gotta get off the bus, okay.

MARTIN: I will. Certainly. (*Pause.* DRIVER *walks off.*) What am I doing here. What the fuck am I doing here. What the fuck am I doing.

Scene Nine

(*An office.* MARTIN *wolfing down sandwich.* KIM *watching him.*)

KIM: Some more?

MARTIN: No, I'm, thank you.

KIM: You're sure.

MARTIN: *Uh*-huh.

KIM: Alright. (*Pause*) So, Martin.

MARTIN: Yes.

KIM: You're not looking your best.

MARTIN: I've been on the road.

KIM: You called me from where?

MARTIN: The Utah region.

KIM: How is it there?

MARTIN: I don't know, Kim. I.... Cold. It was cold.

KIM: Well, you're in New York now.

MARTIN: Yes.

KIM: How long you here for?

MARTIN: I don't know.

KIM: Where are you staying?

MARTIN: I don't know.

KIM: How is business?

MARTIN: I don't know. I don't have a business. I don't have anything. *(Pause)*

KIM: What was it you wanted to see me for, Martin?

MARTIN: Huh?

KIM: When you phoned you said you had to see me.

MARTIN: Yes. *(Pause)* Do you recall our conversation last month?

KIM: On the terrace?

MARTIN: That's right.

KIM: I do indeed.

MARTIN: I felt we made some sort of connection there. That we believed in the same things. That we knew what was important.

KIM: I'm sure that's absolutely true.

MARTIN: I've experienced some...setbacks since we last met. My plan failed. I failed. I won't bore you with the details. I met Dr Waxling. We discussed my proposal at great length and he was very impressed with.... *(Pause)* He couldn't see me as a threat. I didn't present myself as a serious threat and so I failed.

KIM: I regret hearing this.

MARTIN: No. No. It was the best thing that could have happened. Because I'm clean. Now I *know*. It doesn't matter who I am. It doesn't matter what I believe. There's one thing I need. I need to become a threat. I need to become the biggest threat there is. And that's what I'm going to do. *(Pause)*

KIM: What was it you wanted to see me for?

MARTIN: I need half a million dollars now. Later I'll need much more.

KIM: Uh-huh.

MARTIN: I don't care how I get it.

KIM: Right.

MARTIN: Do you understand what I'm saying?

KIM: No. I guess I don't. *(Pause)*

MARTIN: Kim. You have a *nice* office.

KIM: Thank you.

MARTIN: You make a lot of money, don't you.

KIM: I'm comfortable.

MARTIN: Do you need any help in, in what you do?

KIM: I usually work best alone.

MARTIN: But if someone presented himself to you who was prepared to take risks, would you find a person like that useful? *(Pause)*

KIM: You don't know what I do.

MARTIN: I don't care. I mean I do know and it doesn't matter. Whether it's whatever you call it right or wrong, I can't worry about that anymore.

KIM: So this thing that I do, you're saying that you'd like to help me do it, despite its dangers and its possible moral or legal complications?

MARTIN: Yes.

KIM: What is it you think I do? *(Pause)*

MARTIN: At the party—

KIM: Which party.

MARTIN: On the *terrace*, they asked you to leave 'cause...

KIM: Because why?

MARTIN: Because you...you're a dealer. Right? A drug dealer. *(Pause)* Aren't you? *(Pause)* Kim? *(Pause)*

KIM: I undertake freelance market analysis for a consortium of Pacific Rim industrial groups.

MARTIN: What?

KIM: Robot systems. Medical equipment. Information retrieval.

MARTIN: No.

KIM: Yes.

MARTIN: No. Oh Jesus. Oh no. God damn it God fucking damn it. What a fuck up I am. What a fuck up loving asshole. What a shiteating fuckhead. Look at me. Look at me. (KIM *looks at him. Pause.*) Kim. I beg your pardon. I've made some very bad assumptions about...practically everything. And I.... Good seeing you. Take care. *(He starts out.)*

KIM: Martin.

MARTIN: Yes.

KIM: I'd like to offer some advice, if I may.

MARTIN: What?

KIM: There is nothing so valuable in life as a sense of perspective. *(Pause)* I am not what you imagined me to be.

MARTIN: I realize that.

KIM: However, I do know members of my peer group who are. I could arrange for you to meet them. Would you like that?

MARTIN: Yes.

KIM: Alright. *(Pause)* There are many ways of finding money, Martin. Whatever the climate. Whatever the mood.

MARTIN: This is what has to be done.

KIM: Well, you're a big boy. *(Pause)* You don't smoke.

MARTIN: No.

KIM: I need the nicotine. *(He takes out a cigarette pack and unwraps it.)* It's a curious time, isn't it. I find it curious. Curious to be alive. And change... change is *hard*. Honesty, very hard. Leaving your desk...that's hard. We're not free, you know. All of this and we're still not free. *(Pause)* You have faith, don't you.

MARTIN: What?

KIM: Faith. *(Pause)*

MARTIN: Yes.

KIM: I envy that. *(He lights a cigarette and takes a long drag.)* Yes yes yes. I'm sensing *all* sorts of possibilities.

(End of Act One)

ACT TWO

Scene One

(A booth in a restaurant. MARTIN *in new suit,* KIM, RON.*)*

RON: Miami. Miami. Fucking Miami. Fucking skeeve town. Fucking Cubans. Crazed fucking mothers. I hate fucking Miami. You're not safe in Miami. How the fuck you live there I don't know.

KIM: Martin doesn't live in Miami, Ron.

RON: He doesn't.

MARTIN: No.

RON: Where the fuck *does* he live.

MARTIN: Boca Raton.

RON: Huh. Well. *You* go down there, huh? Kim? You go down Miami, right?

KIM: I sometimes go to Miami.

RON: You're fucking *crazy. New* York. *New* York. *New* York. Last night?

KIM: How was it?

RON: The best. the best. Absofuckingwhatley the best. Last night. Okay. We get there. This is at Shea. We get there. In the limo. I got, I'm with, the, *Carol,* she does the, the, *fuck,* you know, that *ad,* the fitness, amazing bod, amazing bod, fucking amazing bod, and I have, for this occasion, I put aside my very best, lovely lovely product, for Carol, who, no, I care about very deeply. So, okay, get to Shea, it's fucking *bat* night, everybody with the bats, fifty thousand bat-wielding sociopaths, security is very tight. *I* have a private booth. In the circle. This is through GE, my little addictive exec at GE. So we entree, me and Carol, and my client, I see, has fucked me over, cause there's already someone there, you know who, that talk show guy, he's always got like three drag queens and a Satanist, and he's there with a girl can't be more than fourteen. "Oops." This fucking guy, my *daughter* watches that show. And between us, heavy substance abuser. I ask him to leave. I mean I come to watch a ball game with my good friend Carol and I'm forced to encounter skeevy baby-fucking cokeheads. One thing leads to the other, politeness out the window he comes at me Mets ashtray in his hand. What do I do.

KIM: You have a bat.

RON: I have a bat, I take this bat, I acquaint this individual in the head with this bat. "Ba-doing." Right, badoing? He doesn't go down. Stands there, walks out the door, comes back two security guards. "Is there a problem here, boys?" "Well sir, this man, bicka bicka bicka," "Yes, I completely understand and here's something for your troubles."

KIM: How much?

RON: How much, Kim? How much did I give these good men to resolve our altercation? I gave them one thousand dollars in U.S. currency. And they were very grateful. Mr Microphone sits down, doesn't speak, doesn't move rest of the night. Moody fucking person. Mets take it, great ball, home with Carol where we romp in the flower of our youth. I win. I dominate. I get all the marbles. And that is why I love New York.

KIM: Yours is a rich and happy life, Ron.

RON: Yeah, it is, it is so fuck you, you bogus Ivy League skank. You spent four years sucking bongwater at Hofstra just like me. That's a nice suit.

KIM: You like it?

RON: How much you pay for it.

KIM: I paid nothing for this suit, Ron. It was a gift.

RON: Fuck *you*.

KIM: From an admirer.

RON: Fuck you. This fucking guy. You know how many times a week he gets laid?

MARTIN: No.

RON: Neither do I. Fifteen years since college I know him, butter wouldn't melt. I don't think it's happened. You ever been laid, Kim?

KIM: No, Ron. Never. What's it like.

RON: Fuck you. You get your horn piped by air hostesses every night. You Protestant bastard. That's a nice suit. I don't look good in clothes. *(Pause)* It's hot. Gonna be a hot summer. *(Pause)* What are we here for, so?

KIM: Martin?

MARTIN: I have a proposition for you, Ron.

RON: This is fine. This is wonderful.

MARTIN: First let me say that I'm a person who's comfortable with risk.

RON: Hmm-*hmm*.

MARTIN: And what I want, what I'd like to *present*, to you, is something we might both find very, um, um....

KIM: Martin's a businessman, Ron. He understands business. He understands the principles of trust and discretion, and he needs to create some wealth. *(RON looks at MARTIN. Pause.)*

MARTIN: Yes. *(Pause)*

RON: Well. This is very nice. This is most lovely for him and I wish him luck. How does he intend to do these things?

KIM: He's going to sell Amway products, Ron. He's going to claw his way to the top of the Amway ladder.

RON: Then fuck *you* with your attitude. I gotta pick up my kid from Dalton twenty minutes, what kind of arrangement you looking for here?

KIM: How are you for blow.

RON: Ooo, "blow," listen to him, we bad, we cool, I don't know what you're talking about, I sell landscaping equipment.

KIM: Really.

RON: You know it.

KIM: Well, Martin's interested in putting in a pond.

RON: Hmm, how big a pond?

KIM: How big a pond, Martin?

MARTIN: I... *(Pause)* I've secured an equity loan of two hundred fifty thousand against my property in Florida. *(Pause)*

RON: How much?

MARTIN: Two hundred fi—

RON: *(To KIM)* I don't find you funny anymore.

KIM: Oh dear.

RON: Fuck you think I am, some TV show?

KIM: No, Ron. You're almost too real.

RON: You fucking bastard.

MARTIN: What's wrong?

KIM: He's considering your offer.

RON: No fucking way.

KIM: Being a little short-*sighted*.

RON: No. No. I'm being smart. We're not hello the Palladium six lines in the toilet anymore. The current event, one key a month close personal friends I am a happy man. Quarter million, that is, that is, that puts you in a room very close to a bunch of crazed implacable Colombians with enough firepower send you to Venus in pieces.

KIM: Gee, Dad.

RON: Hey, these are *serious people*, Kim. They take one look at no offense Mister Rogers here lunchbox full of cash who is he where's he come from the fuck he's *doing* there anyway he wins a prime chance to lose his nut and sit inside a barrel with his dick shoved up his mouth.

KIM: What a dark view of the world, Ron.

RON: You are such a fucking *tourist*.

KIM: That's me.

RON: It is you, it is *you*. I got your history Kim, you messed with all kindsa wack shit, you took lotsa pictures, but you never rolled the windows down and that has made you one fucked-up little unit.

KIM: This is really not interesting.

RON: 'Cause you never played your *chances*, buddy, you got plenty a toys but you never played your chances.

KIM: I'm playing them now.

RON: Too fucking late, you wanna crash and burn go ahead, *I* operate from a position of safety. I don't know why I let myself be seen with you.

KIM: Because I go out of my way introducing responsible people like this man here—

RON: This man, this man, I don't *know* this man.

KIM: I do. And believe me, let him go you'll regret it.

RON: "Oh."

KIM: Yes. Yes. Because someone *else*—

MARTIN: Hold on.

KIM: Someone with vision—

MARTIN: Kim, let me—

KIM: Is going to, just a sec, profit immensely while you're still peddling your little Glad Bags—

MARTIN: Kim. *Kim.* Excuse me. I want to say something. Alright? *(Pause)*

KIM: Please.

MARTIN: Thank you. *(Pause)* Ron. I'd like to see if I can make you understand my, my purpose in coming here, my goals, what I hope to achieve, and the reasons I feel... *(Pause)* No. No. That's pointless. I want you to listen to me. Because this is how it is. Alright. There's something I need to get done. I don't have time to waste on...*individuals* who won't seize an opportunity. I don't resent them. I don't condemn them. But I will not give them my time. *(Pause)*

RON: So?

MARTIN: So here's what you need to know about me. I have a quarter of a million dollars in cash sitting in a briefcase. I'm eager to spend it. Kim has spoken highly of you. You're aware of my proposal. Either on the boat or off, I have to hear now.

RON: *(To* KIM*)* Trying to *threaten* me?

MARTIN: On or off.

RON: "Off." Fuck you. Off.

MARTIN: Fine. Kim, call me? We'll make new arrangements.

KIM: Mmm-hmm. (MARTIN *gets up and starts out.* RON *looks at* KIM.) There you are.

RON: Wait. Wait. Hey. Hey, um, what's his—

KIM: Martin.

RON: Martin. Yo. Martin. Come on. Sit down. Everybody with the attitude. Come on now. Alright. *(Pause.* MARTIN *returns to the table and sits.)*

MARTIN: Yes?

RON: Wanna be a rich man, huh. (MARTIN *shakes his head.)* Doing this for science?

MARTIN: I'm financing a film.

RON: A film.

MARTIN: A *movie.*

RON: Yeah. Well, um, that makes sense.

MARTIN: I believe it does.

RON: No, I mean, hey, who doesn't go for a little entertainment, right buddy?

KIM: Ron, you've captured the matter in its essence. *(Pause)*

RON: I got stuff, I gotta pick up my daughter, I got dry cleaning.

KIM: Righty-o.

RON: This, the thing.

MARTIN: Yes.

RON: I don't know. I'm telling you. I don't know.

MARTIN: What's that mean.

RON: I don't *know*. I'll see what I can *arrange*.

MARTIN: I'm not interested in waiting.

RON: You're not...*interested*.

MARTIN: No.

RON: Then fu—

KIM: Ron.

RON: What.

KIM: I consider us friends.

RON: So?

KIM: Do something big with your life. For once. *(Pause)*

RON: What's it about.

MARTIN: Huh?

RON: Your movie.

MARTIN: It's based.... *(Pause)* This creature goes around cracking people's heads open scooping their brains out.

RON: Well. Whatever. I mean I wouldn't take my kid to see it, you know, what *you* laughing about?

KIM: Nothing, Ron.

RON: Hey, rot in hell, you heartless fuck. I'm serious. Try a little compassion, huh, it gets you through the day. *(Getting up)* Drinks on you. *(He exits. Pause.)*

KIM: Hungry at all?

MARTIN: Goddamn it.

KIM: What's the problem.

MARTIN: Why did I do that. Why did I *do* that. I *threw* it away.

KIM: Ah no no no.

MARTIN: I am just so tired of little *shits* wasting my time when they can't see past their own fear and—

KIM: Martin. You closed this deal. You did. I am very impressed.

MARTIN: Come on.

KIM: Yes. Listen to me. That was perfect with Ron.

MARTIN: Why.

KIM: Because I know him. He's weak and he loves money. *(Pause)* Lesson here for you though.

MARTIN: What.

KIM: Have a little more faith in your own abilities. *(Pause)*

MARTIN: I will. *(KIM looks at menu.)* Kim.

KIM: Hmm.

MARTIN: What...we haven't, what do you want. From this.

KIM: What do you think I should get?

MARTIN: Te— twenty. Twenty percent. *(Pause)* Have I said something wrong?

KIM: No. It's an impressive...number.

MARTIN: You deserve it.

KIM: Let me propose something else.

MARTIN: What.

KIM: Partnership. *(Pause)*

MARTIN: Kim...I...

KIM: Want to do it for yourself.

MARTIN: I thought you knew that.

KIM: Yes. *(Pause)* Most people— I don't mean to be harsh— they have no sense of themselves. They think other people's thoughts. And they waste their lives. That's not for us, Martin. We're better than that and we know it. Now look what we've achieved. Right here at this table, together. I think it's only a start.

MARTIN: Kim. I'm here to get the movie done.

KIM: What happens after that.

MARTIN: I can't think about it now.

KIM: I wish you would. I really wish you would. Because you can make a hundred movies, yes, is that all you came for? You can run a studio, own half of midtown net four hundred million per, it's only a bigger desk. I've been there Martin believe me please it's *nothing*, nothing at all. But to do what matters, I mean really *do* something out there in the world that frees us from this...*junk*...that's a life. It's the life I read about. It's the life I want. Don't you? *(Pause)*

MARTIN: Staying focused...

KIM: Yes.

MARTIN: On what's important.

KIM: It's not easy.

MARTIN: No.

KIM: I'll keep you honest. *(Pause)*

MARTIN: Alright. I.... Yes. Alright.

KIM: *(Lifting his drink)* Well come on then. Let's have an adventure here. *(They toast.)*

Scene Two

(A motel room. MARTIN with briefcase, KIM, RON with kitchen scale, NUÑEZ. Silence.)

RON: What is that out there?

KIM: Van Wyck Expressway.

RON: It's like a major fucking highway, huh? Who knew.

KIM: Get out of Manhattan much, Ron?

RON: Hey, you know how many times I been here Ozone Park? Martin?

MARTIN: How many times.

RON: Never. I *never* been to Ozone Park. Looks like fucking *every*place. I never been in a motel room totally skanked as this. Where'd that guy go? It's fifteen fucking minutes.

KIM: Why don't you ask this gentleman?

RON: 'Cause I don't speak *Spanish.* (NUÑEZ *looks at him.)* Hi. *(Pause)*

KIM: "A boy sat on a bed, wondering who he might turn out to be."

MARTIN: What?

KIM: You know that.

MARTIN: No.

KIM: First line of the book.

MARTIN: It is?

KIM: Look it up.

MARTIN: When this is done I will. *(Pause)* Thank you.

RON: Fuck. Ing. Christ. *(PAMFILO enters.)*

PAMFILO: Okay. The other car is here.

RON: Terrific.

PAMFILO: They were caught in the traffic from the stadium.

RON: Met game, huh, big Met game today, yeah, uh, you like baseball? *(Pause)*

PAMFILO: Who is Ron again?

RON: That's me.

PAMFILO: Okay, I am Pamfilo.

RON: Yeah, right, I know your cousin, we've done business together, I understood he spoke to you, and, ah, how's he doing?

PAMFILO: Eh?

RON: How's your cousin?

PAMFILO: He's good. *(Pause)*

RON: Okay. Well. Ah. This, these are my clients, Mr Feston, Mr Mirkheim.

PAMFILO: Yes.

RON: Your cousin met them. Very reliable, dependable gentlemen.

MARTIN: How do you do. *(Pause)*

RON: So. *(Pause)*

PAMFILO: Los registraste?

NUÑEZ: No son nada.

PAMFILO: Que te dijo, siempre tienes cuidad con todos. *(To the others)* Nuñez, he is my...security man, okay? He is going to see that everything is safe between us. (NUÑEZ *frisks* RON, KIM, *and* MARTIN.)

RON: Very sensible.

PAMFILO: Yes. Because sometimes men are not honorable.

KIM: Isn't that unfortunate.

PAMFILO: For them it is.

RON: Ha. Right right right.

PAMFILO: Who is with the money?

MARTIN: Me.

PAMFILO: Yes. May I look please. (MARTIN *hands him the briefcase.* PAMFILO *opens it but does not look inside.*) We have met before.

MARTIN: Pardon?

PAMFILO: You and I.

MARTIN: I don't think so.

PAMFILO: No? Someone who is like you.

MARTIN: Well.

PAMFILO: That's right. The man I am thinking of, he is a good man. He provides for his family and respects the memory of his mother.

MARTIN: Does he.

PAMFILO: Yes. Are you a good man, my friend?

MARTIN: I hope so.

PAMFILO: You're not sure, huh?

MARTIN: I am.

PAMFILO: Then I know you would never try and cheat me.

MARTIN: No. *(Pause.* PAMFILO *closes the briefcase.)*

PAMFILO: *(To* NUÑEZ*)* Ve al auto y traeme la bolsa. *(To* MARTIN*)* He is going to bring it.

MARTIN: Great. (NUÑEZ *exits. Silence.)*

RON: So, what, you live in the city there, Pamfilo? *(Pause)*

PAMFILO: No. *(Pause)* Hempstead.

RON: Out on the Island, huh. That's terrific. Lot a, lot a, lot a Colombians, Hempstead?

PAMFILO: I'm from Honduras.

RON: Say what?

PAMFILO: Honduras. It's a country. It's in America. *(Pause. Silence.)*

MARTIN: How...

PAMFILO: Yes.

MARTIN: How long have you been in, in our land.

PAMFILO: Three years. Since I'm nineteen.

MARTIN: How do you like it. *(Pause)*

PAMFILO: You work hard...use your head...you can be very big. (KIM *laughs.*) That's funny, huh?

RON: *(Under his breath)* Shut *up*, Kim.

PAMFILO: Hey, you think I'm funny?

MARTIN: Why don't we—

PAMFILO: I'm not so good as you, is that it? Hey.

KIM: No. I'm just enchanted by your optimism. And I sincerely hope that all your dreams come true. *(Pause)*

PAMFILO: Thank you. (NUÑEZ *enters with suitcase.*) Here is what you want. (NUÑEZ *hands the suitcase to him. He opens it and displays contents.*) Okay?

MARTIN: Maybe.

PAMFILO: Try some. *(He takes out a Saran-wrapped package of coke, opens it, and offers it to* MARTIN. KIM *steps up, reaches into the suitcase, and takes out a different package, opens it and samples it.)*

KIM: This has possibilities.

PAMFILO: It's what you're looking for, huh.

MARTIN: Means to an end.

PAMFILO: What's that.

MARTIN: This will...*get* us...where we have to go.

PAMFILO: Yes. I understand.

KIM: I'd like to weigh it.

PAMFILO: It's twelve kilos, what we said.

KIM: I'm sure it is, but....

PAMFILO: You don't trust me?

KIM: We just want to weigh it. *(To* RON) Isn't that what they do on TV?

PAMFILO: What. You think I am trying to cheat you?

RON: Hey, *no* one's saying that.

PAMFILO: He's saying it.

RON: Just, we're, a precaution—

PAMFILO: *(To* MARTIN) I take you on your honor, my friend, this is how you treat me?

RON: Shit...

MARTIN: I'm not doubting—

PAMFILO: This is no good. No. No this is bad business. We don't do it. Here's the money. This is bad, very bad. Nuñez. (NUÑEZ *starts out.* PAMFILO *follows.*)

MARTIN: Wait. Wait. What do we do....

RON: Forget about it.

MARTIN: No. Pamfilo. Come on. Let's— We can make this work. We *can.* Kim? Please. *(Pause.* NUÑEZ *reenters.* PAMFILO *looks at* MARTIN. *He takes suitcase and opens it.)*

PAMFILO: You take one. Whatever one. Take it and weigh it. They all the same. They all a kilo. I don't think like you. (MARTIN *takes a package from the case. He puts it on the scale.* PAMFILO *looks at* NUÑEZ. *Pause.)*

RON: Two and a quarter, touch under.

PAMFILO: That's a kilo. That's exactly a kilo. Here's another one. Go ahead.

MARTIN: It's alright.

PAMFILO: Go on.

KIM: Make the boy happy, Martin.

MARTIN: Kim. That's enough. *(Pause)* Pamfilo. My apologies. Please. (PAMFILO *looks at* MARTIN, *closes suitcase and offers it to him.* MARTIN *takes it. He hands* PAMFILO *the money.)*

PAMFILO: Este payaso no sabe ni papa.

MARTIN: What?

PAMFILO: Always know your friends. *(He exits with* NUÑEZ. MARTIN *takes package off scale, puts it back in case and shuts it.)*

KIM: Well.

MARTIN: Right.

KIM: *(Offering his hand)* We're in it now. *(Pause)*

MARTIN: *(Taking it)* Yes.

KIM: No. We're in it. We're really *in* it. *Everything's* going to happen.

MARTIN: One less thing in the way. (KIM *sees* RON *staring at the floor.)*

KIM: Something on your mind, Ron?

RON: Yeah. Let's give me my cut and get the fuck out of here as rapidly as possible.

Scene Three

(A rec room. MARTIN, KIM *with briefcase. Late.)*

MARTIN: How do you know this guy?

KIM: Shared a house one summer. He was doing three grams a day. *(Pause)*

MARTIN: I grew up around here.

KIM: Did you.

MARTIN: My parents bought a place. Paid cash. Big moment for them. Saved up, fourteen years. 1968.

KIM: Ancient times.

MARTIN: Yeah. *(Pause)* This afternoon, Kim. The motel.

KIM: Mmm-hmm.

MARTIN: Don't act that way again. Okay.

KIM: Why not.

MARTIN: I don't like it. *(Pause)* We have to agree what we're doing stays normal. I am calling it business and that's how I need it be.

KIM: You're just tired.

MARTIN: It's how I need it, Kim.

KIM: I have a business, Martin. It's in an office. I'm there every day. We discussed something else.

MARTIN: That was talking. This has to get *done* I cannot afford any risks. Do we understand each other? *(Pause)* Kim. Do we—

LEE: *(Entering)* Sorry. Had to switch the security system back on. Press the wrong button I get the Short Hills police force storming the pool deck.

KIM: Can't be too safe.

LEE: You can't, you can't. Kim, get you a drink? Marvin?

MARTIN: Martin. No thank you, Lee.

LEE: Fair enough. Serious man. Welcome to New Jersey. You guys have trouble getting here?

KIM: No.

LEE: Hit traffic?

MARTIN: Not this time of night.

LEE: Yeah. Look. I apologize for that. My schedule's been, you don't wanna know, I'm not even getting home 'til eleven. I don't see my wife, the twins, forget it.

KIM: Working you hard, huh, Lee.

LEE: Sucking me dry, Kim. But it's worth it. We got the jump on the primaries. 'Cause the momentum is there. Uh. Uh. Organization is there. Money's there. We're diving straight into the Grown-Up Pool. Really. I mean this one counts, and, uh, uh... *(Pause)* Yeah, I'm sorry, what was I saying?

MARTIN: Something that counts.

LEE: Right, exactly.

KIM: Lee's consulting for Paul Kinsen.

MARTIN: Who?

LEE: Senator Kinsen. Arizona.

MARTIN: You consult on...?

LEE: Chief of Media Relations actually. Got the whole campaign.

KIM: Congratulations.

LEE: And all I had to do was blow him.

MARTIN: Excuse me?

LEE: I'm kidding of course. Great opportunity for me, something *big*.

KIM: Old Mr Stars and Jackboots.

LEE: What are you, some pansy Democrat?

KIM: I'm a registered bystander.

LEE: Look at Kinsen this year. Try Kinsen out. Kinsen could be very very good for you.

KIM: Why's that.

LEE: 'Cause he wants to win and he's primed to kick ass.

KIM: I'm loving it.

LEE: Which is what I'm saying. He's the man for the nineties. This guy takes no prisoners. Is that what you want in a Great White Father? I think so. Check this out, what do you think, dummy ad, national spot, wanna hear it, okay, great. *(He picks up a stack of storyboards.)* What it is, should be, is a *movie*, a little thirty-second movie about something we want to say. Desert, morning light, very pure, very "American." Uh, uh, uh, young boy, blond hair, big horse. Tries to climb on. Can't. Falls off. Hits hard. Eats dirt. You with me?

MARTIN: Yes.

LEE: Voiceover: "There are some who believe the best is behind us. Some who think we've lost the way. Some who feel that fear rules the length and breadth of a once-proud land." Dramatic pause. Kid stands up. Tight on the face. V.O.: "Paul Kinsen believes differently. He believes in a nation whose future means more than its past. He believes in a nation unafraid of its strength. He believes in a nation of dreams. Because dreams can be real." Kid slaps the dust off. Beat. "If we want them to be." Kid grabs the stirrup, whatever. He's up. He's on. He's riding. He's a winner. *And* dissolve to Kinsen, presidential as hell. Super titles: "Paul Kinsen. Believe...the...what." Believe the what, huh. Believe the something. What's good to believe in.

MARTIN: Are you asking me?

LEE: I'm stuck at the tag. Breaking my balls Kinsen this fucking presentation. Know what he's saying? "Why can't it be me on a horse?" I mean I'm on the team ten thousand percent but Wonder Chimp the man isn't, please, I didn't say that. What do we believe in here, *I* don't know, I don't, I honestly don't, no idea. Boom boom boom.

MARTIN: How about possibilities.

LEE: Huh?

MARTIN: Believe the possibilities. We all believe in possibilities, don't we, keeps us going.

LEE: "Believe the Possibilities."

MARTIN: You got it.

KIM: That's amusing, Martin.

LEE: "Paul Kinsen: Believe the Possibilities." Yum dum dum ba dum bum ba bum bum. Hell does that mean.

MARTIN: What do you think it means.

LEE: It means, I don't know, Go for the Gusto, Be All You Can Be, Ram Tough, it means whatever you want it to mean, it doesn't mean anything, it sounds good. Am I right? Is that it? Hello? *(Pause)*

MARTIN: Yes. That's it exactly.

LEE: *(To KIM)* What flew up his ass?

KIM: Past his bedtime.

MARTIN: I'm fine.

KIM: You'd better be, friend. *(They look at each other. MARTIN turns away.)*

MARTIN: Let's get down to business.

LEE: Yes.

MARTIN: This has to be a cash—

KIM: *Martin* and I have something very special here, Lee. I want you to know you're the first person we thought of.

LEE: Thank you. I'm excited.

KIM: You should be.

LEE: Little *surprised...*

KIM: Why's that.

LEE: I didn't know you were dealing.

KIM: Disappointed?

LEE: Well, you know. It's a step. It's a grey area.

KIM: I like me in grey.

LEE: Yeah, right. Boom boom boom.

MARTIN: We discussed possibly a couple of kilos.

LEE: Well, a couple, one, I'm getting off it, but if the quality—

MARTIN: The quality is superb.

LEE: 'Cause what I *been* buying—

KIM: We hear you.

LEE: It doesn't really get me, it just doesn't seem to get me as, it doesn't seem to *give* me the same feeling of...

KIM: Uh-huh.

LEE: The same, uh, uh, uh...

MARTIN: Strength.

LEE: Yeah. Strength. Strength. Yeah. Yeah. *(Pause)* And I won't fuck with crack, you know. I won't. 'Cause that's really, that is a very *bad*, um... problem.

KIM: Then Lee, absolutely is this for you. *(He takes kilo bag out of the briefcase and lays it before* LEE.*)* Look at that.

LEE: Hmm.

KIM: Shines just like mica.

LEE: Yeah, this could be good for me.

KIM: I think so.

LEE: 'Cause I need it.

KIM: Go ahead. *(LEE tries some. Pause.)* What did I tell you? *(LEE says nothing.)* Now I want you to know that there is plenty more if—

LEE: What are you doing here, Kim?

KIM: Excuse me?

LEE: I don't, is this a joke?

KIM: No.

MARTIN: What's the problem?

LEE: This is garbage.

KIM: No. I've *tried* it, Lee.

LEE: You have.

KIM: Yes, and it's the best coke you can—

LEE: Bullshit.

KIM: Lee—

LEE: *Bull*shit. This is what you buy outside the Port Authority before you catch the bus. I'm past this, I'm *way* past it, you think you're gonna fool me? *(Pause. KIM tries some.)*

MARTIN: What's happening, Kim.

KIM: Hold on a second.

LEE: This won't even get my *tongue* high.

KIM: Give me a *second*, Lee.

LEE: Asking for big money you better—

KIM: Shut up. Lee, okay.

LEE: Hey, this is my *house*, buddy, you don't speak to me—

MARTIN: Kim—

KIM: YES, GIVE ME ONE *SECOND* PLEASE THANK YOU. *(Pause)* The cases.

MARTIN: What?

KIM: The motel. They switched cases.

MARTIN: I don't—

KIM: They *switched cases*. They forced the *argument*, he *stepped* into the hall, they came back we weighed the kilo—

MARTIN: No.

LEE: Hey, you wanna keep it down—

KIM: They took us.

MARTIN: No. No.

KIM: We *sucked* it up—

MARTIN: But they, he offered—

KIM: Stupid *white* boys and they *took* us.

MARTIN: No. No. There's a deal. You— We have a *deal*. You're gonna buy this.

LEE: Keep dreaming.

MARTIN: You're buying. God*damn* you. You have to *buy*—
(TERRY, LEE's *wife, enters in robe.*)

LEE: Don't threaten me, Pee Wee, I don't buy jack from you, hi honey, are we too loud?

TERRY: What's going on....

LEE: Hon, ah, you remember Kim Feston from the *summer.*

TERRY: ...Half awake and I, hello...

KIM: How are the twins, Terry.

TERRY: Oh, they're....

LEE: Kim and his friend are very interested in fund raising for Senator Kinsen, we're just connecting on it, they want to help us along see if they can make a difference.

TERRY: It's late, Lee. You're never going to get up.

LEE: I know, I'll, in a minute. Really. *(Pause)*

TERRY: Anybody want tea?

LEE: No sweetie, thank you. *(Pause)*

TERRY: Well come to bed soon. (LEE *nods. She exits. Pause.)*

MARTIN: Oh my god. What have I done.

LEE: Excuse me. Over here. This is *my* rec room you're sitting in. I got a wife and two baby kids upstairs, I got a presentation due nine o'clock in the morning, and I have NO FUCKING WAY of getting high tonight. So would you please leave.

KIM: Lee, I suggest—

LEE: You have nothing to say to me, Kim. You just went belly up.

Scene Four

(A car. MARTIN, KIM *behind wheel. Silence.)*

MARTIN: That was the turnoff.

KIM: What?

MARTIN: That was the turnoff for New York. *(Pause)*

KIM: I'll take the next exit.

MARTIN: Yah.

KIM: We'll turn around.

MARTIN: 'Kay. *(Pause)* I'm fucked, Kim.

KIM: Stop it.

MARTIN: I am. I'm *fucked*. I'm *so* fucked.

KIM: That's not *helping*, alright.

MARTIN: You don't understand the position—

KIM: We had a setback. We were too eager. We made a mistake, that's done. We move on.

MARTIN: Where. Where do we move *to*.

KIM: We can sell the coke. It's a garbage cut but we can sell it.

MARTIN: For how much.

KIM: Less.

MARTIN: To who?

KIM: Somebody stupid.

MARTIN: Who?

KIM: I have to think about it.

MARTIN: You don't *know*.

KIM: I have to *think*. I have to work it *out*.

MARTIN: Do you know what you're doing, Kim? Do you? I really need to find out. Do you have any *idea*?

KIM: There's always possibilities.

MARTIN: The *money*—

KIM: You don't care about money.

MARTIN: But *my* money, Kim. That was *my*— I mean it was a loan. You *know* that. I can't pay that back. I was counting on the, the.... I don't have it. You understand? Anywhere. I'm *already*.... Here it is. Okay. I've been bad about money. I'm in a, a, *situation* with it and I don't see how I can get out. It's going to bury me, Kim. I'm really afraid it's going to bury me and— *(Rotating lights of a squad car start flashing behind them.)* Oh fuck.

KIM: It's alright.

MARTIN: What's happening?

KIM: I don't know.

MARTIN: Were we speeding?

KIM: We'll find out.

MARTIN: It's not us, I'm sure it's not, don't stop, what are you doing—

KIM: Hide the briefcase, would you, Martin.

MARTIN: What?

KIM: *(Pulling car over.)* Hide the briefcase please. Under the seat.

MARTIN: This is not me. This is not where I'm supposed to be....

KIM: It would be a good idea to hurry up right now.

MARTIN: It won't *fit*.

KIM: I'm sure it will.

MARTIN: *(Trying to jam it under)* It won't. It won't. Oh fuck what am I doing here.

KIM: Martin. Stop it. Stop it. Alright. It's just a briefcase. Everybody has one. *(STATE TROOPER approaches with nightstick-style flashlight in hand.)* There is absolutely nothing to get alarmed about. *(TROOPER comes up to driver's side.)* Officer.

TROOPER: Posted speed limit on this parkway is fifty-five miles an hour.

KIM: Yes.

TROOPER: You're clocked on radar at seventy-six.

KIM: Yes. Of course.

TROOPER: See your license, please.

KIM: Certainly. *(TROOPER inspects license. Pause.)*

MARTIN: Just got a little lost on our way back to the city.

TROOPER: Which city is that.

MARTIN: New York.

TROOPER: I've heard of it.

MARTIN: Right. Ha.

KIM: Officer, it's late, I understand the violation, please we'll just take the ticket.

TROOPER: Rushing off to bed, huh.

MARTIN: We have a big presentation to make first thing in the morning.

TROOPER: Do you.

MARTIN: Yes.

TROOPER: Back there in New York.

MARTIN: That's correct. (TROOPER *shines light into car. Briefcase is on* MARTIN's *lap. He looks straight ahead at nothing.*)

KIM: I tell you, next time I set the cruise control and forget about it. *(Pause)* You know?

MARTIN: What?

KIM: *(To* TROOPER*)* Creeps up on you, check the speedometer and—

TROOPER: Could you both step out of the car please?

MARTIN: What for?

TROOPER: I'm asking you to.

KIM: Is this really necessary?

TROOPER: If you want it to be. *(Pause)*

KIM: Fine. Let me turn the engine off.

TROOPER: Uh-huh. (KIM *shuts off engine and drops the keys.*)

KIM: Great. *(Hunching over)* I dropped my keys. I'm sorry. Could you just shine your light here. One sec.

TROOPER: *(Leaning in)* Where.

KIM: Right here. *(Coming up)* Okay. I found them. (*He has a small caliber pistol in his hand.*)

MARTIN: Kim, are you— (KIM *grabs the flashlight and shoots the* TROOPER *point-blank in the face. Pause.*)

KIM: Look what I've done.

Scene Five

(*A field by a road.* MARTIN *with* TROOPER's *flashlight,* KIM *smoking cigarette.*)

KIM: Where are we?

MARTIN: I don't know.

KIM: Sky's lit up in that direction.

MARTIN: It's a refinery. They're all up and down here. We should have stayed on the Parkway.

KIM: You might want to shut that off. (MARTIN *shuts off flashlight. Pause.*)

MARTIN: What are we going to do.

KIM: I'm going to enjoy this cigarette.

MARTIN: Why didn't you tell me Kim.

KIM: You know I've been afraid, I'll say it now, really afraid. Afraid to be *tested*. Afraid I wouldn't be strong. But I *was*. I *was*. You *saw* that I was, god I feel—

MARTIN: Kim, you should have *told* me.

KIM: What did you want to know, I was *ready*, he stood there and— look how this hand's shaking—

MARTIN: That you had a *gun*, a fucking *gun*.

KIM: Can't have an adventure without a gun.

MARTIN: Fuck adventure this was my *business*.

KIM: Whatever you want to call it.

MARTIN: No Kim, no, my *business* we were conducting, not some, some, in the street that you read about, a guy some bracelet he gets...*shot* Jesus *Christ* there's blood on my shirt.

KIM: Would you rather be arrested?

MARTIN: I don't know.

KIM: You must have an *opinion*.

MARTIN: I DON'T KNOW. MY BRAIN'S GONE AND I CAN'T *THINK* ANYMORE. (*Pause*)

KIM: Let me tell you something, Martin. It might help you, because it's true. Everything...*everything* up to this exact moment...is the Past. We're done with it. You're concerned about that policeman? I am not. It's so clear to me.

What did he want to do? Take what we have and punish us. By whose authority? Not mine, Martin. Not mine. This is so *clear* now. It's a dead little planet we're standing on. I'm alive. And I don't need to be forgiven one goddamn thing. Do you? *(Pause)* Now we have several possibilities spread before us. We can go on debating ethics in the middle of a marsh. We can ease up to the next state trooper and turn ourselves in. Or we can drive back to Manhattan secure in the knowledge that we are two polite young white men in well-cut suits and will...not...be...touched. Because we set the standards. And we judge *ourselves* accordingly. *(Pause)* It's freedom, Martin. I am talking to you about being free. *(Pause)*

MARTIN: I'm done.

KIM: What's that mean.

MARTIN: I'm finished with it.

KIM: Just like that.

MARTIN: Yes.

KIM: I thought you wanted to be a threat.

MARTIN: I don't know what I "wanted to *be*." I can't *remember*. I've eaten myself up and there's nothing left. *Nothing*.

KIM: You're very weak. Aren't you.

MARTIN: I *am*, so fuck it. Fuck the coke. Fuck the money, fuck *all* money. And fuck the movie. I won't make it. Who was I kidding. It's shit anyway—

KIM: Is it.

MARTIN: *Yes*, let's say it, that book is just *shit*. Some fucking fantasy about power and, and, "everything is possible," where *are* they, where are these "possibilities," I don't see them, *this* is it, this is life and that's ALL IT WILL EVER BE.

KIM: Where are you going, Martin.

MARTIN: To find the highway. Let go of me.

KIM: That's a bad idea, Martin. (MARTIN *keeps walking.*) Martin. This is your mess.

MARTIN: Fuck it.

KIM: Your *mess*, Martin, I won't get stuck with it... (MARTIN *keeps walking.*) Hey. You. Little man. *(He takes out the gun and shoots.* MARTIN *shouts and falls.* KIM *starts toward him.)* I bet that hurts, huh.

MARTIN: You bastard...we're *part*ners...

KIM: You just changed that didn't you. *(He reaches* MARTIN.*)* Finish what you start. *(He puts the gun against* MARTIN's *head.)*

MARTIN: Kim. Please.

KIM: Hmm.

MARTIN: I can't face it, I can't, I can't, I'm scared, I'm so scared....

KIM: I'm sorry for you. *(He pulls the trigger. Gun jams. Pause.)*
Would you give me that?

MARTIN: What?

KIM: Give me the flashlight please?

MARTIN: No...

KIM: Come on.

MARTIN: HELP ME! SOMEBODY HELP ME!

KIM: Shh. Quiet. Don't be frightened.

MARTIN: *Fuck* you...

KIM: Yes, alright. Just give me the flashlight. Come on. You know you're not
up to this. Give me the flashlight everything will be okay. Nothing to get
alarmed about. You're safe. You are. You really are. *(Pause)*

MARTIN: Here. *(He butts* KIM *in the face with the flashlight.* KIM *staggers back.*
MARTIN *clubs him again, swinging wildly.)* You *want* this? You *want* it? Take it,
take it!

KIM: Martin— okay—

MARTIN: HERE'S YOUR THREAT.

KIM: *(Collapsing)* Uh—

MARTIN: HERE'S YOUR POSSIBLE. HERE'S YOUR SAFETY, YOU FEEL
THAT? *(*KIM *stops moving.* MARTIN *keeps beating him.)* GET UP. GET UP.
I'M READY. I AM NOT AFRAID. I AM NOT AFRAID. *(*KIM *lies face down.*
MARTIN *lowers his arms. Long pause.)* Kim. Hey. Look at this. Look at it you
fuck. *(He pushes* KIM *over with his foot and displays the flashlight barrel.)* That's
your blood. You see it? That's *your* blood. Here's what I know. I'm stronger
than you.

Scene Six

RADIO ANNOUNCER: *(V.O. in blackout.)*...In local Jersey news, police are
pursuing what they call "several promising leads" in last week's brutal
slaying of Officer Thomas Selby, an eight-year veteran of the Highway
Patrol. Selby was shot point blank in the face when he stopped a motorist
just south of the Irvington exit on the Garden State. He will be buried with

full honors tomorrow. In a separate incident, investigators are still hoping
to identify the body of a man found bludgeoned to death near the Linden
refinery fields Wednesday morning. The man was described as white, well
dressed, approximately thirty-five years old. Police are considering the
possibility that the murder was drug related. They have no leads at this time.

Scene Seven

(A private office. Bright sun. Big desk. CARLING *standing with briefcase, waiting.*
MARTIN *enters.)*

MARTIN: *(Extending his hand)* Mr Carling.

CARLING: Mr Powers. *(They shake.)*

MARTIN: Sorry to keep you hanging. Welcome to California.

CARLING: Thank you.

MARTIN: Bet you don't get out here much.

CARLING: First time.

MARTIN: Well. Happy New Year. Make way for tomorrow, huh?

CARLING: Ready or not. *(Pause. He notices poster.)* That one of yours?

MARTIN: Oh yes.

CARLING: *Dead World.*

MARTIN: Buckets of blood quickie. Did it for half a million and it looks it.
Got us started though.

CARLING: Huh.

MARTIN: We're doing a big one now. Big picture. Very proud.

CARLING: What is it.

MARTIN: Based on a book, ah, wonderful wonderful story, about a little guy
overcomes all the odds to make his dream a reality. It's upbeat, it's about
winners, and, uh...it'll be great.

CARLING: Sounds exciting.

MARTIN: Tell you the truth, this point in my life, I'd rather watch my son
play softball. You have children, Mr Carling?

CARLING: Afraid not.

MARTIN: It changes you. Truly changes you. *(Pause)*

CARLING: Mr Powers, I think you know we have a problem.

MARTIN: We seem to, and I thank you for getting in touch with me.

CARLING: Certain evidence has come into my possession that links you to Mr Martin Mirkheim, the subject of my investigation.

MARTIN: What evidence is that.

CARLING: It arises out of a settlement by Far Horizon Films, I believe that's your company, to a Dr Waxling for nonpayment and breach of contract.

MARTIN: Mirkheim.

CARLING: That's right.

MARTIN: Don't know who you're talking about. *(Pause)*

CARLING: Mr Powers. Tax evasion is a serious crime and the State of Florida will vigorously pursue prosecution.

MARTIN: As well they should.

CARLING: I hoped my visit here would give you an opportunity to come to terms with the situation.

MARTIN: You mentioned that on the phone. I'm not sure what your point is.

CARLING: My point...is that back taxes are the least of Mr Mirkheim's concerns. *(He opens his briefcase and removes a manila folder.)* Would you like to see my hobby? *(As he sorts through papers inside)* Notice of seizure, collateral on defaulted equity loan, this is years ago...old credit card statements, also unpaid.... Divorce granted in absentia, Palm Beach County Court...just bits and pieces, nobody bothers with them....

MARTIN: Mr Carling, I have a busy—

CARLING: Sworn deposition, motorist Garden State Parkway, night of April 23, 1991...not my field but I happen to be curious.... *(He picks up a Polaroid photo from folder.)* A New York City businessman. *(He places it on the desk.)* He's dead now. (MARTIN *doesn't look.*) No interest in history, Mr Powers?

MARTIN: I prefer the future. It's more hopeful.

CARLING: Well, at this moment, your future is what you make of it. I'd say.

MARTIN: Would you. *(Pause)* You know the worst thing a man can do, Mr Carling? He can undertake an adventure. He can misjudge his strength. And he can destroy himself. *(He reaches into his desk and brings out a thick envelope and a gun.)* One of these is for you. *(Offering envelope)* Is it this? *(As* CARLING *hesitates)* Check inside to be sure. Go ahead. (CARLING *takes envelope and looks inside.)*

CARLING: This *is* mine. Thank you.

MARTIN: Don't mention it. *(Of file)* That stays.

CARLING: Of course. *(He places the folder on the desk.)*

MARTIN: Is there something else to discuss?

CARLING: I don't think so.

MARTIN: Then you keep *safe* in California. Okay?

CARLING: Yes. *(He exits.* MARTIN *watches him go. Pause.)*

MARTIN: *(Into intercom)* Nothing till I buzz. *(He places the gun back in the desk, then reaches for the folder. He looks through the contents, turning the pages slowly. To himself:)* Focus. Stay *focused...* *(He reaches for the lighter on his desk.)* Keep ready. *(He sets the folder aflame, holding it in his hand.)* Be strong. *(He drops it in the wastebasket as it continues to burn.* MARTIN *sits at his desk, looking straight out. Lights fade.)*

END OF PLAY

SIGHT UNSEEN

Donald Margulies

ABOUT THE AUTHOR

Donald Margulies's WHAT'S WRONG WITH THIS PICTURE? enjoyed
its most recent production in the summer of 1990 at the Jewish Repertory
Theater in New York, where he is a writer-in-residence. Following the
play's development at New York Writers Bloc and at the Sundance Institute
Playwrights' Lab, it was originally presented at the Manhattan Theater Club
in 1985 and on the west coast at the Back Alley Theater in 1988. WHAT'S
WRONG WITH THIS PICTURE was also published by Broadway Play
Publishing in that year.

His other plays include THE LOMAN FAMILY PICNIC (Manhattan Theater
Club, A "Best Play of 1989-90"); THE MODEL APARTMENT (Los Angeles
Theater Center, Drama-Logue Award, NY Foundation of the Arts Grant);
FOUND A PEANUT (New York Shakespeare Festival); PITCHING TO
THE STARS (West Bank Cafe); RESTING PLACE (Theater for the New
City); and LUNA PARK, GIFTED CHILDREN, and ZIMMER all were
produced at the Jewish Repertory Theater.

Donald Margulies has done a number of projects for film and television,
and is currently working on two screenplays. He is a frequent contributor
to the 52nd Street Project, and is a member of both New Dramatists and
The Dramatists Guild.

SIGHT UNSEEN premiered at South Coast Repertory on 17 September 1991. The cast and creative contributors were:

JONATHAN WAXMAN ....Stephen Rowe
NICK ....Randy Oglesby
PATRICIA .... Elizabeth Norment
GRETE .... Sabina Weber

Director .... Michael Bloom
Set design... Cliff Faulkner
Costume design .... Ann Bruice
Lighting design ....Tom Ruzika
Music...Michael Roth
Stage manager .... Andy Tighe
Assistant stage manager .... Randall K. Lum

SIGHT UNSEEN was subsequently produced at Manhattan Theatre Club (Lynne Meadow, Artistic Director; Barry Grove, Managing Director) on 7 January 1992, and moved to the Orpheum Theatre on 26 March 1992, in New York City.

ACKNOWLEDGMENTS

The author wishes to acknowledge the following people for their insight and hard work which contributed to the development and success of SIGHT UNSEEN: all the folks at South Coast Rep, particularly Jerry Patch, Elizabeth Norment, Stephen Rowe, Randy Oglesby, Sabina Weber, Michael Roth, Cliff Faulkner, Daniel Reichert, Kamella Tate, Kris Logan, Anni Long, and Jarion Monroe; David Kranes and the actors at the Sundance Playwrights Conference who worked on an early version of the play, most notably Evan Handler, Kevin Kling, Mia Dillon, Daniel Jenkins, and Kathy Hiler; New Dramatists; Kate Nelligan, Anthony Heald, Peter Friedman, Wendy Makkena; Bruce Whitacre, Kate Loewald, and everybody who worked on the Manhattan Theatre Club production, most especially Michael Bloom, Dennis Boutsikaris, Deborah Hedwall, Laura Linney, Jon DeVries, and Lou Liberatore. Special thanks also to my wife, Lynn Street.

This play is for
Jonathan Alper
(1950-1991)
and
Laura Kuckes
(1961-1990)

CHARACTERS

JONATHAN, 35-40
PATRICIA, 35-40
NICK, 40s
GRETE, 25-30

JONATHAN and PATRICIA are American; NICK is English. GRETE is German; her English is excellent, if accented. JONATHAN has maintained his working-class Brooklyn accent; NICK's rural, working-class speech finds its way into his university accent, particularly when he's been drinking; and PATRICIA's dialect suggests that of an expatriate New Yorker living in England.

SCENES

Act One

1. A cold farmhouse in Norfolk, England. The present.
2. An art gallery in London. Four days later.
3. The farmhouse. An hour before the start of Scene One.
4. A bedroom in Brooklyn. Fifteen years earlier.

Act Two

5. The farmhouse. A few hours after the end of Scene One.
6. The art gallery. Continued from the end of Scene Two.
7. The farmhouse. A few hours after the end of Scene Five.
8. A painting studio in an art college, New York state. Seventeen years earlier.

Ideally, a turntable should be used to ensure quick transitions between the four discrete settings.

The play is performed with an intermission after Scene Four.

ACT ONE

Scene One

(Lights up: The kitchen of a cold farmhouse in England. Dusk. Jonathan, overnight bag on his shoulder, stands at the open door. Nick is eating a hard roll.)

JONATHAN: You must be Nick.

NICK: Mm.

JONATHAN: Jonathan Waxman. *(He extends his hand.* NICK *doesn't shake it, but takes a bite of his roll instead.)* Is Patricia...? *(*NICK *shakes his head.)* Oh. You *were* expecting me?

NICK: Mm.

JONATHAN: *(Meaning, Where is...?)* Patricia...?

NICK: A lamb roast.

JONATHAN: Ah. Well! Nick! Nice to meet you. *(*NICK *says nothing. A beat.)* I left the car right outside. That alright? *(*NICK *looks out the door, shrugs.)* 'Cause I'll move it.

NICK: No no. *(A beat)*

JONATHAN: Uh, I think I'm kind of freezing. You mind if I— *(*NICK *gestures for him to come in.)* Thanks. *(A beat)* I made really good time, by the way. Left London 'round one; not bad, huh? *(*NICK *shrugs. A beat.)* Her directions were really good Patricia. *(A beat)* Boy, this driving on the wrong side of the road stuff!—Ever drive in America? *(*NICK *shakes his head.)* Ever *been* to America? *(*NICK *shakes his head again.)* Uh huh, well it's *weird* cars coming at you like that. A simple thing like the way you perceive the flow of traffic, the way you're used to seeing, gets challenged here, it all gets inverted. You've got to keep reminding yourself, over and over, remember what side of the road you're on. 'Cause all you need's to zone out for one second on the M4 and that's it, you're fucken wrapped in twisted metal. *(*NICK *just looks at him. A beat.)* Will she be long Patricia?

NICK: God, I hope not.

JONATHAN: Oh, I'm sorry, am I interrupting something?

NICK: *(Gestures to a room)* Well...

JONATHAN: Please. Do what you have to do. I want to hear all about your work, though.

NICK: Hm?

JONATHAN: Your work. I really want to hear about it.

NICK: Oh.

JONATHAN: Archeology's one of those things I've always found fascinating, but I don't know much about it.

NICK: Well, I...

JONATHAN: Not now. Whenever. Over dinner. I brought you some good wine; we should drink it. *(Takes out bottles of wine)* Maybe later I'll get you to show me the dig you're working on.

NICK: Uh...

JONATHAN: No, really, I'd like to see it. Hey, I know how obnoxious it is when people say they want to see my studio and then I show them and they're not really into it?, all they're thinking about is *after*, telling their friends they were there? No, I mean it, I'd really love to see it.

NICK: It's.... It's rather dull.

JONATHAN: I'm sure it isn't. What are you working on right now?

NICK: *(A beat)* A Roman latrine. *(A beat. PATRICIA enters wearing a bulky sweater and carrying a bag bursting with groceries.)*

PATRICIA: Well! You're here!

JONATHAN: *(Over "You're here")* Hi. Yeah. *(She moves around the room, unpacks groceries, prepares dinner.)*

PATRICIA: Fancy car.

JONATHAN: Rented. *You* know. What the hell.

PATRICIA: Must be fun whipping round these country roads in a thing like that.

JONATHAN: Yeah, as a matter of fact I was just telling Nick....

NICK: Um...

PATRICIA: What. *(He gestures to his office.)* Go. *(NICK hesitates, goes. A beat.)* He has work. *(JONATHAN nods. A beat.)* So. Arrived in one piece I see.

JONATHAN: Your directions...

PATRICIA: What.

JONATHAN: Excellent. Just terrific.

PATRICIA: Oh, good. I'm glad you liked them.

JONATHAN: Great spot.

PATRICIA: Yeah? Looks like a lot of mud most of the time. *(Pause)*

JONATHAN: Good to see you, Patty.

PATRICIA: Is it? Well, good. *(Pause)*

JONATHAN: So you got a lamb roast?

PATRICIA: Ground veal, actually. It was on special. I've become quite a resourceful little cook over here, you know.

(NICK returns, gets a bottle of scotch, gestures offstage, exits.)

PATRICIA: Nick is painfully shy. Was he shy with you?

JONATHAN: *(Lying)* Nick? No. *(A beat)* So you've become a good cook you said?

PATRICIA: I didn't say good, I said resourceful. No one's a good cook here, so no one notices. Stews are the answer, I've discovered. The meat quality is so awful, you stew the stuff for hours till it all falls apart and it's unrecognizable as meat. Bet you can't wait for dinner, hm? *(She puts on water for tea, etc.)*

JONATHAN: Mmm. Can I help with anything?

PATRICIA: *(Over "with anything")* No. Sit. Pretend you're comfortable. Take off your coat.

JONATHAN: *(Meaning the cold)* No, I'll keep it if you don't mind....

PATRICIA: It's so funny having Americans visit, watching their teeth chatter.

JONATHAN: I think it's warmer out*side*.

PATRICIA: Probably. You get used to the cold and the damp, strangely enough. You get used to anything.

JONATHAN: You've kept your accent.

PATRICIA: For the most part. You'll notice little things here and there.

JONATHAN: It struck me on the phone; I thought by now you'd sound totally....

PATRICIA: I don't know, I like sounding American. It works to my advantage, really. You have no idea how hard it is being a woman running an excavation.

JONATHAN: I'll bet.

PATRICIA: The sexism here... If you think the *States* are bad.... Being an American woman gives me license to be rude, aggressive, demanding. It comes in handy.

JONATHAN: Don't you ever miss it?

PATRICIA: What?

JONATHAN: Home.

PATRICIA: This is my home.

JONATHAN: What, you don't miss Disneyland, or the Grand Canyon, or Zabar's?

PATRICIA: No.

JONATHAN: You don't miss Zabar's? Now I know you're full of it.

PATRICIA: I don't. I don't get choked up when I see the flag, or Woody Allen movies. I've stopped reading about politics. Reagan, Bush, they're interchangeable. No, I prefer my bones and coins and petrified cherry pits.

JONATHAN: You must miss *some*thing. Insulated housing, *some*thing.

PATRICIA: No. I'm an expatriate now.

JONATHAN: An expatriate.

PATRICIA: Yes.

JONATHAN: Gee, I've never known an expatriate before, someone who could just turn their back....

PATRICIA: On what. I've turned my back on what? America? VCRs and microwaves? If that's what I've "turned my back on".... We work hard here. It's not like the States. Everything is a struggle. It shows on our faces, on our hands. I haven't bought myself new clothes in years. We have to save for everything. The electric fire started smoking?

JONATHAN: Yeah...?

PATRICIA: It'll be weeks before we can buy a new one. Everything's a struggle. The weather is hard. Leisure is hard. Sleep is hard.

JONATHAN: Do you ever think about leaving?

PATRICIA: God! What have I been saying! I like it!

JONATHAN: Oh.

PATRICIA: You're just like my mother! I *like* it here! I *like* the struggle! I *like* surviving obstacles. Hell, I survived you, didn't I. *(He reaches for her hand; she pulls away. Pause.)* Who are you to talk about turning one's back.

JONATHAN: What do you mean?

PATRICIA: You with your shiksa wife in Vermont.

JONATHAN: Upstate.

PATRICIA: Whatever.

JONATHAN: I don't understand. What does my wife have to do....

PATRICIA: *(Over "have to do")* You're an expatriate, too, and you don't even know it.

JONATHAN: How?

PATRICIA: You made a choice. When you married your wife, you married her world. Didn't you? You can't exist in two worlds; you've got to turn your back on one of them.

JONATHAN: I hadn't thought of it like that.

PATRICIA: See? We're more alike than you thought. *(Pause)* God, when I think of all the angst, all the, what's the word?, "cirrus"?

JONATHAN: *Tsuris.*

PATRICIA: After all the tsuris our young souls went through.... Your wife should thank me.

JONATHAN: You're right; she should.

PATRICIA: I laid the groundwork. I was the pioneer.

JONATHAN: Yeah.

PATRICIA: The sacrificial shiksa.

JONATHAN: You're looking beautiful, Patty.

PATRICIA: Stop.

JONATHAN: You are.

PATRICIA: I look fat.

JONATHAN: No.

PATRICIA: All the meat and potatoes, and nights at the pub. Don't look at me. I'm afraid this place is perfect for women like me, who've let themselves go.

JONATHAN: You haven't.

PATRICIA: We can blend right in with the mud.

JONATHAN: You look beautiful.

PATRICIA: And *you* look rich.

JONATHAN: I don't even. I'm the same old Jonathan.

PATRICIA: Don't be coy. You're rich and famous. How does it feel to be rich and famous?

JONATHAN: It's meaningless. Really.

PATRICIA: Oh, yeah, right.

JONATHAN: No, the whole scene is meaningless bullshit. You know that. It's all timing and luck.

PATRICIA: Timing and luck.

JONATHAN: Yeah. The party's over for me already; I'm not making now what I made two years ago.

PATRICIA: But you still have your millions to keep you company.

JONATHAN: The numbers don't mean anything. I mean, I'm not crying poverty or anything....

PATRICIA: Oh! Well!

JONATHAN: My gallery takes fifty per cent. Okay? Remember that. Fifty. And then the government on top of that...

PATRICIA: Don't you think you're protesting just a little too much?

JONATHAN: Okay, so maybe I've enjoyed a little recognition—

PATRICIA: "A little recognition"?! Jonathan! You're "it"....

JONATHAN: No, no, not anymore.

PATRICIA: *(Continuous)* the cat's pajamas. You can't fool me. I read all about you in *The Times.*

JONATHAN: The New York *Times*? You read the New York *Times*? Hypocrite. You were just telling me how you....

PATRICIA: *(Over "telling me how you")* My mother sent it to me.

JONATHAN: You talking about the Sunday Magazine piece? Couple of years ago?

PATRICIA: "Jonathan Waxman: The Art Scene's New Visionary."

JONATHAN: Oh, please...

PATRICIA: *(Overlap, laughs, then)* Is that what it was? "New Visionary"?

JONATHAN: "Bad Boy or Visionary"?

PATRICIA: "Bad Boy or Visionary," excuse me.

JONATHAN: What do you want from me?

PATRICIA: Cover story and everything. Wow, Jonathan, how'd you manage that? I was quite impressed. You on the cover, the very model of messy, Jewish intensity.

JONATHAN: They shot me in my studio. That's how I look when I'm working.

PATRICIA: I know how you look when you're working. *(They look at one another. Pause.)* My mother's always sending me clippings about you.

JONATHAN: Oh, yeah? Why?

PATRICIA: I don't know, I'd say she's trying to tell me something, wouldn't you? The *Vanity Fair* piece was fun. "Charlatan or Genius?"

JONATHAN: I don't believe this.

PATRICIA: Every time she sends me something, I take it as some sort of indictment, some sort of accusation: *"See what you could've had? See what could've been yours if you weren't so crazy?"*

JONATHAN: Is that what *you* think or is that what *she* thinks?

PATRICIA: Me? No. *(Pause)* So tell me about your show. How's it going in London? *(That English inflection slips in)* Is it going well?

JONATHAN: Yeah. Pretty much. Oh, I brought you a catalogue. *(Hands her one from his bag)*

PATRICIA: Hefty.

JONATHAN: There are a couple of gaps I'm not too happy about. Particularly in the early stuff. It's supposed to be a retrospective.

PATRICIA: A retrospective? At your age?

JONATHAN: Are you kidding? I'm almost passe.

PATRICIA: You know, I still have that very first painting you did of me, remember?

JONATHAN: Of course I remember. Where is it?

PATRICIA: Over the mantle. Go and see.

JONATHAN: No shit. You didn't just haul it out of the attic, knowing I was coming?

PATRICIA: There is no attic. And, no, Jonathan, I wouldn't do anything at this point to feed your ego. *(He goes to the doorway leading to the living room and sees his painting; it's like seeing a ghost. She watches him in silence while he looks at the painting.)*

JONATHAN: Jesus. Look at that. I can't believe you saved it. How old could I have been? Twenty-two, tops? *(She nods; a beat.)* You know? It's not bad. I threw out most of my student work years ago. I couldn't stand looking at anything. But this, this one's different. It's really not bad.

PATRICIA: When do you open?

JONATHAN: What? Oh. Tuesday. *(Re: the painting)* Look at that: see what I was doing with the picture plane?, how it's sort of tipped? I didn't think I started doing that till like much later.

PATRICIA: Nervous?

JONATHAN: No. I don't know. What can I do? It's my first solo show outside of North America, okay?, my European debut.

PATRICIA: Yeah...?

JONATHAN: So the critics are salivating, I'm sure. Ready to chomp into me like their next Big Mac.

PATRICIA: And what if they do?

JONATHAN: I don't know, I can't worry about it. Press is press. Good or bad. My father, God!, my father loved seeing my name in print.

PATRICIA: Oh, yeah?

JONATHAN: *My* last name, after all, was *his* last name. Got such a kick out of it. Eight pages in the Sunday *Times*. He couldn't believe The New York *Times* could possibly have that much to say about *his* kid. "All these words," he said, "are about *you*? What is there to say about *you*?" *(She laughs.)* He was serious; he wasn't just teasing. Oh, he was teasing, too, but it threatened him. No, it did. It pointed up the fact that he could be my father and still not know a thing about me. Not have a clue. What did the fancy-schmancy art world see that he didn't? What were those big dirty paintings about, anyway? So then when all the hype started...

PATRICIA: "New visionary"?

JONATHAN: Yeah, and that's very seductive in the beginning, I got to admit. Vindicating, even: "Ah ha! See? I *am* a genius. *Now* maybe my father will respect me." But it had the opposite effect on him. It didn't make him proud. It bewildered him. It alienated him. How could *he* have produced a "visionary"? It shamed him somehow. I can't explain.

PATRICIA: How's he doing?

JONATHAN: Oh. Didn't I tell you on the phone?

PATRICIA: What.

JONATHAN: He died.

PATRICIA: Oh, no.

JONATHAN: Right before I flew to London.

PATRICIA: You mean last week?

JONATHAN: What's today? Yeah, last Thursday it happened.

PATRICIA: Oh, Jonathan.... What happened?

JONATHAN: It was long in coming. Did I not mention this on the phone?

PATRICIA: No.

JONATHAN: Sorry, thought I did. Strange to think, four days ago I was in Flushing, Queens, burying my father under the Unisphere. *(Pause)*

PATRICIA: *He* was sweet to me, your Dad.

JONATHAN: Yeah, I know.

PATRICIA: What about shiva? Didn't you have to sit shiva?

JONATHAN: There was no time.

PATRICIA: Oh.

JONATHAN: I mean, they were mounting the show.

PATRICIA: Couldn't they have waited? I mean, your *father...*

JONATHAN: No. I had to be here. I mean, there was nothing more I could do; he was dead. What could I do?

PATRICIA: I don't know.

JONATHAN: It was good for me, getting away, I think. Therapeutic. Bobby's doing it, though, shiva. He wanted to. I don't know, I just couldn't. It didn't seem like the thing to do. It's like I'd been sitting shiva for him for fifteen years, since my mother. I'd done it already. *(A beat)* I wasn't a very good son.

PATRICIA: That's not true; I'm sure you made him very proud.

JONATHAN: No no, that's not what I need to hear. I wasn't. *(A beat)* I went to pack up his house the other day? My parents' house? All his clothes, my old room, my mother's sewing machine, all those rooms of furniture. Strange being in a place where no one lives anymore.

PATRICIA: I know; I do that for a living.

JONATHAN: Yeah, I guess you do. Anyway, what I found was, he'd taken all the family pictures, everything that was in albums, shoved in drawers—hundreds of them—and covered an entire wall with them, floor to ceiling, side to side. I first saw it years ago, when he'd started. It was his Sistine Chapel; it took him years. He took my hand *(I'll never forget this)* he took my hand—he was beaming: "You're an artist," he said to me, "*you'll* appreciate this." He was so proud of himself I thought I was gonna cry. Proud and also in a strange way competitive?

PATRICIA: Uh-huh.

JONATHAN: So, there was this wall. The Waxman family through the ages. Black-and-white, sepia, Kodachrome. My great-grandparents in the shtetl, my brother's baby pictures on top of my parents' courtship, me at my bar mitzvah. Well, it was kind of breathtaking. I mean, the sweep of it, it really was kind of beautiful. I came closer to examine it—I wanted to see how he'd gotten them all up there—and then I saw the staples.

PATRICIA: What?

JONATHAN: Staples! Tearing through the faces and the bodies. "Look what you've done," I wanted to say, "How could you be so thoughtless? You've ruined everything!" But of course I didn't say that. How could I? He was like a little boy. Beaming. Instead I said, "Dad! What a wonderful job!" (*A beat*) So, there I was alone in his house, pulling staples out of our family photos. These documents that showed where I came from. Did they *mean* anything to him at all? I mean as artifacts, as proof of a former civilization, when my mother was vibrant and he was young and strong and we were a family? (*A beat*) That's all gone now, Patty. It's all gone. (*Pause*)

PATRICIA: You have your wife. (*He nods. Pause.*) She must trust you a lot.

JONATHAN: Why?

PATRICIA: Letting you pop up to see how the old lover made out? Or, ah-ha!, you didn't tell her you were coming!

JONATHAN: No, I told her.

PATRICIA: Too morbid for her taste, huh?, she decided to stay in London?

JONATHAN: No. Actually, she didn't come over.

PATRICIA: Oh?

JONATHAN: She stayed home. Up near New Paltz. We moved out of the city a couple of years ago.

PATRICIA: I know. The article said. I thought it said Vermont.

JONATHAN: No. We bought a farm.

PATRICIA: I know. Some "turn of the century" thing; here we have to ask "turn of *which* century?" So why isn't she here *with* you, your wife? Your big European debut.

JONATHAN: She wanted to. (*A beat*) She's pregnant.

PATRICIA: (*A beat*) Ah. Well. A baby. My! Aren't you full of news!

JONATHAN: She's pretty far along.

PATRICIA: Congratulations.

JONATHAN: Thanks. I mean, flying was out of the question. Third trimester.

PATRICIA: Of course. So I've heard. Well. Isn't that nice. You'll be a father soon.

JONATHAN: Yeah. Nine weeks or something, yeah.

PATRICIA: Well. This *is* something: Jonathan Waxman a father. Just as you've lost your own.

JONATHAN: Yeah. The irony hasn't escaped me. *(A beat. Going to his wallet.)* Would you like to see a picture?

PATRICIA: Of the child already?

JONATHAN: No, of Laura.

PATRICIA: *(Continuous)* My God! American technology...

JONATHAN: *(Over "technology")* I *did* have a sonogram I carried around. It's a boy.

PATRICIA: A boy.

JONATHAN: You can tell. You can see his, you know, his scrotum.

PATRICIA: Yes.

JONATHAN: I meant a picture of Laura. Would you like to...

PATRICIA: I've already seen her.

JONATHAN: How?

PATRICIA: The article.

JONATHAN: Oh, right.

PATRICIA: Remember? Gazing at you like an astronaut's wife?

JONATHAN: *(Returns the picture to his wallet)* Oh, well, I thought you might've liked to...

PATRICIA: No, I will, show me.

JONATHAN: It's okay.

PATRICIA: *Show* me. *(He shows her the photo. A beat.)*

JONATHAN: That was our wedding.

PATRICIA: I figured, white dress and everything. How long ago was that?

JONATHAN: A year ago May. We waited a while. How about you?

PATRICIA: Me?

JONATHAN: You and Nick, you've been married *how* long?

PATRICIA: I don't know, eight or nine years?

JONATHAN: Eight or nine?, what do you mean?

PATRICIA: We didn't have much of a wedding. I like her dress. She's so thin. A dancer, right? *(He nods. She returns the photo.)* She seems nice.

JONATHAN: Yeah, thanks, she is, you'd like her.

PATRICIA: I'm sure.

JONATHAN: And Nick seems...

PATRICIA: Don't do that.

JONATHAN: What.

PATRICIA: I tell you I like *your* spouse, you tell me you like *mine.* You don't have to do that.

JONATHAN: I wasn't.

PATRICIA: The fact is...Nick may seem...odd...

JONATHAN: No...

PATRICIA: *(A small laugh)* Yes. But he absolutely adores me.

JONATHAN: That's *good.* I'm glad he does. He should. *(A beat. They look at one another.)* And you?

PATRICIA: Look, what do you want?

JONATHAN: What do you mean?

PATRICIA: Do you have some sort of agenda or something?

JONATHAN: No.

PATRICIA: You just happened to be in the neighborhood?

JONATHAN: I wanted to see you again.

PATRICIA: Why?

JONATHAN: I don't know, it felt somehow...incomplete.

PATRICIA: What did?

JONATHAN: We did. I did. *(A beat)* I came...I wanted to apologize.

PATRICIA: *(Smiling)* Not really.

JONATHAN: What did you think when I called?

PATRICIA: I don't know, I was nonplused. I buried you years ago, then all of a sudden a call from London. You caught me off guard.

JONATHAN: So why did you invite me up?

PATRICIA: You caught me off *guard,* I said. I don't know, what *should* I have done?

JONATHAN: You could've said it was a bad time, you were busy, you had other plans...

PATRICIA: None of which was true.

JONATHAN: You could've said you had no interest in seeing me again. *(Pause)* Patty... *(He makes a conciliatory gesture; she rebuffs him.)*

PATRICIA: I'll give you dinner and a place to spend the night, but, no, Jonathan, I won't forgive you. *(Pause. He goes for his bag.)*

JONATHAN: Look, maybe this wasn't such a good idea. I should go to a hotel.

PATRICIA: No! *(A beat)* Hey, no one here calls me Patty. It's a novelty. *(He drops his bag; she picks up a basket.)* I'm going foraging in my garden for dinner.

JONATHAN: I'll come with you.

PATRICIA: You aren't invited. *(A beat)* You're cold. I think it actually is warmer inside. *(She puts on her jacket and goes.* JONATHAN *soon gravitates toward the painting and looks at it for a while.* NICK *enters, the depleted bottle of scotch in his hand.)*

NICK: Oops. *(*JONATHAN *sees him. A beat.)* You've spotted your painting.

JONATHAN: Yes.

NICK: I can't tell you how many nights I've stared at the fire and imagined that painting in the flames.

JONATHAN: Excuse me?

NICK: Oh, I wouldn't dream of damaging it. It's a work of art. And I am a preservationist by nature. *(A beat)* It makes Patricia happy to have a piece of you on the wall. Did I say a *piece of you*? I meant a piece *from* you. Or perhaps I *meant* a piece *of* you. A piece of *yours,* at any rate. She gazes at it sometimes, when we're sitting by the fire. It doesn't move me in the same way. No, the eye of the beholder and all that. Drink?

JONATHAN: No. I painted it a long time ago. When Patty and I were at school. It's strange seeing something I did like twenty years ago and see all these things I couldn't possibly have seen when I painted it.

NICK: You're rich now, aren't you?

JONATHAN: What?

NICK: Patricia tells me you're rich.

JONATHAN: Oh, God.

NICK: Read it in some magazine.

JONATHAN: Well, we talked about that. Actually, I...

NICK: *(Over "Actually, I")* She said you're rich. You're successful.

JONATHAN: Those are two different things, really.

NICK: Are they?

JONATHAN: Yes, I think—

NICK: How much do you make in a year?

JONATHAN: Well, I don't—

NICK: Am I out of line?

JONATHAN: Well, maybe.

NICK: How much then?

JONATHAN: It's difficult to say. I've had years in which I've made almost nothing. It's only in the last couple of years—

NICK: *(Over "couple of years")* How much would you get for something like that, for instance? *(Meaning the painting on the wall)*

JONATHAN: A student painting? I have no idea.

NICK: Guess.

JONATHAN: I really don't know.

NICK: Come on. A pivotal work. You said so yourself. A seminal work. How much would a seminal work, given your current currency, if you will, your current notoriety, how much would an old, young Waxman bring?

JONATHAN: I really have no idea.

NICK: Come on, guess.

JONATHAN: In the thousands, certainly. I don't know.

NICK: *(Over "I don't know")* Oh, I would think more than that.

JONATHAN: Look, I really don't pay much attention to this stuff.

NICK: Don't pay attention to money? Surely you must.

JONATHAN: No, I let my gallery worry about it.

NICK: Art for art's sake, eh? Well, even I, even I who knows, or for that matter, *cares* very little about contemporary values in art, or, even, the value *of* contemporary art, even I would guess you're being awfully stingy on yourself. Considerably more than in the thousands, I would say. More like in the *tens* of thousands, wouldn't you agree?

JONATHAN: Maybe. I really don't know.

NICK: Oh, I would think. A pivotal, precocious painting like this? A seminal masterpiece?

JONATHAN: I don't know. What do you want to hear? Whatever you want to hear.

NICK: You.

JONATHAN: What.

NICK: I feel as though I've known you all along.

JONATHAN: Oh, yeah?

NICK: Your picture. She has this snapshot.

JONATHAN: What snapshot?

NICK: A Polaroid. The two of you. Patricia the co-ed. The party girl. Lithe and sunny. Her tongue in your ear. You, squirming like a boy caught in a prank. With gums showing. You don't look at all handsome. She assured me you were. A costume party of some kind.

JONATHAN: A costume party?

NICK: Mm. Patricia in a swimsuit dressed as Miss America. You're dressed like a jester. A clown. A clown or a pimp.

JONATHAN: A what?

NICK: Loud clashing plaids, a camera round your neck. Sunglasses.

JONATHAN: Oh. Halloween. I was a tourist.

NICK: Hm?

JONATHAN: A tourist. I went dressed as a tourist.

NICK: A tourist.

JONATHAN: A visitor, a stranger. An observer. The camera, the Hawaiian shirt.

NICK: It doesn't read. (JONATHAN *shrugs.*) You look like a pimp.

JONATHAN: The idea was a tourist.

NICK: Hm?

JONATHAN: Never mind.

NICK: Patricia had forgotten what you'd dressed up as. (*A beat*) She thought a pimp.

JONATHAN: No.

NICK: Mm. (*A beat*) What was the idea?

JONATHAN: The idea?

NICK: What did it mean? Was there some symbolic value?, dressing as a tourist?

JONATHAN: I don't know...

NICK: Symbolic of your perception of yourself at that time, perhaps?
A transient person? Dislocated?

JONATHAN: That's interesting. I wonder if—

NICK: Rubbish. Now, that picture, that photo. Was all I had to go on.
For years. Until that New York *Times* article. That one Polaroid she keeps
in a box with letters. *(Confidentially)* I've snooped. There's a postal card from
you in that box. One picture postal card. No letters.

JONATHAN: I didn't write much.

NICK: Hm?

JONATHAN: There was no need to write. We were in school together. We saw
each other all the time.

NICK: No, I imagine there *were* letters. Painful collegiate prose. Heartsick
poems. Declarations of lust.

JONATHAN: Sorry.

NICK: I imagine there *were* letters, but she burned them. Like Hedda Gabler
or somebody. Watched with glee while the missives went up in flames.

JONATHAN: No.

NICK: I think there *were*. I prefer to think there *were*. And all that remains is
an innocuous postal card. From Miami Beach, Florida or someplace.

JONATHAN: Yes. A visit to my grandparents. Fort Lauderdale.

NICK: Then there are the stories. Tales of Waxman. The Jonathan Stories.
Faraway sounding, exotic. Like from the Old Testament, if you will.
Patricia's voice becomes especially animated while telling a Jonathan story.
She achieves a new range in a different key. A new tune, a new music
entirely. Fascinating. I watch her face. The dimples that sprout! The
knowing smiles! Remarkable behavioral findings. *(A beat. He moves his chair
closer.)* I've become a Waxmanologist, you see. A Waxmanophile. No, a
Waxmanologist. It's my nature. Beneath this reticent exterior lies a probing,
tireless investigator. A detective. An historian. And I'm good at my work.
I'm compulsive. I'm meticulous. I study the past in order to make sense of
the present.

JONATHAN: I understand.

NICK: You're smaller in person than I imagined. I held out for a giant.
A giant among men. Instead, what's *this*? You're medium-sized. Compact.
Razor burn on your neck. Pimple on your cheek. She said you were
handsome; you're alright. Perhaps your appeal lies below the belt,
but I doubt I'd be surprised.

JONATHAN: Look, I think I'll— *(Pointing to the door)*

NICK: Circumscision isn't common practice in the UK, you know. *(*JONATHAN *stops.)* Jews still do it the world over, don't they. On religious grounds. Here the risk is too great. Too many accidents. Too many boy sopranos. Here we hold on to our overcoats. *(*PATRICIA *returns with her basket filled with vegetables and herbs.)*

PATRICIA: Oh. Good. You're getting acquainted. *(*JONATHAN *and* NICK *look at one another.)*

(End of scene)

Scene Two

(In the black, we hear the din of people chatting in a large room. Lights up: four days later. An art gallery in London. A polished wood floor and a white wall upon which "Jonathan Waxman" is spelled in display letters. It is after JONATHAN's *opening; plastic cups of wine are scattered about. An attractive, European new-wave-looking young woman (*GRETE*) arranges two Mies van der Rohe-style chairs and sets up a mini tape recorder on a table between them.* JONATHAN *enters.)*

JONATHAN: Can we do this quickly?

GRETE: Yes. Please. Sit down.

JONATHAN: It's just I promised Antony—

GRETE: *(While setting up her recorder)* No, no, sit, let us start immediately.

JONATHAN: *(Over "immediately")* There's another reception for me in Hampstead, I really—

GRETE: *(Over "Hampstead")* I am ready. Please. We can begin. *(She gestures for him to sit; he does. She takes a deep breath.)* Now: First may I congratulate you, Mr Waxman, on such a provocative exhibition.

JONATHAN: Thank you.

GRETE: It has been eagerly awaited and does not disappoint.

JONATHAN: Thank you very much. Can we get to the questions?

GRETE: Of course.

JONATHAN: *(Overlap)* I really don't have time to schmooze, I'm sorry.

GRETE: You were kind enough to agree to—

JONATHAN: Well...

GRETE: It is a thrill and an honor to finally meet—

JONATHAN: Thank you. Really, could we please—?

GRETE: *(Takes out a stack of index cards)* Forgive me, I have prepared some questions.... I will begin with the more important ones first.

JONATHAN: However you want to work it.

GRETE: *(After a deep breath)* Mr Waxman.

JONATHAN: Yes.

GRETE: Your depiction of the emptiness and spiritual deadness of middle-class American life in the closing years of the twentieth century have earned you both accolades and admonishment in your own country. Your large, bold canvases of nude men and women who seem as alienated from one another as they they do from their environment have been generating controversy in the art community in the United States for the better part of the last decade. They have also been commmanding huge price tags in the art market. How do you reconcile the success of your work with its rather bleak subject matter?, and, do you think your work speaks as effectively to the rest of the world?, or, like a joke that loses something in translation, is its popularity purely an American phenomenon?

JONATHAN: *(A beat)* Your English is very good.

GRETE: Thank you. I was a year at N.Y.U.

JONATHAN: Ah. Now: Do I think my work is intrinsically American? Yes. Do I think that it's the equivalent of an inside joke that excludes the rest of the world? Definitely not. Whether the rest of the world *likes* it is another question. I'm not gonna worry too much about it. What was the first part of your question? How do I, what?, reconcile....

GRETE: The success of your work with its rather bleak subject matter.

JONATHAN: Right. Well, I like to think that people are responding to good art. By good art I mean art that effectively tells the truth, effectively *reflects* the truth, and the truth is often rather bleak, so...I mean, you're German, right?

GRETE: Yes...

JONATHAN: Germany's been way ahead of us on this. American art is just starting to get politicized again. Before AIDS, it was all about style and cleverness; we didn't know what to make art *about*. Your country, in Germany, you had guys like Beuys, and Kiefer, making art that terrified and revolted you. *Because they knew what they were making art in response to.*

GRETE: To...?

JONATHAN: To the most horrible event of our time. Yeah, that old thing. They were dealing with a society that had literally gone to hell. They were looking for clues among the ashes, looking for answers.

GRETE: Yes, but is it not arguable that events such as America in Vietnam, America in Central America, the failure of the American civil rights movement, to name a few, should have been sufficiently powerful premises for making art during the last generation?

JONATHAN: Yeah, but we're talking about the Holocaust. The horror by which all other horrors are judged.

GRETE: Horror is horror, is it not? How can you say that one horror is more terrible than another? All societies are guilty of injustice—

JONATHAN: Whoa. Look, maybe we shouldn't get into this. Let's just talk about the work. Okay? Let's talk about the work.

GRETE: Very well.

JONATHAN: Um.... What was I gonna say? Oh, yeah. So anyway, I don't really see my work as bleak. I'm responding to situations that exist in American society that are bleak, maybe, but I'm presenting them in allegorical ways that I hope are provocative and entertaining, even. I mean, I don't set out by saying to myself, "I'm gonna make this really *bleak* painting of an interracial couple trying to make love in a vandalized cemetery." Bleak never comes into it. It's just an image. Just a story.

GRETE: I'm glad you brought up that painting. *Walpurgisnacht*, no? 1986. A very shocking painting. Some critics have suggested that the couple isn't making love but that the woman is being raped.

JONATHAN: That's what some critics have said, yes. They've accused me of being racist for showing a black man raping a white woman, but I say it's *their* problem 'cause *they're* the ones who can't fathom a naked black man on top of a naked white woman without calling it rape.

GRETE: Yes, I've read that explanation before. Some people have suggested that you were being disingenuous in your protestations.

JONATHAN: Some people would be wrong.

GRETE: But wouldn't you agree that the title, which means "Witches' Night," could easily mislead?

JONATHAN: No. If those people were to look beyond their own fears and knee-jerk attitudes toward miscegenation and actually look at the painting, they'd see that the lovers are in a Jewish cemetery that's been desecrated. Stones are toppled, spray-painted with swastikas. That's what the title refers to. I thought I was really hitting people over the head but I guess not.

Everyone saw red and failed to see the painting. Just when things quieted down, *feminists* got on my case 'cause the man was on top of the woman!

GRETE: *(A beat)* While *Walpurgisnacht* is probably your most famous work— certainly it is your most controversial—and, fittingly, the centerpiece of this exhibition, the talk of the show here today seems to be a painting that to my knowledge has never before been shown.

JONATHAN: Yes.

GRETE: A student work. *The Beginning*, it is called.

JONATHAN: Uh huh.

GRETE: Painted while you were in your early twenties.

JONATHAN: Yeah. I only recently came across it again. I'd figured it must've gotten lost or destroyed; student work is *supposed* to get lost or destroyed. But when I found it again, this thing I thought I'd lost, it was like a rush. Every painting I ever did suddenly made sense.

GRETE: Hm. It is the only painting from your personal collection, I see.

JONATHAN: Yes.

GRETE: A very curious painting, Mr Waxman.

JONATHAN: Curious how?

GRETE: On the surface, it appears to be a fairly commonplace, rather youthful study of a seated figure.

JONATHAN: *(Over "of a seated figure")* Yeah, but you can't fault the painter for being young. The painting may not be brilliant, but it is inspired. I mean, I look at it and I feel the excitement and the, the *danger* of that day all over again.

GRETE: What was it about that day?

JONATHAN: I don't know, it was one of those days artists kill for. The kind we always hope we're waking up to, but which rarely comes to pass. I wish I knew what I'd had for breakfast that day or what shirt I was wearing or what I'd dreamed the night before. Burning leaves; I remember the room smelled of burning leaves. Whatever it was, something clicked that day. I was born. My life began. I starting seeing things I'd never seen before.

GRETE: There is a kind of...*openness*, yes?, present in this painting that is virtually absent in your later work. The way the model engages the viewer, for instance. Her penetrating, unwavering eye contact. Nowhere else in your work does one find that kind of...connection.

JONATHAN: *(A beat. She's right.)* Hm.

GRETE: *(Rhetorically)* I wonder about the model. Who *was* this woman? What role did *she* play? I wonder where she is today?

JONATHAN: *(A beat)* I have no idea.

(End of scene)

Scene Three

(The farmhouse. An hour before the start of Scene One. PATRICIA is sweeping the floor. NICK watches while preparing tea for the two of them. After a long silence.)

PATRICIA: We'll give him our bed. *(He doesn't respond.)* Nick?

NICK: Yes?

PATRICIA: We'll give him our bed. *(A beat)* Alright?

NICK: Fine. *(Pause)*

PATRICIA: I'll *offer* it. How's that? I'll *offer* him the bedroom. It'll be up to him. Alright?

NICK: Alright.

PATRICIA: We can sleep on the futon down here. Don't you think? *(NICK shrugs. A beat.)* Don't you think it would be easier?

NICK: Fine.

PATRICIA: Do you? Do you think it would be easier?

NICK: *(Over "would be easier")* Fine. Whatever.

PATRICIA: Tell me.

NICK: Yes, I think it would be easier. *(Pause)*

PATRICIA: God, I should change the sheets. Don't you think?

NICK: Patricia...

PATRICIA: I really just changed them, should I bother to change them?

NICK: For one night?

PATRICIA: That's what *I* thought: it's only one night. No, I'm not going to change them.

NICK: Don't.

PATRICIA: We can get away with it. He doesn't have to know.

NICK: No.

PATRICIA: They're clean. Tomorrow I'll change them. When he leaves. In the morning.

NICK: Yes. Bright and early. When he leaves. In fifteen hours, eight of which will be spent sleeping. Come have tea. *(Pause. She continues sweeping.)* Patricia, come have your tea.

PATRICIA: Do you mind about the bed?

NICK: What do you mean?

PATRICIA: Do you mind about us giving him the bed?

NICK: Mind?

PATRICIA: I mean, don't you think it would be more comfortable? It's warmer in the bedroom. He'll be cold. Americans are always cold. *(Pause)* Nick? Do you mind about the bed.

NICK: Have your tea.

PATRICIA: *Do you*? Tell me. *(Pause)*

NICK: It's only for one night. *(A beat. He reminds her.)* Tea. *(She continues puttering.)* We'll be fine downstairs. We'll light a fire. Warm it up. We've spent nights downstairs in front of the fire before. Right? Haven't we?

PATRICIA: What am I going to do with him?

NICK: What do you *mean* what are you going to do with him? You should have thought about that before.

PATRICIA: *(Over "You should have")* I mean it's been fifteen years. What am I going to do with him? What do I say?

NICK: Patricia. Really.

PATRICIA: This is foolish. Stupid. Let's go and leave a note.

NICK: Alright, love. Let's.

PATRICIA: "Called away suddenly."

NICK: Yes. Okay. "Dramatic findings in Cotswolds require our presence."

PATRICIA: *(Laughs, then)* What time is it?

NICK: Nearly half past four.

PATRICIA: Damn. I've got to get to the butcher.

NICK: Have your tea. He's not bloody royalty, you know. *(She puts on her coat.)* Where are you going?

PATRICIA: To get a lamb roast.

NICK: Why don't I come *with* you?

PATRICIA: Someone has to be here.

NICK: You don't expect *me* to....

PATRICIA: I'll be right back.

NICK: *I* shouldn't be the one who....

PATRICIA: Please, Nick. Please.

NICK: Wait for him to get here.

PATRICIA: Nick...

NICK: No, take him with you. Show him the town. He'll be here any time.

PATRICIA: The butcher will be closed.

NICK: *I'll* go to the butcher, you stay.

PATRICIA: You won't know what to get.

NICK: A lamb roast, you said. Let *me* go. You can be here when he arrives. He's *your* friend.

PATRICIA: You're mad about the bed.

NICK: I am not mad about the bloody bed!

PATRICIA: *(Over "the bloody bed")* If you don't want him to have our bed, *tell* me! Tell me you don't want him to! *(Pause)*

NICK: *(Simply)* He has it already. *(Pause)*

PATRICIA: Why didn't you tell me not to invite him?

NICK: Me? Tell you? What do you mean?

PATRICIA: *(Over "What do you mean")* Why didn't you forbid me from seeing him again?

NICK: Forbid you? How, Patricia? How could I forbid you? *Why* would I? I wouldn't presume to forbid you to do anything.

PATRICIA: *Why*? *Why* wouldn't you? *(They look at one another. Pause. She starts to exit; he calls.)*

NICK: Patricia. *(She stops and turns. Pause.)* Come home soon?

(End of scene)

Scene Four

(Fifteen years earlier. Late afternoon. Spring. Blinds drawn. JONATHAN's *bedroom in his parents' house in Brooklyn, complete with the artifacts of a lower-middle-class boyhood, the notable exception being a sewing machine. Wearing a vest, suit*

trousers, and socks, JONATHAN *is curled up on a bed. His hair is long. There is a tentative knock.* PATRICIA *enters. A beat. She whispers:)*

PATRICIA: Jonathan? *(She waits, whispers again.)* Jonny? *(She looks around the room, gravitates toward the bookshelf, and begins scanning the titles. After a while, he sits up and sees her looking at a paperback.)* I love your little-boy handwriting. So round. The loopy "J" in "Jonathan," the "o," the "a"s. "This book belongs to Jonathan Waxman." *(Laughs, shows him the book) The Man From UNCLE.* I wish I knew you then, Jonny. *(She returns the book to the shelf and continues looking.)*

JONATHAN: What are you doing?

PATRICIA: I love looking at people's books.

JONATHAN: *(Still awaiting a response)* Patty...?

PATRICIA: It's like looking into their brain or something. Everything they ever knew. Everything they ever touched. It's like archeology. Lets you into all the secret places.

JONATHAN: Patty, what are you doing here?

PATRICIA: Only took me two years to get in the front door. Hey, not bad.—Why isn't *Franny and Zooey* at your place?

JONATHAN: It is. I have doubles.

PATRICIA: Oh. *(Pause. They look at one another.)* You look handsome in your suit.

JONATHAN: *(He begins to put on his shoes.)* Thanks.

PATRICIA: I don't think I've ever seen you in a suit. Have I? I must have. Did you wear a suit at graduation? No, you wore a cap and gown. What did you wear underneath it? Anything?

JONATHAN: What time is it?

PATRICIA: I don't know. *(A beat)* Your dad kissed me. When I came in? He kissed me. On the lips. He's very sweet, your dad. Said he was glad to see me, he was glad I came. See? He wasn't upset to see me. I told you you were overreacting. He's always kind of had a crush on me I think. *You* know the Waxman men and their shiksas. They're legend.

JONATHAN: *(Fixing his shirt)* I should go back down.

PATRICIA: No. Why? Stay. *(She tries to touch his hair; he moves away. On his rebuff:)* So this is where you and Bobby grew up. *(She sits on a bed.)*

JONATHAN: That's right...

PATRICIA: Funny, it's just how I pictured it. Like one of those Smithsonian recreations? *You* know: those roped-off rooms? "Jonathan Waxman's

Bedroom in Brooklyn, Circa 1970." "The desk upon which he toiled over algebra." "The bed in which he had his first wet dream..."

JONATHAN: That one, actually.

PATRICIA: *(She smiles; a beat.)* I loved the oil painting bar mitzvah portraits of you and Bobby over the sofa by the way.

JONATHAN: What can I tell ya?

PATRICIA: Oh, they're great. *(A beat; she sees the incongruous sewing machine.)* *Sewing* machine?

JONATHAN: She moved it in when I moved out.

PATRICIA: Ah.

JONATHAN: The only woman on record to die of empty nest syndrome. *(She goes to him and hugs him.)*

PATRICIA: Oh, Jonny, I'm sorry...

JONATHAN: *(Trying to free himself)* Yeah. You know, I really should go back down. My father... *(They kiss, again and again; he's bothered as her kisses become more fervent. Protesting.)* Patty...Patricia... *(She tries to undo his belt.)* Hey! What's the matter with you?

PATRICIA: Lie down.

JONATHAN: Patricia, my father is sitting shiva in the living room!

PATRICIA: Come on, Jonny...

JONATHAN: NO, I SAID! Are you crazy?! What the fuck is the matter with you?!

PATRICIA: You won't let me *do* anything for you.

JONATHAN: Is this supposed to cheer me up?!

PATRICIA: I want to do something.

JONATHAN: I don't want sex, Patricia.

PATRICIA: I've never known anyone who *died* before; tell me what I should do.

JONATHAN: This isn't about you. Do you understand that? This is *my* problem, *my*...loss, *mine*.

PATRICIA: But I'm your friend. Aren't I? I'm your lover, for God's sake. Two years, Jonathan...

JONATHAN: *(Over "for God's sake")* I thought we went *through* this...

PATRICIA: I want to be with you. I want to help you.

JONATHAN: You can't help me, Patty. I'm beyond help.

PATRICIA: Don't say that.

JONATHAN: It's true. I am beyond help right now. You can't help me. Your *blow*jobs can't help me.

PATRICIA: You don't know how I felt not being at the funeral.

JONATHAN: I'm sorry.

PATRICIA: No you're not. I was in agony. Really. I couldn't concentrate on anything all day. Knowing what you must've been going through? What kind of person do you think I am? I wanted to be with you so much.

JONATHAN: So you came over.

PATRICIA: You didn't say I couldn't. You said the funeral. I came over *after*.

JONATHAN: I meant the whole thing.

PATRICIA: What whole thing?

JONATHAN: The funeral, shiva...

PATRICIA: You mean I was supposed to keep away from you during all *this*?, like for a *week*?—isn't shiva like a week?

JONATHAN: Patty...

PATRICIA: Do you know how ri*dic*ulous this is? Don't you think you're taking this guilt thing a little too far? I mean, your mother is dead—I'm really really sorry, Jonny, really I am—and, okay, we know she wasn't exactly crazy about me...

JONATHAN: I'm so burnt out, Patty.... My head is...

PATRICIA: (*Continuous*) Not that I ever did anything to *offend* the woman *per*sonally or anything. I just happened to be born a certain persuasion, a certain incompatible persuasion, even though I'm an atheist and I don't give a damn *what* religion somebody happens to believe in. But did she even bother to get to know me, even a little bit?

JONATHAN: Oh, Patty, this is—

PATRICIA: It's like I was invisible. Do you know how it feels to be invisible?

JONATHAN: What do you think?, my mother's dying wish was keep that shiksa away from my funeral?! Come on, Patty! Grow up! Not everything is about *you*. I know that may be hard for you to believe, but not everything in the world—

PATRICIA: (*Over "in the world"*) Oh, great.

JONATHAN: (*A beat*) Let's face it, Patricia, things haven't exactly been good between us for months.

PATRICIA: What do you mean? Your mother's been *sick* for months. How can you make a statement like that?

JONATHAN: What, this is a surprise to you what I'm saying?

PATRICIA: Hasn't your mother been dying for months.

JONATHAN: I don't really have the strength for this right now.

PATRICIA: Hasn't she? So how can you judge how things have been between us? Her dying has been weighing over us, over both of us, for so long, it's colored so much...

JONATHAN: *(Over "it's colored so much")* Look...if you *must* know—

PATRICIA: What.

JONATHAN: If you must know... *(A beat)* I was the one who didn't want you there. It wasn't out of respect to my mother or my father or my grandmother, it was me. I didn't want to see you. I didn't want you there, Patty. I didn't want to have to hold *your* hand and comfort *you* because of how cruel my mother was to you, I didn't want that...I didn't want to have to deal with your display of—

PATRICIA: Dis*play*?

JONATHAN: Your display of love for me. Your concern. It was all about *you* whenever I thought about how it would be if you were with me! I didn't want you there, Patty. I'm sorry. *(A beat)* I guess when something catastrophic like this happens.... You get to thinking.

PATRICIA: Yes? Well? *(Pause)*

JONATHAN: I don't love you, Patty. *(He smiles lamely and reaches for her as if to soothe her as she goes to get her bag. She groans, punches his arm, and goes. He stands alone for a long time before moving slowly over to the sewing machine. He clutches a pillow and gently rocks himself. As he begins to cry: lights fade to black.)*

(End of Act One)

ACT TWO

Scene Five

(Lights up: The farmhouse. A few hours after the end of Scene One. PATRICIA and JONATHAN are seated at the table after dinner. The wine is nearly finished; they are all somewhat disinhibited. NICK is standing nearby, looking through the exhibition catalogue.)

JONATHAN: Drive down with me tomorrow.

PATRICIA: I don't go to London, I try to *avoid* London.

JONATHAN: *(Over "avoid London")* You can take the train back Tuesday night, after the opening.

PATRICIA: *(Over "after the opening")* The crowds, tourists, everything so bloody expensive.

JONATHAN: Don't worry about money; everything is on me.

PATRICIA: Why should everything be on you? I don't want everything to be on you.

JONATHAN: *(Over "I don't want everything")* What, you think I'd invite you down and make you pay for it?

PATRICIA: God, Jonathan...

JONATHAN: Let me treat you to a couple of days in London!

PATRICIA: You sound like such an American!

JONATHAN: Come on, we'll hang out for a couple of days, it'll be fun.

PATRICIA: What are you talking about?

JONATHAN: We'll do the museums, you'll come to the opening, I'll introduce you to people...

PATRICIA: I don't need to meet people, I know enough people.

JONATHAN: *(Over "enough people.")* I mean artists. Writers, actors. You wouldn't believe the people coming.

PATRICIA: Uh-huh.

JONATHAN: Hey, I'll take you to Caprice.

PATRICIA: Is that a restaurant?

JONATHAN: *Yes*, it's a restaurant.

PATRICIA: I *told* you, your name-droppings are wasted on me.

JONATHAN: Patty, let me do this. I want you to be my *guests, both* of you.

PATRICIA: Well, I don't know about Nick; he *completely* falls apart in London, don't you, Nick.

NICK: Hm?

PATRICIA: *(Continuing, to* JONATHAN*)* That's never any fun, holding his hand as we brave the crush on the pavement. Besides, he couldn't get away.

JONATHAN: Then *you* come.

PATRICIA: No. I couldn't. What are you saying? I don't like big cities anymore either, they get me nervous. I don't even remember the last time I was there.

JONATHAN: Then you're due for a visit. It's really changed, London. Even in the five or six years since I was last over.

PATRICIA: You were here? Five or six years ago?

JONATHAN: Yeah, just a...quick thing, *you* know. Passing through.

PATRICIA: Uh-huh. *(A beat)* I know: must have been a year ago Christmas. Whenever my mother comes, she drags me to every bit of crap on the West End; Lloyd Webber's latest ditty. Do you know what they get for that slop?

JONATHAN: Patty.

PATRICIA: I can't just take off and go; some of us have to work for a living, you know.

JONATHAN: Oh, well! Excuse *me!*

PATRICIA: *(Over "Excuse me")* I have data to collect. I have responsibilities, people who count on me; I can't just come and go as I please.

JONATHAN: I'm not asking you to quit your job and run away with me. Two or three days!

PATRICIA: Two or *three*? A minute ago it was a couple.

JONATHAN: Patty...

PATRICIA: I can't get away. This is a very exciting time for us. Has Nick told you about the project?

JONATHAN: A Roman latrine?

PATRICIA: Is that all he told you? Nick! *Tell* Jonathan.

NICK: What.

PATRICIA: About the project. *(To* JONATHAN*)* He loves to minimize. *(*JONATHAN *nods. To* NICK.*)* Tell him what you found.

NICK: Patricia...

PATRICIA: Oh, you! *(To* JONATHAN*)* He's impossibly modest. Nick found, not only the latrine, but a late medieval rubbish pit.

JONATHAN: A garbage dump?

PATRICIA: Yes!

NICK: *I* didn't find it, Patricia, we *all* found it....

PATRICIA: Do you have any idea what a valuable find that is, medieval rubbish? Seriously. Shoes, rags, broken plates. It was one of those happy accidents and Nick led us to it.

NICK: I *didn't*. I wish you wouldn't...

PATRICIA: Everything you need to know about a culture is in its rubbish, really. What they wore, what they ate. It's a treasure trove. Tons of it. I sift through parcels of ancient rubbish every day, analyze it, catalog it. That's what I do. Every day. Now you know. I shouldn't have told you.

JONATHAN: Why not?

PATRICIA: Sounds fascinating.

JONATHAN: No, it does. *(She gives him a look. He laughs.)* It does. —Come to my opening.

PATRICIA: Stop it.

NICK: Um... *(They look at him. A beat. Referring to the catalogue:)* I'm looking at your paintings....

JONATHAN: Yes...?

NICK: And, honestly...I don't get it.

JONATHAN: What don't you get?

NICK: I don't get...what's all the fuss about?

JONATHAN: What fuss?

PATRICIA: Oh, Nick. Be nice.

NICK: I mean, is this all it takes to set the art world ablaze?

PATRICIA: Nick's idea of art is the *Mona Lisa*.

NICK: My idea of art, in point of fact, Patricia, begins and ends with the Renaissance. Everything before it was ceremonial, arts-and-crafts—hardly "art," really; everything since, well, everything since has been utter rubbish.

JONATHAN: Are you kidding? How can you say that? *(To* PATRICIA*)* All of modern art, he's dismissing just like that?

NICK: *(Over "just like that")* But it's all been done, hasn't it. The so-called modern age, as far as I can tell, has been one long, elaborate exercise, albeit a futile one, to reinvent what had already been perfected by a handful of Italians centuries ago.

JONATHAN: But the world is constantly reinventing *itself.* How can you say that Leonardo's world view expresses our world, or Picasso's even?

NICK: Picasso. Now *there* was an energetic little bloke.

JONATHAN: Am I supposed to shrink in the shadow of the great masters and pack it all in? Say the hell with it, why bother?

NICK: If you had any sense? Yes. (PATRICIA *giggles naughtily.*) Absolutely. Why bother, indeed? *(To* PATRICIA*)* How is it that all the artists I've ever known feel that what they do is so vital to society? *(She laughs some more.)* Does it ever occur to them that if they were wiped off the face of the earth the planet would survive intact?

JONATHAN: *(To* PATRICIA*)* Gee, you didn't tell me you'd married such an art lover.

NICK: Art was devised as a celebration of beauty, was it not? I mean, does *this* celebrate beauty? *(Waving the catalogue)* This, this...pornography?

PATRICIA: Nick!

JONATHAN: *(Smiling, to* PATRICIA*)* That's okay.

NICK: *(Over "That's okay")* Because as far as I can tell that's precisely what this is. And not very *good* pornography at that.

JONATHAN: Really. Well.

PATRICIA: Nick was raised by a puritanical mother.

NICK: *Fuck* that, Patricia. I look at this..."art" and I see pornography. Tell me what's there that eludes me.

JONATHAN: I'm not gonna *tell* you what to see. If you see pornography...

NICK: I don't *get* it, is what I'm saying. If I don't get it, is it my failure or yours? Enlighten me. Help me see.

JONATHAN: You know, you usually don't have the luxury of painters whispering in your ear when you're looking at their paintings, telling you what to see. That's not the job of the artist. The job of the artist is not to spell everything out. *You* have to participate.

NICK: Participate.

JONATHAN: Yes. You play an active role in all this; it's not just me, it's not just the artist.

NICK: Alright...what's this, then? *(Flips the catalogue to a particular painting)*

JONATHAN: You can't judge the work like *that*, black-and-white reproductions in a catalogue...

NICK: *(Over "in a catalogue")* What is this if not pornography?

JONATHAN: Come on, Nick, use your head a little. What do you see?

NICK: You actually want me to tell you?

JONATHAN: Yeah. Describe to me what you see.

NICK: Alright. I see what *appears* to be a painting...

JONATHAN: Oh, man...

NICK: *(Continuous)* executed with minimal skill in terms of knowledge of basic anatomy...

JONATHAN: You really have to see the *paint*ing...

NICK: *(Continuous)* of what *appears* to be a couple of mixed race fornicating in what *appears* to be a cemetery, is it?

JONATHAN: Don't be so literal! Yes, that's what it appears to be on the surface, but what's it really saying?

PATRICIA: Let me see. (NICK *shows it to her.*)

JONATHAN: *(Continuous)* What's going on there? It's an allegory, it's telling a story. Use your imagination!

PATRICIA: The woman is being raped.

JONATHAN: Ah ha. Is she?

PATRICIA: Well, yes, look at her hands. They're fists.

NICK: They aren't necessarily fists; they're just poorly drawn hands.

JONATHAN: Jesus.

NICK: That's what I mean by the apparent disregard for basic traditions in art like knowing the skeletal structure of the human hand.

JONATHAN: But you know what hands look like.

NICK: What?! Is that your response? I *know* what hands...?

JONATHAN: What I'm saying is, it's not my job to photographically recreate the skeletal structure of the human hand.

NICK: What *is* your job? You keep talking about what isn't your job; what *is* your job? Is it your job to paint well, or not?

JONATHAN: What do you mean by "paint well?" You obviously have very limited ideas about painting. I'm telling you, if you guys came down to London, I'll take you around, we'll look at art, I could *show* you...

NICK: If one were to *buy* one of these...paintings—presuming, of course, one could afford to—where would one put it?

JONATHAN: What?

NICK: I mean, they're quite large, aren't they.

JONATHAN: Fairly.

NICK: One would have to have quite a large wall on which to hang such a painting and, preferrably, an even larger room in which to view it properly. *(Art is meant to be seen, no?)* And that room would undoubtedly have to sit in an even more capacious house. Not your standard taxpayer, I take it.

JONATHAN: No.

NICK: Say *I* wanted to buy one of these.

JONATHAN: You? One of those?

NICK: Mm. What would I do?

JONATHAN: Well, for starters, you couldn't; they're already sold.

NICK: *All* of them?

PATRICIA: *(Leafing through the catalogue; sotto)* "Saatchi Collection," "Union Carbide Collection," "Mobil Corporation Collection..."

JONATHAN: All of the existing ones, yes.

NICK: The "existing" ones?

JONATHAN: Yes. And there's a waiting list for the paintings I have yet to paint.

PATRICIA: A waiting list? You're joking.

JONATHAN: No.

NICK: You mean there are people on Park Avenue or in Tokyo, who have walls in their living rooms especially reserved for the latest Waxman, Number 238?

JONATHAN: Yeah.

NICK: It doesn't matter which painting, as long as they get their Waxman?

JONATHAN: It's not like this is new, you know; artists have always lived off of commissions.

NICK: So, wait, these art lovers, these poor, unsuspecting—rather, *rich*, unsuspecting—patrons of the arts have bought, sight unseen, a painting you have not yet painted?

JONATHAN: Yes.

PATRICIA: Amazing, Jonny. Pre-sold art.

NICK: What happens if they don't like it?

JONATHAN: What?

NICK: The painting. Say it doesn't please them. The colors clash with the carpet; the image makes madam blush. What then? Are they entitled to a refund? Can they hold out for the next one off the line?

JONATHAN: If they really dislike it, I guess, but it hasn't happened.

NICK: So how many can you expect to do in a year?

JONATHAN: One every five or six weeks? Figure ten a year.

NICK: Ten a year. At roughly a quarter million dollars per painting...

JONATHAN: *(Over "per painting")* Now, wait a minute. What is this fascination with my finances? Ever since I got here you've been hocking me...

NICK: *(Over "Ever since I got here")* Patricia, are you aware of how fortunate we are to be the proud owners of our own, actual, *already painted* painting by Jonathan Waxman? And a seminal Waxman at that!

JONATHAN: Look, why should I have to *apologize* for my success?

PATRICIA: Nobody's asking you to.

JONATHAN: *(Continuous)* What am I supposed to do? Reject the money? Lower my price? What would *that* accomplish? Would it make me a better artist if I were hungry again?

NICK: I don't know. Would it?

PATRICIA: *(A beat; looking at the catalogue)* They *do* look like fists, Jonathan.

JONATHAN: What if they are fists? What difference does it make?

PATRICIA: It makes a very big difference. It changes everything. If they're fists, then that suggests that she's being taken against her will. If they're not.... Is the painting about a black man raping a white woman, or is it about a couple screwing in a cemetery?

JONATHAN: Oh. You're saying it's ambiguous.

PATRICIA: I'm saying it's confusing. You can't have intended both things.

JONATHAN: Why not? I've got you thinking about it haven't I?

NICK: But thinking about what? What does it *mean*? If *you* can't say, unequivocally...

PATRICIA: *(To* JONATHAN*)* He has a point. It's all about shock, then. Effect. You can't *mean*, "What difference does it make," Jonathan, that just isn't good enough.

JONATHAN: *(Over "isn't good enough")* You know I don't entirely mean that. I mean, *my* intention is irrelevant; it's all about what you make of it.

NICK: Either way you look at it, it has about as much impact as a smutty photo in a porno mag.

JONATHAN: You can't get past the flesh, can you.

NICK: What?

JONATHAN: This is very interesting. All you see is the flesh. Of course! You surround yourself with *bones* all day. I mean, here you are, freezing your asses off....

PATRICIA: Jonathan...

JONATHAN: *(Continuous)* ...cataloguing bones whose flesh rotted away centuries ago. No wonder my paintings scare you!

NICK: Scare me, did you say?

JONATHAN: Yes. They're...voluptuous, dangerous. They deal with unspeakable things, fleshy things. *That's* what's going on in my paintings. The lengths people go to, living people go to, in order to feel something. Now. Today. *(Pause)*

PATRICIA: We thought we'd put you in our bedroom.

JONATHAN: What?

PATRICIA: We thought we'd put you....

JONATHAN: In *your* room? No, you don't have to do that.

PATRICIA: No bother.

JONATHAN: Where are *you* gonna sleep?

PATRICIA: Down here.

JONATHAN: No no, I'll sleep down here.

PATRICIA: The bedroom is actually warmer.

JONATHAN: I don't mind.

NICK: Are you sure?

JONATHAN: Yeah.

PATRICIA: No, trust me, the bedroom, it's really no problem.

NICK: *(Over "no problem")* Patricia, he said he doesn't mind.

JONATHAN: I don't.

NICK: See? *(To* JONATHAN*)* Yes, why *don't* you stay downstairs?

JONATHAN: Fine.

PATRICIA: But the electric *blank*et is upstairs. He's going to need the electric blanket.

JONATHAN: *(Over "electric blanket")* Don't worry about me.

NICK: I'll bring it down.

PATRICIA: The mattress-warmer, actually. It's under the sheet. You'll have to strip the bed. It really would be easier....

NICK: *(Over "easier")* So I'll strip the bed. The bed needs stripping anyway.

PATRICIA: *(A beat; to* NICK*)* Are you sure?

NICK: Yes. I'll take care of it. Leave it to me.

JONATHAN: Thank you. (NICK *goes. Pause.)* I hope I'm not....

PATRICIA: You hope you're not what?

JONATHAN: I don't know, it seems that my being here...

PATRICIA: Yes?

JONATHAN: *You* know.... Things seem a little, I don't know...prickly, maybe? I mean with Nick?

PATRICIA: I haven't seen this much life in him in years.

JONATHAN: Really. *(Pause)*

PATRICIA: I married Nick to stay in England.

JONATHAN: *(A beat)* Oh.

PATRICIA: They would've deported me. After my degree.

JONATHAN: Ah.

PATRICIA: My visa, *you* know, it was a student visa. It expired. I couldn't go home. How could I go home? Back to my broken-down mother? I couldn't. My skeptical father, who humored me through all my crazy pursuits? I had no one to go home to. No, this made sense. I found that I could survive here. I had to stay.

JONATHAN: *(A beat)* Does he know?

PATRICIA: I'm sure he does. You mean why...? (JONATHAN *nods.)* I'm sure he knows. It was certainly no secret. He knew I needed a way to stay.

JONATHAN: I don't understand you. How can you be so cool about this?

PATRICIA: What?

JONATHAN: The man is obviously crazy about you; he's like a blushing *school*boy around you...

PATRICIA: I know.

JONATHAN: How can you do this? I never thought you'd be capable of something like this. You were such a passionate girl, Patty....

PATRICIA: Oh, God, spare me...

JONATHAN: You were the "student of the world"! Remember? No, really, how do you...I mean, passion, sex, love.... You just decided, what, you don't need those things anymore?, you just shut that part of you all out?

PATRICIA: Yes. Exactly. My "passion" nearly did me in, now, didn't it.

JONATHAN: Oh, come on, don't lay this on me. That's bullshit. You call yourself an expatriate? You're no expatriate, you're just hiding!

PATRICIA: Who the hell are *you* to judge—?!

JONATHAN: Why do you live with him?

PATRICIA: Why? He's my husband.

JONATHAN: That's not a reason. Why do you live with him if you don't love him?

PATRICIA: Who said I don't love him?

JONATHAN: You just said yourself, you married Nick....

PATRICIA: *This is the best I can do*! *(Pause)*

JONATHAN: Don't say that. It isn't even true. I know you too well.

PATRICIA: *Knew* me. You *knew* me. You don't *know* who I am. *(A beat. NICK appears with a bundle of bedding. They look at him. Pause.)*

NICK: Um.... Shall I.... Would you like me to make your bed?

(End of scene)

Scene Six

(The gallery in London. This scene is the continuation of Scene Two.)

GRETE: You just said your definition of good art is "art which effectively reflects the truth." Do you think it is your responsibility as an artist to always tell the truth?

JONATHAN: In my work? Yes.

GRETE: And in your personal life?

JONATHAN: My personal life is my personal life. Look, if my work tells the truth, then I think people are compelled, they *have* to deal with it, they can't not. I like to shake 'em up a little, I admit it. People see my stuff at a gallery, a museum, and the work *competes* for their attention. They're preoccupied, overstimulated. All I can hope is maybe—*maybe*—one night, one of my images'll find its way into their unconscious and color their dreams. Who knows? Maybe it'll change their perception of something forever. I mean, in art, as in life, we tend to affect people in ways we can't always see. You can't possibly know what that other person has taken away with her. *(A beat)* You can't see it. And just 'cause you can't see it doesn't mean it didn't happen.

GRETE: Hm. Getting back to "good art..."

JONATHAN: Okay, let me ask you something: When we talk about good art, what are we talking about? Stuff we like? Stuff our friends make? We're talking about value judgments. Most people, do you think most people, most Americans—my *father*—do you think most people have any idea what makes good art?

GRETE: Hm.

JONATHAN: The little old lady who paints flowers and pussycats at the YMCA—and *dazzles* her friends, I'm sure—I mean, does that little old lady make good art? I mean, why not?, her cat looks just *like* that. I'm not putting her down; I think it's great she's got a hobby. But is what she does good art? See, most people...I remember, years ago, the big van Gogh show at the Met?, in New York? The place was packed. Like Yankee Stadium. Buses emptied out from all over; Jersey, Westchester. All kinds of people. The masses. Average middle-class people. Like they were coming into the city for a matinee and lunch at Mamma Leone's. Only this was Art. Art with a capital A had come to the shopping mall generation and Vincent was the chosen icon. Now, I have nothing against van Gogh. Better him than people lining up to see the kids with the big eyes. But as I braved that exhibit—and it was rough going, believe me—I couldn't help but think of Kirk Douglas.

Kirk Douglas should've gotten a cut of the house. See, there's this Hollywood packaging of the artist that gets me. The packaging of the mystique. Poor, tragic Vincent: he cut off his ear 'cause he was so misunderstood but still he painted all these pretty pictures. So ten bodies deep they lined up in front of the paintings. More out of solidarity for Vincent (or Kirk) than out of any kind of love or passion for "good art." Hell, some art lovers were in such a hurry to get to the postcards and prints and souvenir placemats, they strode past the paintings and skipped the show entirely! Who can blame them? You couldn't *experience* the paintings anyway, not like that. You couldn't *see* anything. The art was just a backdrop for the *real* show that was happening. In the gift shop!

GRETE: Hm.

JONATHAN: Now, you got to admit there's something really strange about all this, this kind of *frenzy* for art. I mean, what is this thing called art? What's it for? Why have people historically drunk themselves to death over the creation of it, or been thrown in jail, or whatever? I mean, how does it serve the masses? *Can* it serve the—I ask myself these questions all the time. Every painting I do is another attempt to come up with some answers. The people who crowded the Met to look at sunflowers, I mean, why *did* they? 'Cause they *thought* they should. 'Cause they thought they were somehow enriching their lives. Why? *'Cause the media told them so*!

GRETE: You seem to have such contempt...

JONATHAN: Not contempt; you're confusing criticism with contempt.

GRETE: *(Continuous)* ...for the very same people and the very same system that has made you what you are today.

JONATHAN: What I am today? What *am* I today? I just got here. People like *you* suddenly care what I have to say.

GRETE: I *do* care.

JONATHAN: I know you do. It cracks me up that you do; it amuses me. You know, up till like eight or nine years ago, let's not forget, I was painting apartments for a living. Apartments. Walls. Rooms. I was good at it, too. I'd lose myself all day while I painted moldings, then I'd go home and do my own painting all night. A good, simple, hard-working life. Then, like I said, like nine years ago, my world started getting bigger. I couldn't even retrace the steps; I can't remember how it happened. All I know is I met certain people and got a gallery and a show and the public started to discover my work. The night of my first opening, it's like these strangers witnessed a birth, like the work had no life before they laid eyes on it. We know that's ridiculous, of course, but this is what happens when you take your art out of your little room and present it to the public: it's not yours anymore, it's *theirs*, theirs to see with their own eyes. And, for each person who sees your work for the first time, you're discovered all over again. That begins to take its toll. You can't be everybody's discovery. That gets to be very demanding. Who are these people who are suddenly throwing money at you and telling you how wonderful and talented you are? What do *they* know? You begin to believe them. They begin to want things from you. They begin to expect things. The work loses its importance; the importance is on "Waxman".

GRETE: Would you prefer to have remained an outsider?

JONATHAN: Preferred? No. It's cold and lonely on the outside.

GRETE: And yet being cozy on the inside...

JONATHAN: "Cozy"?

GRETE: *(Continuous)* ...seems to make you uncomfortable as well. Is this not an illustration of that Jewish joke?

JONATHAN: What Jewish joke?

GRETE: Forgive my paraphrase: Not wanting to be a member of a club that would also have you as a member?

JONATHAN: That's not a Jewish joke, that's Groucho Marx.

GRETE: Groucho Marx, then. Is he not Jewish?

JONATHAN: Yeah, so?

GRETE: Well, does not that joke apply to the problem Jews face in the twentieth century?

JONATHAN: What problem is that?

GRETE: The problem of being on the inside while choosing to see themselves as outsiders...

JONATHAN: Is that a Jewish problem?

GRETE: *(Continuous)* ...even when they are very much on the inside?

JONATHAN: "Very much on the inside"? What is this?

GRETE: *(Over "What is this")* Perhaps I am not expressing myself well.

JONATHAN: No, I think you're probably expressing yourself very well.

GRETE: All I am suggesting, Mr Waxman, is that the artist, like the Jew, prefers to see himself as alien from the mainstream culture. For the Jewish *artist* to acknowledge that the contrary is true, that he is not alien, but rather, *assimilated* into that mainstream culture—

JONATHAN: *(Over "mainstream culture")* Wait a minute wait a minute. What is this *Jewish* stuff creeping in here?

GRETE: You are a Jew, are you not?

JONATHAN: I don't see what that—

GRETE: *(Over "what that") Are* you?

JONATHAN: Yeah; so?

GRETE: I am interested in the relationship between the artist and the Jew, as Jonathan Waxman sees it.

JONATHAN: Who *cares* how Jonathan Waxman sees it? I'm an *American* painter. *American* is the adjective, not *Jewish, American.*

GRETE: Yes, but your work calls attention to it.

JONATHAN: How?

GRETE: The Jewish cemetery in *Walpurgisnacht,—*

JONATHAN: *One* painting.

GRETE: One *important* painting—the depictions of middle-class life, obviously Jewish—

JONATHAN: How can you say that? "Obviously" Jewish.

GRETE: I have studied your paintings, I have done research on your upbringing...

JONATHAN: Oh, yeah?

GRETE: *(Continuous)* I have written many critical studies for art journals in my country. The middle-class life you explore— It is safe to say that your paintings are autobiographical, are they not?

JONATHAN: In what sense? Of course they're autobiographical in the sense that they come from *me*, they spring from *my* imagination, but to say that the subjects of my paintings are *Jewish* subjects, because a Jew happened to paint them, that's totally absurd.

GRETE: Mr Waxman, I cannot tell to what you have most taken offense: the suggestion that was made, or that it was made by a German.

JONATHAN: *(A beat)* Look, maybe we should...

GRETE: Please, just one more question...

JONATHAN: Can we please move on? Let's move on.

GRETE: Of course. *(A beat)* Mr Waxman, you speak with charming self-effacement about your much-celebrated career. You say you are amused by your sudden fame...

JONATHAN: Yes.

GRETE: *(Continuous)* ...and seem to view it as an unwanted but not unwelcome bonus, that making good art is all you have ever wanted to do.

JONATHAN: Yes.

GRETE: And yet—forgive me, Mr Waxman—I am confused. If, as you claim, you had no interest in celebrity, why would you hire a public relations firm?

JONATHAN: This is how you change the subject?

GRETE: There have been whispers, Mr Waxman. *(She says "vispers".)* Why would you hire a publicist if—

JONATHAN: You think I'm the only painter who has a publicist? This is the reality. You reach a certain point in your career, an *artist* reaches a certain point, where he achieves a certain amount of recognition—

GRETE: Yes, I know, you said. I do not question that.

JONATHAN: Will you let me finish please? If you're gonna make a statement like that...

GRETE: I am sorry.

JONATHAN: *(Continuous)* ...then at least let me make my point.

GRETE: Please.

JONATHAN: An artist who's achieved a certain amount of celebrity, very quickly, there are suddenly all these demands being placed on him. I've talked about that.

GRETE: Yes.

JONATHAN: People want you. Interviews, parties, schools. The problem becomes *time*. Where do you find the time to work?, to do the thing that made you famous? This is where having a publicist comes in. The publicist helps manage your social obligations. And if the painter doesn't have one, the gallery does, so what's the big deal?

GRETE: No, no, I understand. Perhaps I did not phrase my question correctly.

JONATHAN: Cut the crap, Miss; your English is impeccable.

GRETE: Mr Waxman, the whispers I have heard....

JONATHAN: Again with the "vispers"!

GRETE: Is it true that you hired a public relations firm *two years* before your first success....

JONATHAN: Oh, come on. What is this, the Inquisition? Art is a business, you know that.

GRETE: Two years *before*, to promote your standing in the art community—

JONATHAN: My "standing"—?

GRETE: *(Continuous)* More importantly, in the art-buying community.

JONATHAN: What are you saying?, I bought my career? I bought my reputation?, what?

GRETE: Mr Waxman...

JONATHAN: *(Continuous)* What about the work? Why aren't we talking about the work? Why must it always come down to business? Huh? *I'm* not doing it, and yet you accuse *me*...

GRETE: *(Over "and yet you accuse me")* Is it true or is it not true?

JONATHAN: That's irrelevant. True or not true, who cares?

GRETE: *(Over "who cares")* It *is* relevant.

JONATHAN: How? How?

GRETE: It is relevant if you espouse to be a visionary of truth.

JONATHAN: *(Over "visionary of truth")* I espouse nothing! What do I espouse? I paint pictures! You're the one who comes up with these fancy labels, people like you!

GRETE: *(Over "people like you")* How can you talk about truth? Mr. Waxman, how can you talk about truth when your own sense of morality—

JONATHAN: What do *you* know about morality?

GRETE: *(Continuous)* When your own sense of morality is so compromised and so—

JONATHAN: Huh? What do *you* know with your sneaky little Jew-baiting comments.

GRETE: I beg your pardon.

JONATHAN: Don't give me this innocence shit. You know exactly what I'm talking about.

GRETE: *(Over "what I'm talking about")* No, I am sorry, I have no idea.

JONATHAN: You think I haven't picked up on it? Huh? You think I don't know what this is all about?

GRETE: Mr Waxman, this is all in your imagination.

JONATHAN: My imagination?! I'm imagining this?! I'm imagining you've been attacking me from the word go?

GRETE: Mr Waxman!

JONATHAN: You have, Miss, don't deny it. You expect me to sit here another minute? What do you take me for? Huh? What the fuck do you take me for? *(He abruptly goes.)*

GRETE: Mr Waxman... *(Pause. She presses a button on the tape recorder. We hear the tape rewind.)*

(End of scene)

Scene Seven

(The farmhouse. A few hours after the end of Scene Five. The middle of the night. JONATHAN, bags packed, his coat on, tears a sheet of paper out of his sketchbook, turns off the tea kettle before its whistle fully sounds, and prepares a cup of tea. The painting, wrapped in newspaper, leans against the kitchen table. He takes six fifty-pound notes out of his wallet and leaves them under the honey pot on the kitchen table. Nick has quietly come downstairs and lingers in the darkness. He emerges from the shadows. Jonathan is startled when he sees him and spills his tea.)

JONATHAN: Oh. Shit. Hi.

NICK: Sorry.

JONATHAN: I didn't see you.

NICK: My fault. *(A beat)* Are you alright?

JONATHAN: A little wet; I'm alright.

NICK: *(A beat)* Couldn't sleep.

JONATHAN: No.

NICK: I mean *I* couldn't.

JONATHAN: Oh. Me, neither.

NICK: Was the futon...?

JONATHAN: No, it's fine. Did the kettle—? I'm sorry if the whistle...

NICK: No. *(A beat)* Shall I get the fire going again?

JONATHAN: No, you don't have to do that, I could've done that. No, I think I'll just head back early.

NICK: Oh. I see.

JONATHAN: Yeah, I think I'll, *you* know...

NICK: Back to London.

JONATHAN: Yeah.

NICK: Hm. *(A beat)* You won't even wait until breakfast?

JONATHAN: No, I'd better not.

NICK: Patricia will be disappointed.

JONATHAN: Yeah, I'm sorry about that.

NICK: She had planned something, I think. Breakfast.

JONATHAN: Oh, that's too bad.

NICK: *(A beat)* So you won't get to see the dig.

JONATHAN: I guess not.

NICK: I was going to take you.

JONATHAN: Next time.

NICK: Yes. Next time.

JONATHAN: *(A beat)* It's just, I've got so much to do when I get back.

NICK: *(Nods; a beat)* Did I...? Was I...? I mean I hope I wasn't too... *(A beat)* You weren't...sneaking out, were you?

JONATHAN: Sneaking—? No. No, I just thought I'd get an early start.

NICK: It's half past three. You'll be in London before seven. That's quite an early start you're getting.

JONATHAN: I couldn't sleep. I thought I might as well hit the road.

NICK: I see. Well. Patricia will be so disappointed. *(A beat)* You weren't sneaking out on Patricia.

JONATHAN: No. Of course not. I was gonna leave her a note.

NICK: I'll give it to her.

JONATHAN: I haven't written it yet.

NICK: Oh.

JONATHAN: I was just gonna sit down and write it.

NICK: Please. Carry on. (JONATHAN *sits. Pause.)* What were you going to say?

JONATHAN: Hm?

NICK: In this note. What were you going to *say*?

JONATHAN: I'm not sure.

NICK: What were you going to tell her? That would be difficult. Finding the right words. Patricia will be *so* disappointed. She was so looking forward to breakfast. I don't know what she'll do. I might have to comfort her. *(A beat)* She doesn't sleep with me, you know.

JONATHAN: Oh.

NICK: Not that I was ever her type. There was a certain challenge to be found in that. I thought she would *never*, not with me. She was so... *attractive*, you know, so confident, so American. The first time she slept with me I thought it must have been because I was her supervisor. I'm sure that was why. When it happened a second time, well, I didn't know *what* to think; I chose to think there was hope. Yes, I opted for hope. In a moment of uncharacteristic brazenness, I asked her to marry me. She accepted. I don't know why. I have my suspicions. *(A beat)* From time to time, I'll fortify myself with stout and kiss her neck, feel her tit, lay with my head there.

JONATHAN: Nick.

NICK: Sometimes she'll let me. She'll even stroke my hair. Once she kissed my head. I wanted to reach up and kiss her mouth, but why get greedy and piss her off?

JONATHAN: Why don't you go back to bed?

NICK: Some nights she'd respond—oh, she'd respond, or initiate even— and I would rush into it foolishly, trying not to feel I was somehow being rewarded. I take what I can get; I'm English. *(A beat)* She succumbed to my charms tonight, though. Tonight she acquiesced. Did you hear us? *(JONATHAN shakes his head; he's lying.)* Oh. What a shame. It was brilliant. *(A beat. He sees the money.)* What's this?

JONATHAN: What.

NICK: Under the honey pot. Money is it? A gratuity? Leaving a gratuity?

JONATHAN: No. Just a little cash.

NICK: A little cash? This is three hundred pounds. Why are you leaving three hundred pounds?

JONATHAN: I thought...

NICK: What.

JONATHAN: I thought it could be useful.

NICK: Useful? Of course it could be useful. Money is always useful. Why are you leaving three hundred pounds?

JONATHAN: I thought I could help you out.

NICK: Me?

JONATHAN: You and Patricia.

NICK: With three hundred pounds?

JONATHAN: Yeah. I happened to have a lot of cash on me, I thought I....

NICK: *(Over "I thought I")* You thought you could help us out, unload some cash....

JONATHAN: You know what I mean.

NICK: *(Continuous)* ...lend us a hand, by leaving three hundred pounds.

JONATHAN: I wanted to say thank you.

NICK: *Thank* you?! *Thank* you?!

JONATHAN: *(Over "you")* Don't be offended.

NICK: Who's offended? Who even suggested offense had been taken?

JONATHAN: I thought maybe.... You sounded....

NICK: Do you wish for me to be offended?

JONATHAN: Oh, please. Look, can we—

NICK: Do you *wish* for me—

JONATHAN: No. I'm sorry; you're taking it the wrong way.

NICK: Am I? You leave three hundred pounds under my honey pot...

JONATHAN: Nick. Jesus. I can't win with you, can I. Please. Just accept my thanks.

NICK: Your thanks for what?

JONATHAN: For letting me spend the night.

NICK: Three hundred pounds? For "letting" you? Three hundred pounds for letting you spend the night? If I'd known there was a price, I'd have charged you considerably more than three hundred pounds. Considering the damages to my home and happiness. Yes, like German reparations after the war. I should thank *you*. Your proximity served as a welcome marital aide. Interesting going at it like that. Each for his or her own reasons, yet mutually satisfying just the same. It is kind of like war, isn't it.

JONATHAN: I never meant you any harm.

NICK: Never meant me...?

JONATHAN: You act as if I'm to blame for your unhappiness. I'm sorry if you're unhappy. I never meant you any harm. We only met this afternoon...

NICK: Have I spoiled the surprise?

JONATHAN: What surprise?

NICK: Were we to awaken to find you gone but three hundred pounds in your stead, under the honey pot? Economic aid, is that it? Jonathan Waxman: Our American Cousin. Our Jewish uncle.

JONATHAN: Enough with the "Jewish", Nick.

NICK: You're right; cheap shot. A Robin Hood for our time, then. Stealing from the rich and giving to the poor. Hey, not entirely off the mark, is it?, stealing from the rich and giving to the— You are quite the charlatan it turns out.

JONATHAN: Am I?

NICK: Oh, yes. You shit on canvas and dazzle the rich. They oo and ah and shower you with coins, lay gifts at your feet. The world has gone insane. It's the emperor's new clothes.

JONATHAN: *(Reaching for it)* Look, if you don't want my money...

NICK: Uh uh uh. Don't get me wrong: I will take your money. Gladly. *And* insult you. I will bite your hand. With relish. Your money is dirty, Wax Man. Hell, I don't care; I could use a few quid. (PATRICIA, *awakened from a deep sleep, enters wearing a robe.*)

PATRICIA: What is happening?

NICK: Our guest is leaving. Getting an early start. He left a gratuity.

PATRICIA: What?

NICK: *(Shows her the money)* Three hundred quid.

JONATHAN: Look, I thought it would be best for everyone if I was gone in the morning.

PATRICIA: Is that what you thought? Why? Was the evening so unbearable?

JONATHAN: No...

PATRICIA: I thought it went pretty well, considering.

JONATHAN: *(Over "considering")* It did.

PATRICIA: It could have been excruciating.

JONATHAN: I know; it could've been. I was gonna write you a note.

PATRICIA: A note. You know, Jonathan?, you have this incredible knack for dismissing me whenever I've finished serving whatever purpose you've had in mind for me. Just incredible.

JONATHAN: Patty.... Look: It was really good to see you.

PATRICIA: What kind of shit is that?: "good to see you." I'm not one of your fucking patrons. (NICK *slips out of the room.*)

JONATHAN: Alright, already! What do you want me to say? Did you think it was easy, calling you and coming up here like this?

PATRICIA: Nobody asked you to!

JONATHAN: I had to! Okay? I had to see you again; I had to face you.

PATRICIA: This is how you face me? By sneaking out? *(She sees the painting. A beat.)* What are you doing with *that*? Oh, no you don't. Absolutely not.

JONATHAN: I'm only talking about a loan.

PATRICIA: Why?

JONATHAN: For the show.

PATRICIA: But it's my painting.

JONATHAN: I know.

PATRICIA: You gave it to me.

JONATHAN: I know I did. I'd like you to *loan* it to me. For the show. My gallery'll send you all the legal...

PATRICIA: *(Over "all the legal")* What the hell do you want with this painting? It isn't even that good.

JONATHAN: I don't care how good it is. It's missing something, the show. *I'm* missing something. I've been looking for a link, a touchstone. When I saw this painting...

PATRICIA: It's *me* in that painting, Jonathan. You gave it to *me*.

JONATHAN: Don't worry about privacy, the loan can be anonymous...

PATRICIA: I sat for that painting. The day we met. You gave me that painting.

JONATHAN: *(Over "You gave me that painting")* It'll be anonymous, nobody has to know your name.

PATRICIA: That's not the point. I don't want my painting hanging in a gallery!

JONATHAN: It's only for five weeks. In five weeks, they'll ship it back to you.

PATRICIA: It doesn't mean anything to anyone else; it means something to me. I don't understand— Is *this* why you came?

JONATHAN: What? No.

PATRICIA: *(Continuous)* Hoping I'd provide the missing link?

JONATHAN: I wanted to *see* you. I had no idea you'd even have it. As far as I knew you'd hacked it to bits fifteen years ago.

PATRICIA: Why didn't I?

JONATHAN: You tell me.

PATRICIA: So, what was your plan, you were just going to pack it up and go?

JONATHAN: I was going to write you a letter. To explain.

PATRICIA: What, that you were stealing it?

JONATHAN: Borrowing it.

PATRICIA: Taking it. Without my knowledge. That's stealing! You were stealing my painting!

JONATHAN: I didn't think it would matter so much to you. I thought you'd be, I don't know, flattered.

PATRICIA: Flattered?!

JONATHAN: To be in the show.

PATRICIA: God, Jonathan, the arrogance! So you just take what you want now, hm? Is that what fame entitles you to? I don't understand what's happened to you, Jonathan, what's happened to your conscience? You had a conscience, I know you did. Guilt did wonders for you. It made you appealing. Now I don't *know*. You've lost your *good*ness or something. Your spirit. (NICK *has slipped back in.*)

JONATHAN: You're right; I have. I *have* lost something. I've lost my way somehow, I don't know.... I've been trying to retrace my steps.... Ever since my father died...I'm nobody's son anymore, Patty. They're all gone now, all the disappointable people. There's no one left to shock with my paintings anymore. When I saw this painting, though, it was like all of a sudden I remembered where I came from! There's a kind of purity to it, you know?, before all the bullshit. Patty, I just need to hold onto it.

NICK: How much is it worth to you?

JONATHAN: What?

NICK: (*Gets the painting*) Start the bidding. What's it worth?

PATRICIA: Nick. For God's sake...

JONATHAN: I'm only talking about borrowing it.

NICK: Borrowing is no longer an option. Either you buy it outright...

JONATHAN: You're not serious.

PATRICIA: Nick! This is none of your business!

NICK: None of my—? It most certainly *is* my business.

PATRICIA: It isn't yours to sell!

NICK: Oh, let him have the bloody painting and let's be on with it!

PATRICIA: No!

NICK: Please, love. Let him take it out of our home. At long last, please.

PATRICIA: It isn't for sale!

NICK: *Let* him, Patricia. Let him take it to London.

PATRICIA: No, Nick!

NICK: Let him buy it. Doesn't it make sense, love? Think of it: This one painting...

PATRICIA: No!

NICK: We'll make some money, love. Tens of thousands.

PATRICIA: This painting doesn't have a price!

NICK: It's our future, love! Our future was sitting on the wall all along. Think of it: We can *save* some money, we can pay our debts. We can get on with it. *(Pause. Softly.)* Let him take the painting, love. (NICK *and* PATRICIA *look at one another for a long time. She lets him take the painting; he gives it to* JONATHAN.) There you go.

JONATHAN: *(To* PATRICIA, *who is facing away)* You're sure this is what you want?

NICK: Yes. Absolutely. Send us a check. Pounds or dollars, either is acceptable. As long as it's an obscene amount.

JONATHAN: It will be.

NICK: Good. *(A beat)* Goodbye, Jonathan.

JONATHAN: Goodbye.

NICK: *(To* PATRICIA*)* I think I'll...go back to bed. *(He starts to go. She takes his hand.)*

PATRICIA: Soon. (NICK *leaves. Long pause.)* I can't describe the pleasure I had being your muse. The days and nights I sat for you. It thrilled me, watching you paint me. The connection. The connection was electric. I could see the sparks. I never felt so alive as when I sat naked for you, utterly still, obedient. I would have done anything for you, do you know that?

JONATHAN: Patty...

PATRICIA: Isn't that shameful? A girl so devoid of self? I would have done anything. *(A beat)* You know, even after that last time in Brooklyn, I never actually believed that I'd never see you again.

JONATHAN: No?

PATRICIA: No, I always held out the *possibility*. But *this time*... *(A beat)* We won't be seeing each other again. Will we. *(A beat. He shakes his head. A beat.)* Hm. I wonder what that will be like. *(They continue looking at one another as lights fade.)*

(End of scene)

Scene Eight

(About seventeen years earlier. A painting studio at an art school. Easels in motley array. We can see the model dressing behind a screen. A class has just ended; all who remains is a youthful, shaggier JONATHAN, *who continues to paint. Soon, the model, the young* PATRICIA, *enters and finishes dressing in silence. Finally:)*

PATRICIA: How's it going?

JONATHAN: Hm?

PATRICIA: How's it—

JONATHAN: Oh. Fine. *(Pause)*

PATRICIA: You want me to shut up?

JONATHAN: What? No.

PATRICIA: Can I see?

JONATHAN: Uh...

PATRICIA: Please? I won't—

JONATHAN: It's.... It's really not there yet.

PATRICIA: Oh, come on...

JONATHAN: You'll get the wrong idea.

PATRICIA: I won't say anything.

JONATHAN: I don't know, I'm still...

PATRICIA: Not a peep.

JONATHAN: *(A beat)* Alright. *(She goes to the easel, stands beside him for a long time trying not to show her reaction.)* I'm playing around with the point of view. See how the—

PATRICIA: Shhh... *(She takes a long beat, then walks away, resumes dressing. Pause.)*

JONATHAN: Well...?

PATRICIA: What. *(He looks at her expectantly.)* You told me not to say anything.

JONATHAN: You can say *some*thing...

PATRICIA: I'm going on a diet effective immediately.

JONATHAN: I knew you'd take it the wrong way. It's purposely distorted. I'm trying something. You see how it looks like I'm looking *down* at you and *at* you at the same time? That's why the figure, your figure, looks a little...

PATRICIA: Huge. No, I'm kidding, it's good. Really. It's me. I have this mental image of myself...I think I'm a Botticelli, but I always come out Reubens. *(A beat)* You're very good, you know.

JONATHAN: I am?

PATRICIA: Oh, come on, you know it. I looked around during the break. You're the best in the class.

JONATHAN: Nah, I'm just having a good day.

PATRICIA: You want me to shut up so you—?

JONATHAN: That girl Susan's the best I think.

PATRICIA: She is not. Are you kidding?

JONATHAN: She's very slick, I know, but her color...

PATRICIA: I'm Patricia, by the way.

JONATHAN: I know.

PATRICIA: I mean, we haven't been formally introduced; you've been staring at my *bush* all *day* but we haven't....

JONATHAN: I'm Jonathan.

PATRICIA: I know. *(They shake hands. Pause.)*

JONATHAN: You're a good model.

PATRICIA: Yeah? This is my first time ever.

JONATHAN: Is it really? I wouldn't have known.

PATRICIA: You mean it?

JONATHAN: Yeah. I really wouldn't have known. You're good.

PATRICIA: What makes a model good?

JONATHAN: I don't know. You're very steady.

PATRICIA: Steady.

JONATHAN: *You* know, you keep the pose.

PATRICIA: Oh.

JONATHAN: *You* know what I mean.

PATRICIA: So that's all it takes? Steadiness?

JONATHAN: No. I don't know, I mean, when you're working from a model...

PATRICIA: Yeah...?

JONATHAN: *(Continuous)* ...you kinda have to distance yourself.

PATRICIA: Uh huh.

JONATHAN: I mean, just because one of you is naked, it's not necessarily a sexual thing.

PATRICIA: It's not?

JONATHAN: No. It's.... You have to maintain a certain objectivity, a certain distance. See, it's the whole *gestalt*.

PATRICIA: The *gestalt*.

JONATHAN: Yeah. It's the room and the pose and the canvas. It's the *moment*. The light, the way you look...

PATRICIA: You like the way I look?

JONATHAN: *(A beat)* Yes.

PATRICIA: *(A beat)* I can't believe I actually signed up to do this *(my mother would die)*. It isn't hard, all I have to do is sit still and let my mind wander. I do that all the time anyway. Why shouldn't I get paid for it? I was watching them burn leaves out the window. The fire was beautiful. —Hey, you want me to get undressed?

JONATHAN: What?

PATRICIA: So you can work.

JONATHAN: No you don't have to do that...

PATRICIA: I don't mind...

JONATHAN: Your time is up; you don't get paid overtime.

PATRICIA: I don't care.

JONATHAN: No, really, I can paint from memory. Really.

PATRICIA: Why should you paint from memory? I'm *here*...I mean, I *do* have my film history class...

JONATHAN: Is that your major? Film?

PATRICIA: No, I have no major. I'm a dilettante.

JONATHAN: Oh.

PATRICIA: You want to know what I'm taking this semester? I'm taking American Film Comedy from Chaplin to Capra, Women in Faulkner's South, Poetry Workshop *(talk about dilettantes)*, Introduction to Archeology. And, you know what? It's wonderful, I am having such a wonderful time. I never thought being a dilettante could be so rewarding. I'm interested in a lot of different things so why should I tie myself down with a major, you know?

JONATHAN: *(Humoring her)* Uh huh.

PATRICIA: You're humoring me.

JONATHAN: *(Lying)* No.

PATRICIA: My *father* always humors me; you're humoring me.

JONATHAN: I'm not.

PATRICIA: What's wrong with someone admitting she's a dilettante?

JONATHAN: Nothing.

PATRICIA: All it means is that I see myself as a student of the world. A student of the world. I'm young, I have time. I want to try a *lot* of things. Is that something to be ashamed of?

JONATHAN: No. It's just.... I've never been able to do that. I mean, all I ever wanted to do was paint. I wanted to be an artist, ever since I was a little kid. I was like four and I could copy amazing. I don't know, if I could just paint all the time, maybe once in a while go out for Chinese food...that's all I want out of life. *(Pause)*

PATRICIA: You know?, you do this *thing*...

JONATHAN: What.

PATRICIA: *(A beat)* I've been *watch*ing you. While you work?

JONATHAN: You've been watching me?

PATRICIA: Uh huh. There's this *thing* you do I've noticed. With your mouth.

JONATHAN: What do I do with my mouth?

PATRICIA: When you're painting.

JONATHAN: What do I *do*?!

PATRICIA: *(A beat)* You sort of stick your tongue out.

JONATHAN: Oh. So you're saying I look like an idiot?

PATRICIA: *(Laughing)* No, it's... I'm sorry.... It's *cute*...

JONATHAN: Oh, great...

PATRICIA: It *is*. I mean, your concentration... *(A beat)* It's sexy.

JONATHAN: Oh, I'm sure. This dribbling down my...a real turn-on.

PATRICIA: *(Laughing)* It is... *(She suddenly kisses his mouth.)*

JONATHAN: *(Surprised, he recoils.)* Hey!

PATRICIA: Sorry. I'm sorry.... Look, why don't you just paint... *(Quickly gathers her things)*

JONATHAN: No, wait...I didn't mean "Hey!" I meant "Oh!" It came *out* "Hey!"

PATRICIA: Are you gay or something?

JONATHAN: No.... Surprised. I'm not used to having girls...

PATRICIA: What.

JONATHAN: I don't know. Come on so strong.

PATRICIA: Sorry. It won't happen again. *(She goes.)*

JONATHAN: Oh, great...

PATRICIA: *(Returning)* Let me ask you something: If I hadn't kissed you, would you have kissed me?

JONATHAN: No.

PATRICIA: What *is* it with you?! We're staring at each other all day.... I'm *naked*, totally exposed to you...your tongue is driving me insane— the attraction is mutual, wouldn't you say? I mean, wouldn't you say that?

JONATHAN: Yeah...

PATRICIA: Then what is it? *(Pause)*

JONATHAN: You...scare me a little.

PATRICIA: I scare you.

JONATHAN: You do. You scare me.... A lot, actually...

PATRICIA: How could I scare you? I'm the scaredest person in the world.

JONATHAN: Oh, boy... *(Takes a deep breath; a beat)* You scare me...'cause of what you represent. I know that sounds....

PATRICIA: *(Over "I know that sounds")* For what I r— What do I represent? Dilettantism? Nudity? Film studies?

JONATHAN: *(A beat)* You aren't Jewish. *(He smiles, shrugs. A beat.)*

PATRICIA: You're kidding. And all these years I thought I was.

JONATHAN: Look, this is hard for me. It's a major thing, you know, where I come from...

PATRICIA: What, your mother?

JONATHAN: Not just my mother. It's the six million! It's, it's the diaspora, it's the history of the Jewish people! You have no idea, the *weight*. You got to remember I come from Brooklyn. People where I come from, they don't like to travel very far, let alone intermarry. They've still got this ghetto mentality: safety in numbers and stay put, no matter what. It's always, "How'm I gonna get there?" *(She smiles.)* No, really. "How'm I gonna get there?" and "How'm I gonna get home?" "It'll be late, it'll be dark, it'll get cold, I'll get sick, why bother? I'm staying home." This is the attitude about the world I grew up with. It's a miracle I ever left the house! *(She laughs. They look at one another for a long beat.)*

PATRICIA: So now what do we do?

JONATHAN: What do you mean?

PATRICIA: This is it? No discussion? The end?

JONATHAN: I *told* you. I'm sorry. I can't...get *involved* with you.

PATRICIA: "Involved"? What does that *mean*, "involved"? You can't *look* at me?, you can't *talk* to me? What are you so afraid of?

JONATHAN: I don't even know.

PATRICIA: We're talking about a *kiss*, Jonathan, a kiss, some coffee, and maybe spending the night together.

JONATHAN: Uy.

PATRICIA: We are not talking about the future of the Jewish race.

JONATHAN: See, but I think we are.

PATRICIA: My God, they've got you brainwashed! Is this what they teach you in Hebrew school?

JONATHAN: This is how it starts, though, Patricia: a kiss.

PATRICIA: You make it sound like a disease!

JONATHAN: Well, maybe it is. Maybe it's wrong and destructive and goes against the natural order of things. I don't know. Maybe it just shouldn't be.

PATRICIA: And maybe it's the greatest adventure!

JONATHAN: Assimilation as Adventure. Sounds like one of your courses.

PATRICIA: *Don't humor me!* It's very condescending, Jonathan, it really is.

JONATHAN: *(Over "it really is")* I'm sorry I'm sorry.

PATRICIA: I come from a tribe, too, you know. Maybe not one with the same history as yours, but still.... You're as exotic to me as I am to you! You're an artist! An artist has to experience the world! How can you experience the world if you say "no" to things you shouldn't have to say "no" to?!

JONATHAN: *(A beat. He smiles.)* Do me a favor?, get my mother on the phone? *(He gestures to the easel with his brush, meaning: "I should get back to work." A beat. She kicks off her shoes. Quietly.)* No, no, don't, really.... What are you doing?

PATRICIA: Don't paint from memory. *I'm* here, Jonathan. *(A beat)* Paint *me*. *(They're looking at one another. As she slowly unbuttons her blouse, and he approaches, lights fade to black.)*

END OF PLAY

A Short History

South Coast Repertory was founded in 1964 by David Emmes and Martin Benson, who continue to serve as the theatre's artistic directors in 1993. Since its inception SCR has devoted itself to developing and producing new plays by America's finest emerging and established playwrights, while balancing each season with selections from the classic and modern repertoires. Five founding members serve as SCR's core company, their talents supplemented by a large extended company and by guest artists new to SCR's collaboration.

SCR's new play endeavors have flourished since 1984, when the Collaboration Laboratory (Colab) was established as a comprehensive program to commission, develop, and produce new work. Among Colab's projects are NewSCRipts, a public play-reading series that has a success rate of better than 80% in sending new plays on to production, and the Hispanic Playwrights Project and California Playwrights Program, whose specific emphases enable SCR to serve special constituencies. Colab also has funded commissions for forty new plays since 1985.

SCR's work with new plays has had a notable impact on a national level. Since 1982, three out of four plays premiered at SCR have gone on to subsequent productions at such major theaters as the New York Shakespeare Festival, Yale Rep, Playwrights Horizons, Circle Rep, Steppenwolf, Manhattan Theatre Club, and Berkeley Rep. Largely because of its efforts on behalf of playwrights and their work, SCR received the 1988 Tony Award for outstanding achievement by a resident theater.

SCR produces a six-play season on its Mainstage and a five-play season on its Second Stage, for a total subscription audience of more than 20,000 people. The theater also produces a three-play children's series, and two touring shows that annually reach nearly 100,000 students in area schools.

South Coast Repertory's World Premieres

1992-93

GREAT DAY IN THE MORNING, by Thomas Babe
LET'S PLAY TWO, by Anthony Clarvoe
SO MANY WORDS, by Roger Rueff

1991-92

NOAH JOHNSON HAD A WHORE, by Jon Bastian
BOUNDARY WATERS, by Barbara Field
THE EXTRA MAN, by Richard Greenberg
SIGHT UNSEEN, by Donald Margulies
HOSPITALITY SUITE, by Roger Rueff

1990-91

ALEKHINE'S DEFENSE, by Robert Daseler
PIRATES, by Mark W. Lee
EL DORADO, by Milcha Sanchez-Scott

1989-90

THE RAMP, by Shem Bitterman
ONCE IN ARDEN, by Richard Hellesen
SEARCH AND DESTROY, by Howard Korder
MAN OF THE FLESH, by Octavio Solis

1988-89

DRAGON LADY, by Robert Daseler
ABUNDANCE, by Beth Henley
THE GEOGRAPHY OF LUCK, by Marlane Meyer
AT LONG LAST LEO, by Mark Stein

1987-88

V & V ONLY, by Jim Leonard
PRELUDE TO A KISS, by Craig Lucas
DOG LOGIC, by Thomas Strelich

1986-87

COLD SWEAT, by Neal Bell
BIRDS, by Lisa Loomer
THREE POSTCARDS, by Craig Lucas and Craig Carnelia
HIGHEST STANDARD OF LIVING, by Keith Reddin

1985-86

BEFORE I GOT MY EYE PUT OUT, by Timothy Mason

1984-85

SHADES, by David Epstein
THE DEBUTANTE BALL, by Beth Henley

1983-84

BING AND WALKER, by James Paul Farrell
MEN'S SINGLES, by D.B. Gilles
LIFE AND LIMB, by Keith Reddin

1982-83

SHE ALSO DANCES, by Kenneth Arnold
GOODBYE FREDDY, by Elizabeth Diggs
APRIL SNOW, by Romulus Linney
CLOSELY RELATED, by Bruce MacDonald
BROTHERS, by George Sibbald

1980-81

SCREWBALL, by L.J. Schneiderman
CHEVALIERE, by David Trainer

1979-80

POINTS IN TIME, by Elias Davis and David Pollock
TIME WAS, by Shannon Keith Kelley

1972-73

IN THE MIDST OF LIFE, by Ron Thronson, Toni Shearer, and
Bryant McKernan

1971-72

OLI'S ICE CREAM SUIT, by Richard Ploetz

1970-71

MOTHER EARTH, by Ron Thronson and Toni Shearer
SNOWMAN IN THE EMPTY CLOSET, by Gary White

1968-69

THE INCREDIBLE REIGN OF GOOD KING UBU, by Ron Thronson

1967-68

ADVENTURES IN A PAPER BAG, by John Arthur Davis and Ron Thronson
PICTURES FROM THE WALLS OF POMPEII, by Tim Kelly

1966-67

LAST DAY OF THE YEAR, by Peter Renno

1965-66

CHOCOLATES, by Ian Bernard

1964-65

THE TRIAL OF GABRIEL KAPUNIAK, by Mel Shapiro